BEYOND EXPRESSION
A systematic study of the foundations of linguistics

Albert Weideman
University of The Free State

PAIDEIA PRESS
2009

This book is a revision of a dissertation originally submitted, in June 1981, to meet the requirements for the degree of Master of Arts in English in the Faculty of Arts of the Free State, Bloemfontein.

Beyond Expression
© 2009
The Reformational Publishing Project
2123 Godwin Ave. S.E.
Grand Rapids, MI 49507
www.reformationalpublishing project.com

ISBN 978-0-88815-204-6

ACKNOWLEDGEMENTS IN THE ORIGINAL

I wish to thank Dr. D. S. Albertyn for his advise and guidance in planning this dissertation, as well as for his many helpful suggestions which greatly assisted me in preparing this study. I would also like to express my gratitude to my family and all relatives, friends, students, colleagues and other scholars who have supported and encouraged me.

Contents

Prologue ix

Chapter one
Philosophy and the special sciences
The 'objectivity' of linguistic theory	1
The relationship between philosophy and the special sciences	2
The foundational character of philosophy	3
Philosophical linguistics	4

Chapter two
Developing a linguistic methodology
The structural-empirical method	6
The limits of method-borrowing	8
General properties of language as linguistic universals in Chomsky's theory	10
Similarity and difference between languages	11
Norm and fact	12
Structures and facts in Chomsky's thought	13
Chomsky and Kant	17
Freedom and determinism	20
Linguistic ideas	25
Lingual principles	25
Elementary and complex linguistic concepts	27

Chapter three
Sample of a previous attempt 30

Chapter four
Material lingual spheres
Introduction	39
Formal and informal	41
Reduction of typical structures to general concepts of function	42
Material lingual spheres	47
Register	49
Attempts at distinguishing between material lingual spheres	50
The material lingual sphere of conversation	52
The typical characteristics of certitudinal discourse	54
Scientific language	55
The language of art	56
The material lingual sphere of legal language	57
Applications of material distinctions in language teaching	58

Chapter five
The expressive character of language
Communication versus expression	60
The field of investigation of linguistics	63
A typological linguistic classification	65
Speech as object of inquiry	67
Speech and writing	69
Verbal language	70
Some remarks on terminology	71
Anthropological foundations of linguistics	72

Chapter six
The elementary linguistic concept of lingual unity and multiplicity
Introductory remarks	75
Lingual system and its formal and material aspects	76

The lingual unity and diversity of lingual subjects
and objects   78
The lingual unity and diversity of lingual facts   81

Chapter seven
Spatial analogies in the lingual aspect
External and internal coherence   84
The lingual sphere of applicability of
a lingual system   86
The lingual dimensionality of a lingual system   90
The lingual position of lingual facts   91
Structuralism as relationism   92
Lingual extension on the factual side of
the lingual aspect   97

Chapter eight
Lingual constancy as an elementary linguistic concept
The theoretical problem   104
The consistency of lingual norms   108
The period of appeal to authority   109
Arguments against   114
The 'mechanical' elements of language   117
The relative constancy of lingual facts in their
lingual extension   119

Chapter nine
The operation of lingual norms in factual lingual processes
Physical analogies in the structure of the
lingual aspect   124
Factual lingual process and normative
lingual procedure   127
Transformations as normative lingual operations   133
The validity of lingual norms   135
Changes in lingual norms   135
Factual lingual maintenance and change   136

Chapter ten
Lingual development and organization
Language and biology	139
Normative lingual development and maturity	140
Factual lingual growth and differentiation	141
Factual lingual organization	144

Chapter eleven
Lingual volition and sensitivity
Linguistics and psychology	147
Lingual volition and intention	149
Factual lingual will	152
The factual perception of lingual objects	155

Chapter twelve
Lingual identification and distinction
Language and thought	161
Normative lingual concurrence and contradiction	162
Language and logic	164
Factual lingual identity	168

Chapter thirteen
Formative retrocipations in the lingual aspect
The internal molding of language	170
The normative dimension of lingual competence	171
Other normative analogies	178
The factual dimension of lingual competence	179
The constitutive structure of the lingual aspect	181

Chapter fourteen
Discourse, text and other social anticipations
Linguistic concept and linguistic idea	185
Sociolinguistics as a study of the social anticipations in the lingual aspect	187
Normative anticipations	189
Material lingual spheres as normative types of discourse	191

Typical specifications of the general modal norm of acceptability	194
The appropriativeness, relevance and informativeness of utterances	196
'Text' as factual lingual unit	198

Chapter fifteen
The idea of lingual economy

Other linguistic issues	201
The idea of lingual economy	202
A system for lingual sharing	203
A broadening of the concept of objective factual lingual unit	213
A minimum unit for conversation	214
Opening and closing conversations	216
The overall organization of conversation	218
Some other factual lingual units	219
The remainder of the agenda	220

Chapter sixteen
A linguistic alternative

	221

Epilogue   225

Bibliography   230

Abstract   236

Prologue

When Kerry Hollingsworth first approached me in August 2005 with the idea of publishing my dissertation on *Systematic concepts in linguistics*, I was understandably reluctant. I had, since the time it was conceived and written, changed my professional, disciplinary focus to the field of applied linguistics, and had neither worked in linguistics since the late 1980's, nor had I kept fully abreast of its development. Kerry's argument, as well as that of my former colleague Danie Strauss, was that, even though some of it may now be slightly out of date, the material might still be worthwhile as an example of the application of the systematic insights of the philosophy of the cosmonomic idea to a special science. The enormity of the task of updating my knowledge of developments in linguistics nonetheless seemed to be a little too daunting. It was suggested, then, that we do not go this route, but lightly edit and then publish the text as an historical example of what contribution Dooyeweerd's systematics might make to a special discipline.

A number of professional commitments and technical difficulties — the text was, for example, not available electronically, since its writing predated the use of word processing by a number of years — prevented me from seriously considering Kerry's proposal. Eventually, in July 2006, the text was scanned and there was an opportunity of devoting some attention to the proposed project.

When I started working through the material, experimentally converting it into a slightly more current style, also as regards referencing, I realised that Kerry and Danie may, at least in broad terms, have been right. The initial work contains analyses that I know have not been made elsewhere, and that might be useful both as an example and as a starting point by other academics who are struggling to come to grips with the same or similar concepts. Moreover, in the introductory discussion relating to Chomsky in the second chapter, a relationship is identified between his thought and that of Kant — a still largely unexplored theme in discussions of the history of linguistics. This is important for various reasons, not the least of which is that Chomsky himself (cf. e.g. Chomsky 1966) linked his work more closely to that of Descartes, and may have been unaware of his debt to Kant (or of having encountered Descartes through some Kantian filter). Perhaps of even greater interest is the remarkable similarity of the concerns raised by Carnap in his work in the late 1930's, and that of Chomsky a good twenty years later, in the late 1950's — another neglected topic, as far as I am aware, in the history of linguistic thought. This debt, if that is what it is, is a puzzle that still has not been solved, as far as I am aware. Did Chomsky as a young student perhaps hear Carnap lecture? Did he perhaps take notes, and, when it came to starting out on his own as a scholar, not realise the remarkable similarities in their terminology and approach? In the several works of Chomsky (1957, 1965, 1966, 1970, 1972a, 1972b, 1974, 1975, 1978a, 1978b, 1979) that I analysed for the original book, there was simply no substantial acknowledgment of his indebtedness to Carnap (1937).

It is no coincidence that Chomsky's work features so prominently in the discussion of the original. Reformational philosophy has always proceeded in close interaction with other approaches and viewpoints, challenging them on their starting points and in this way attempting to open up — not always successfully — a line of communication with theoretical opponents. The prominence of Chomsky in the original discussion is therefore simply a reflection of how important his work was at the end of the 1970's. In some sense, that prominence has endured in spite of the various technical revisions and subsequent versions of his syntax, and the proposal of alternative views. Indeed, the influence of Chomsky's conceptions was challenged from other quarters as well, and most seriously so in respect of the social dimensions of linguistic analysis. This brings me to a third, and perhaps even more important reason why the original discussion may still yield worthwhile results and comment.

In re-reading and editing the manuscript, I realized something that was not apparent at the time that the original book was written. This is that the systematic analysis almost exactly predicted what is certainly the most major fault line within the discipline of linguistics: the separation at that time of the ways of theoretical linguistics (given the influence of transformational syntax) and of sociolinguistics. I know today that the robustness with which the analysis of the elementary linguistic concepts articulated this separation of the ways was one of the main reasons I never took seriously Seerveld's (1968) experimentation with the rearrangement of the temporal order of the different modalities of our experience. There was evidence in this analysis, in other words, that it could robustly identify one of the most important events on which the history and development of linguistics literally hinged, and that for me was as strong a validation of the theory as one could wish or hope for.

Though the analyses therefore appeared to contain some promise still, what to do with the less than current nature of some of the linguistic analyses referred to remained a problem. The one consolation to me was that, in the years since I wrote the original, I had done some further analyses (Weideman 1984, 1985a, 1988, 1991, Weideman & Visser 1986, Weideman, Raath & Van der Walt 1986, Weideman & Verster 1988) that articulated some of the points originally made, for example, in the identification of different material lingual spheres or discourse types in the earlier study. I resolved to refer to these in the revision, wherever it was relevant and appropriate, to achieve a measure of currency. In addition, I decided that I would add at least this prologue and, having done that, an epilogue: the former to articulate the reasons for my decision to continue with a revision of the original, along with its possible weak points, and the latter to spell out what I think still needs to be done to complement these initial analyses.

All of these considerations therefore eventually persuaded me that it was worthwhile to proceed. I resolved in the end to let the original analysis stand much as it was, and to present it for scrutiny to those who today continue to struggle either with the understanding of these elementary linguistic concepts, or with doing scientific work, also in other disciplines, responsibly.

Pretoria
August 2006

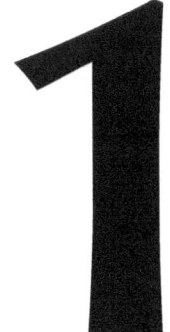

Philosophy and the special sciences

The 'objectivity' of linguistic theory

One of the die-hard myths of modern thought is the so-called neutrality or objectivity of our subjective theorizing. It is a dogma of scientific endeavor that has survived almost every major shake-up in the history of Western thinking. But it is nonetheless recognized today more than ever before that the dogma of objectivity is exactly that: an unverified and indeed unverifiable dogma. It has remained as much an illusion as the intellectual mirage of the attendant belief in the progressive discovery of truth. As Robins (1967: 3) remarks:

> It is tempting, and flattering to one's contemporaries, to see the history of a science as the progressive discovery of truth and the attainment of the right methods. But this is a fallacy. The aims of a science vary in the course of its history, and the search for objective standards by which to judge the purposes of different periods is apt to be an elusive one. 'The facts' and 'the truth' are not laid down in advance, like the solution to a crossword puzzle, awaiting the completion of discovery. Scientists themselves do much to determine the range of facts, phenomena, and operations that fall within their purview, and they themselves set up and modify the conceptual framework within which they make what they regard as significant statements about them.

Much the same point is made by Palmer (1976: 16) when he says that "in linguistics ... the facts are so intangible ... Indeed what we consider as facts will to a large extent depend on the framework, i.e. the model within which we describe them."

One of the aims of this study is to show how one can account for the serious differences between various trends in linguistics by accepting them as differences, and by working within the assumption that a theory always fits into a framework of ideas that is never neutral or objective, but related to the subjective human thinking process of which it is the outcome. To see this requires a clarification of the relation between philosophy and the special sciences.

The relationship between philosophy and the special sciences

A new interest has arisen in the relationship between philosophy and the field of linguistic inquiry in recent times. Chomsky himself has to a certain extent been instrumental in drawing our attention to the nature of this relationship, especially since the publication of his *Cartesian linguistics*. "It should be borne in mind", Chomsky remarks in an early note to the introduction of this work (1966: 76, note 4), that the period he wishes to deal with "antedates the divergence of linguistics, philosophy and psychology. The insistence of each of these disciplines on 'emancipating itself' from any contamination by the others is a peculiarly modern phenomenon." He concludes this remark, significantly, by pointing out that "current work in generative grammar returns to an earlier point of view, in this case, with respect to the place of linguistics among other studies" (Chomsky 1966: 76). In *Language and mind,* Chomsky (1972a: 1) echoes this point of view when he remarks:

> There have been signs in the past decade that the rather artificial separation of disciplines may be coming to an end. It is no longer a point of honor for each to demonstrate its absolute independence of the others, and new interests have emerged that permit the classical problems to be formulated in novel and occasionally suggestive ways ...

In short, the remarkably similar interests of philosophers and linguists make it foolish "to insist on a sharp separation of these disciplines, or for either to maintain a parochial disregard for the insights achieved in the other" (Chomsky 1972a: 161; cf. too Chomsky's criticism of the artificial separation of linguistics and psychology in *Reflections on language* [1975: 160-161]).

Chomsky's remarks in this regard serve to characterize the spirit in which I wish to approach the present study. Not only is philosophy "bound to be unproductive if it is not done in close co-operation with the special sciences", as Carnap (1937: 332) believed, but the reverse is just as true: the various scientific disciplines, including the special field of linguistics, are always implicitly or explicitly informed by some philosophical trend. It is sheer foolishness to disregard this in one's specialist field today.

The foundational character of philosophy

An image might be useful to clarify further the relation between linguistics and philosophy. If we compare our scientific endeavor with a house, then the foundations would be the philosophical perspective that underlies our theory of what is happening in the various rooms, one of which may be called 'linguistics'. The various special sciences are necessarily founded upon philosophical presuppositions (Dooyeweerd 1953 vol. 1: 545-566; see also vol. 2: 556-557).

It has been ably demonstrated by others (e.g. Strauss 1970) that all academic disciplines proceed from explicit or implicit assumptions that are of a philosophical nature. The mere existence of various schools of thought within the same academic discipline points to divergences that can ultimately be related to the different philosophical answers that such schools, trends or approaches give to questions concerning the nature or field of their investigation. Applied to linguistics, this means that differences between the structuralist school (in all its varied forms) and the generativist approach are related to diverging philosophical perspectives. This divergence can be explained only in part, as will become clear later, by relating them to empiricist and rationalist trends in linguistic thought, as Chomsky proposes. It is not my intention to repeat here all the arguments that have been produced in the cited literature — not the least of which is that the statement that linguistic theory is independent of philosophical assumptions is itself demonstrably an expression of a particular philosophical assumption. However, such arguments have seemed sufficiently persuasive to me to attempt an explanation of a systematic linguistic methodology that takes them seriously, especially in stating explicitly my reliance on a particular philosophical perspective. The development of this explanation is the major aim of this study.

Perhaps one's acceptance of the foundational character of philosophy is only possible if, with many other theorists, one has been persuaded that the goal of objectivity in academic studies is unattainable, and that any theory, even though it depends on facts, implies a selection and sifting of those facts that are relevant to the theory. Robinson (1975: 7) correctly assumes that unless "one knows what one is looking for there is nothing to find, and such knowing is not the result of objective observation", adding that the supposedly 'objective' approach might well be suffering from "the belief that if one stares long enough at the bits, at the sounds as sounds, they will somehow cohere ..." (1975: 8). Not only do the facts speak because practising scholars know the language that they speak, and can therefore give a fact its place in the coherent story of their discipline (Robinson 1975: 155), but we must also note that the facts speak to the scholars only because the coherence of their theoretical model is guaranteed by an integral philosophical framework.

If this is correct, the most one can hope to achieve in the development of a theoretical method is to spell out explicitly what the philosophical assumptions are that underlie it, and then proceed to consider the different arguments for or against the validity of the theory. Without any doubt these arguments will always have to revolve around the question whether the theory does justice to the facts — in the case of linguistics, in other words, whether the linguistic perspective that is adopted does not constitute a violation of our experiential knowledge of language. In the next chapter this requirement will be dealt with more fully.

Philosophical linguistics

If we now take the image that was used in the last section a little further, and apply it to the academic interest there may be in the philosophical groundwork of a particular room, say that of linguistics, one might say that the linguistic philosopher is concerned not so much with the shape of the furniture in the room (which would be of particular interest to the morphologist), but rather with the structure of the walls that separate and simultaneously link the room ('linguistic studies') with other rooms.

Properly speaking, one must distinguish between philosophy (as the foundational theoretical framework), philosophical linguistics[1] and the various linguistic sub-disciplines like semantics, syntax, morphology and phonology (or graphology in the case of written language).

The *linguistic methodology* that I wish to outline tentatively in this study belongs to what may be called philosophical linguistics. What one is looking for in such a methodology is not merely a question of linguistic technique or method, but the explanation and discovery of "new questions ..., new contributions to understanding, achieved perhaps with new 'methods'. And finally, new ideas and new principles ..." (Chomsky 1979: 179).

---

1. This is a term that must not be confused with the terms 'philosophy of language' or 'linguistic philosophy', both of which indicate theoretical studies with aims different from that of philosophical linguistics.

2 Developing a linguistic methodology

The structural-empirical method

The lingual aspect of experience analogically reflects the other modalities of or our world, and these analogies constitute the structural basis or transcendental conditions for language. The scientific investigation of these analogies is guided by a theoretical idea of language. The analysis that I wish to offer will attempt to clarify systematically the structural conditions for language and the factual lingual expressions that are regulated by these conditions in light of this theoretical idea. This is why the approach has been called the transcendental-empirical or structural-empirical method. I shall also attempt to demonstrate that this method constitutes a more adequate methodological explanation of linguistic theory than any empirical-inductive method, since the latter method of finding the 'universals of language' presupposes an insight into the systematic linguistic concepts that can only be discovered through an application of the transcendental-empirical method (Hommes: 1972: 2-16, 389).

Applied to linguistics, the structural-empirical method does not entail the vacuous categorization associated with an academic pigeon-holing exercise, but is an attempt to come to a systematic theoretical understanding of facts that have been dealt with in linguistic theory in the past. It comprises a linguistic methodology that tries "to discover how the categories recognized by everyone (under their different names) are to be integrated into a general theory, and to

Developing a linguistic methodology

refine and elaborate these categories" (Chomsky 1979: 155-156). It is a method that, therefore, entails a confrontation with and challenge to traditional and current linguistic theory on the basis of a discussion of the systematic relevance of these facts as they have been clarified in other theories.

Such a discussion of the systematic significance of other theories within the scope of one's own theory cannot — even though it strives to do complete justice to these theories — fail to entail also an aspect of reinterpretation. To Hjelmslev's earlier acknowledgement of this state of affairs (1963: 7) needs to be added only that a methodological reinterpretation may justifiably also *broaden* the empirical scope of the interpreted theory.

This aspect of reinterpretation is also the difficulty that Chomsky encountered in his 'reasonable' interpretation of structuralist linguistics. He observes (Chomsky 1979: 114) that, after selecting their corpus of lingual facts, these linguists *might* have claimed that their discovery procedures constitute the theory which, applied to the corpus, produces the grammar, and, furthermore, that such a discovery procedure is part of the speaker's genetic equipment. But, as Chomsky explains, structuralist linguists did in fact *not* make this claim. It nevertheless seems that this interpretation is a legitimate reconstruction, even though it conflicts with what most structuralist linguists intended (Chomsky 1979: 155); legitimate, too, because it is only within the scope of their own theories that linguists can explain what they believe to be the contribution, even if only implicit, in another theory (see the discussion of the term 'transformation', below, Chapter 9, as an instance of methodological reinterpretation). In the event of such a reinterpretation we have an example of giving new significance to old concepts (Chomsky 1979: 177).

What Greimas (1974: 67-68) has to say about the 'elementary structure of meaning' will go some way towards explaining what the theoretical intentions of the structural-empirical method are. This elementary structure, according to Greimas, contains abstract lingual categories which are indefinable universals such as 'relation', 'identity', 'difference', and 'generation'. These universals have 'interdependent' definitions organized in relational networks.

The structural-empirical method proposed in this study seeks to clarify and explain exactly these 'undefined or nondefinable universals of language' or meaning. Its hypothesis is that there are relational networks that exist between the lingual and other experiential aspects, and that these networks express the interdependence of the lingual aspect and the other aspects of our experience. The theoretical clarification of these interrelationships proceeds firstly from an analysis of various elementary linguistic concepts. The 'elementary structure' of the lingual aspect is not, as Greimas has it, of a logical nature, nor is it a mere theoretical 'construction' (Greimas 1974: 67, 68, 77, 78, 79), as will be shown; even though these networks of relationships may receive theoretical articulation in linguistic theory, they remain always the very real conditions for the production of concrete language on which such theorizing depends.

In short, the structural-empirical method is in the first place a systematic method, in that it is an attempt to systematize lingual facts and lingual norms, but it is also a method that is relevant to the history of linguistics as a discipline, because it offers a systematic discussion of how language theorists have contributed to an understanding of lingual norms and lingual facts. The systematic phase of the application of the method must therefore be complemented by a fully fledged historical study, but the latter lies outside the scope of the present study.

The limits of method-borrowing

One of the most complete and successful attempts at applying the structural-empirical method must surely be that of Hommes (1972), and, together with the earlier work of Strauss (1967), this is a study on which I have heavily relied. One must not conclude, however, from the successful application of the transcendental-empirical or structural-empirical method in other disciplines, that it is an intrinsically juridical, sociological or aesthetic method. It can, as a philosophically-conceived method, be applied to the fields of jurisprudence, sociology, aesthetics, linguistics or in fact any other discipline with equal validity, since it entails a particular view (cf. above, Chapter 1) of the relationship between philosophy and the various academic disciplines.

Therefore our employment of the structural-empirical method does not borrow from legal, sociological or aesthetic theory, but shares a philosophical basis with its application in those fields. Applied to our field of investigation, it is a method belonging to that particular zone of linguistic enquiry that may best be called philosophical linguistics, because it deals with the basic questions of linguistic theory — questions concerning the nature of language and the elementary and complex systematic linguistic concepts that must receive theoretical formulation in linguistic theory.

If one accepts that the methodology of any branch of theoretical enquiry necessarily involves giving answers to philosophical questions directly related to it, there need be no fear that one is adopting a method that is foreign to one's field of investigation. If philosophy forms the trunk of the academic tree, and linguistics one of the branches, then the posing of questions concerning the relation between linguistics and philosophy is perfectly in order. One must naturally be careful of borrowing from other disciplines. The effects of such borrowing have in the past sometimes tended to obscure instead of clarify linguistic phenomena, and the introduction of definitions employed by logic to semantics is an example of this (see below, Chapter 12).

The methodology of jurisprudence cannot, however, develop phonological distinctions, neither can semantic theory clarify theoretically the relation between legal cause and legal effect. But there are questions that are common to all fields; for example, sociology, jurisprudence and linguistics must all have a notion by which to distinguish between norm and fact, and although a legal norm will differ from a social convention or grammar rule, the jurist will discover that certain factual legal (juridical) events are regulated by a set of legal norms in the same way that the sociologist may find that people subject themselves to social conventions and patterns, or that the linguist may discover that people regard their lingual behavior as being subject to rules of grammar. There is nothing surprising to this: it is a common feature of diverse types of human action that it is governed by rules or norms.

In spite of the commonness of the concepts at a fundamental level, however, the account of the way in which the distinction between norm and fact operates will have to take into consideration the specified juridical, social, aesthetic or lingual context within which it occurs.

Only when the distinction between what is juridical, social or lingual in nature is honored, can one begin to formulate the limits of method-borrowing between jurisprudence, sociology and linguistics. If linguistics is to borrow from mathematics or logic, the linguist must therefore realize what the intrinsic limitations of such borrowing are. The facts of mathematics are of a numerical character, and the distinction between the numerical and lingual aspects is not an arbitrary one. The same applies to the employment of the categories of logic in linguistics. Linguists must not be surprised if they find that their use of a mathematical method in linguistic enquiry involves the imposition of severe restrictions necessitated by the lingual nature of the facts they are describing, restrictions that do not apply in the original field. The reason for this is that the required restrictions that appear to apply whenever there is a true case of method-borrowing are but an assertion of the limits of the various fields involved.

In short, linguistics must never be "a mere ancillary or derivative science ... Linguistics must attempt to grasp language, not as a conglomerate of non-linguistic (e.g. physical, physiological, psychological, sociological) phenomena, but as a self-sufficient totality, a structure *sui generis*" (Hjelmslev 1963: 5-6), because it is guided, characterized, indeed uniquely qualified by the lingual aspect of our experience.

General properties of language as linguistic universals in Chomsky's theory

General properties of language are to Chomsky biotically determined mechanisms (also see below, Chapter 10), if they are not to be merely historical accident and of no linguistic relevance (Chomsky 1978a: 37). And Chomsky says of the theory of language that he has developed since the conception of *The logical structure of linguistic theory* (Chomsky 1978a: 45):

> The principles of this theory ... define the linguistic universals that constitute 'the essence of language' (as distinct from accidental properties or properties determined by the exigencies of language use), and thus can be taken as one fundamental element in the characterization of the innate 'language faculty'.

From this observation it is clear that a rationalistic starting point, which entails that linguistic investigation should primarily be concerned with a theoretical analysis of normative lingual competence, is what prevents Chomsky from including in his definition of language universals 'properties determined by the exigencies of language use.'

But Chomsky's contribution is that — with other, statistically inclined approaches — he has unashamedly brought up the topic of linguistic universals, and if the above statements are stripped of their rationalistic overtones, they contain very concise and accurate remarks about the nature of linguistic investigation. One may quarrel over the question whether the linguistic 'schematism' that he identifies is of a genetically determined, biotic character, but the fact remains that the topic has been broached, and linguistic theory has been enriched as a result, because it can again tackle one of the basic theoretical issues of the discipline. After setting out our own position in the next two sections, we shall return to this theme in Chomsky's thought.

Similarity and difference between languages

"The similarity between languages," writes Hjelmslev (1963: 76), "is their very structural principle; the difference between languages is the carrying out of that principle *in concreto*," and with certain reservations the observation appears to me to be sound.

If the 'structural principle' of language is viewed as the lingual function of expression by means of signs (see below, Chapter 5), then it is certainly true that the lingually qualified structure of any conceivable concrete language has a structural similarity with every other language. The lingual qualifying function of language indeed operates also as a normative structure for concrete usage, and this explains why linguistic theory has to take into consideration the remarkable similarities between languages in spite of the fact, for example, that the normative requirements of inflexional and non-inflexional languages also embody distinct variations.

The concrete factuality of language is always made possible by a transcendental condition; it always entails the realization of a structural lingual principle, 'the carrying out of that principle *in concreto*.' As Hjelmslev (1963: 77) says: "Differences between languages ... rest on ... different realizations of a principle of formation ..."

This relationship between factual language and the normative structural lingual principle, called 'process' and 'system' respectively by Hjelmslev, is the point dealt with in the next section.

Norm and fact

I am in agreement with Dooyeweerd (1953 vol. 2: 8) that norm and fact, or "law and subject are mutually irreducible, notwithstanding the opinions of rationalists and irrationalists. Law and subject are only possible in their indissoluble correlation. The functional subject-side of the law-sphere is determined and delimited by the functional laws of the sphere." Translated into the terminology I have adopted, this means that norm (law) and fact (subject) are always distinct, but nonetheless unbreakably correlated (cf. too Dooyeweerd 1953 vol. 3: 97, and Hjelmslev 1963: 39), and the nature of this correlation is such that norms determine and regulate the facts within a given aspect (law-sphere) of experience.

The distinction between lingual norm and lingual fact has been formulated in various ways in linguistics: as 'langue' and 'parole' by De Saussure, or as 'competence' and 'performance' by Chomsky. For Chomsky's own view of the similarity between his and De Saussure's distinction, see his discussion with Parret (Chomsky 1974: 35). Greimas (1974: 57; cf. too Chomsky 1970: 10, 23 and Hjelmslev 1963: 39-40) very neatly summarizes Hjelmslev's position on this:

> Hjelmslev interpreted the opposition between langue and parole as a general opposition, common to all scientific approaches, between system and process, or, in linguistics, between paradigmatic and syntagmatic ... The opposition concerns both modes of organization of language considered as a semiotic system. But parallel to this, there exists another problem — the mode of existence of semiotic systems; there the Saussurean opposition between langue and parole was expressed, in Europe, by the opposition of the virtual to the actual, which corresponds *grosso modo* to Chomskyan competence and performance.

And Greimas makes another important interpretative addition to this by mentioning (1974: 57) that European linguistics reflects a social, collective idea of language as opposed to the psychological, individualistic conception of the Americans.

Lingual norm and lingual fact, in their mutual correlation and unbreakable coherence, are two aspects of what must be theoretically clarified, *viz.* both the normative structures or conditions for language and the factual, concrete language that is regulated by these structures. This is already implicitly stated by the name of the scientific methodology proposed by reformational philosophy, *viz.* the structural-empirical method. If the theoretical view is thus drawn too narrowly, the resulting method will be structurally and empirically inadequate.

In view of this last remark, it is significant to note that Chomsky's grammatical theory explicitly provides for the exclusion of certain lingual facts or data (an exclusion which, as will become clear in the subsequent discussion, is the result of a rationalistic starting point). Chomsky says that what is observed may often be irrelevant and insignificant, and that the relevance of data is in part determined by a systematic theory (Chomsky 1970: 28). Essentially the same point is made in his *Language and responsibility* (Chomsky 1979: especially 107-108).

Yet, in a sense, all theories of language proceed from a structural-empirical method. Though rationalist theories might be inclined to emphasize the one aspect and empiricist theories the other, the fact remains that even the most confident rationalist theory will have to make use of at least certain 'factual' data of language, gleaned, say, from an idealized native speaker's lingual competence; and even the most ardently persuasive empiricist theory has to recognize sooner or later that the order which the theorist finds in language cannot simply be disguised as an arbitrary order, because it is a *given* orderliness regulated by a normative lingual order, and not an orderliness that is created by the linguistic investigator. Expressed somewhat differently (Sampson 1979: 26): "*Both* experience *and* innate faculties are necessary to account for human knowledge" of language.

Structures and facts in Chomsky's thought

The relevance of the distinction between normative lingual structure and the factual data of language becomes even clearer when we explore this theme in Chomsky's thought a little further. If our definition of rationalism is that it entails an absolutization of the norm-side of reality, Chomsky's position on the relation between normative structures and factual data has a distinctly rationalist inclination. Whereas the actual data are degenerate, the grammar in Chomskyan terms remains an idealization (Chomsky 1978a: 12).

Like Carnap before him, who also attempted an outline of a general syntax applicable to any language (Carnap 1937: Foreword, p. xiv), Chomsky holds a rationalistic belief in the degeneracy of verbal languages; In 1937, Carnap (1937: 2) stated in that in "consequence of the unsystematic and logically imperfect structure of the natural word-languages (such as German or Latin), the statement of their rules of formation and transformation" would be extremely complicated. He therefore advocated, as Chomsky was to do twenty years later, a syntactic study concerned with the formal structure of language, and distinguished between pure and descriptive syntax. The latter is concerned with what Chomsky has termed 'performance', since it accounts for "the syntactical properties and relations of empirically given expressions" (Carnap 1937: 7), while the former is concerned with the possible arrangements of elements that need not be actually realized (Carnap 1937: 6-7).

Since, for Carnap, the "difference between syntactical rules ... and the logical rules of deduction is only the difference between *formation rules* and *transformation rules*, both of which are completely formulable in syntactical terms" (1937: 2; emphases in the original), we must first "leave aside the question of the formal deficiencies of the word-languages, and, by the consideration of examples, proceed to convince ourselves that rules of formation and transformation are of like nature, and that both permit of being formally apprehended" (Carnap 1937: 2).[2] Carnap then proceeds to give an example that antedates the now infamous Chomskyan sentence "Colorless green ideas sleep furiously." The fact that "Pirots karulize elatically" is a sentence, says Carnap, can be gathered from the form of the words in a well-constructed language (1937: 2).

Chomsky's position is thus one of 'R' (rationalist) rather than 'E'

---

2. I am unable to say whether, among the formidable technicalities of Carnap's theory, there are further parallels between his and Chomsky's work and points of view. This would require a further and more detailed study.

Developing a linguistic methodology

(empiricist) (see Chomsky 1975: 146 ff.), and his view of the relation of lingual structures and lingual facts is embedded within the contours of 'knowledge' and 'intuition' (Chomsky 1978a: 37; cf. too 1965: 8-9):

> A grammar determined by a linguistic theory (given data) constitutes a hypothesis concerning the speaker-hearer's knowledge of his language and is to be confirmed or disconfirmed in terms of empirical evidence drawn, ultimately, from investigation of the linguistic intuitions of the language user ...

Put like this, Chomsky's remarks appear merely to restate the point of view of a structural-empirical method. The point is, however, that although Chomsky may be credited with views closely allied to this type of theory, the rational formalization of linguistic knowledge that he attempts eventually expels the idea of a subjective (factual) intuition from his theory: " ... an investigation of the adequacy of a proposed general theory is of course possible only under the condition that 'intuition' and similarly obscure terms do not appear in the theory itself," he remarks (Chomsky 1978a: 63-64).

It is therefore apparent that Chomsky restricts his analysis to the restrictive elementary linguistic concepts (lingual knowledge and competence), while refusing to investigate 'obscure' notions (linguistic ideas) such as (a pre-theoretical) lingual intuition — although these ideas are a necessary stepping stone for the initial formulation of his field of investigation (see below, pp. 25, 44).

It is not unlikely that the theoretical restriction to what can be rigorously applied after formulation is the result of a more thoroughly rationalist turn that Chomsky's thought underwent in the shift from testing the adequacy of the theory by means of the acceptability of an utterance to an adult native speaker (and such a person's lingual intuition), to its abandonment in favor of the ideal speaker's lingual competence (cf. Reichling 1969: 78).

This rationalism is also responsible for causing Chomsky to deny that his generative grammatical model is a model for the production of speech, or a statement on how a speaker would proceed to construct a derivation (Chomsky 1965: 9; cf. too 139-140). Even though Chomsky may understand the device of the internalized generative grammar to be actually put to use in the understanding of utterances (1970: 10), the questions of production and construction of lingual utterances belong to him to a theory of language use (performance).

Chomsky strives, in other words, to separate effectively lingual competence and performance, by insisting that the system of linguistic competence which underlies behavior is not realized in any direct or simple way in behavior (Chomsky 1972a: 4).

The rules of grammar, then, sometimes have in Chomsky's theory the peculiar quality of not always determining or regulating lingual facts that are subject to them, since they only aim at describing a normative lingual competence (Chomsky 1975: 189):

> The rules of English grammar do not determine what speakers will do in anything remotely like the sense in which the law of falling bodies determines that if people jump from a building, they will hit the ground in a specifiable time. All the rules of grammar tell us is that a person will (ideally) understand and analyze a sentence in certain ways, not others — a very different matter.

This seems to be quite a crucial point, for at least two reasons: (a) Indeed, physical laws do not determine the movement of physical subjects in the same ways as a grammar determines what lingual subjects (speakers) will do, but factual lingual utterances are nevertheless determined (be it in a lingual way) by grammar rules. Of course there are differences between physical laws and grammar rules, not the least of which is that lingual subjects will have freedom of choice between various alternative possibilities that may all be grammatically acceptable (in the sense of being applications of the same valid rules of grammar), whereas the movement of physical subjects and objects is determined strictly by physical laws. But then physical laws and grammatical rules will be similar in having (physical or lingual) facts which are *subject to them* in the sense of being determined by them. It is only on the basis of this *similarity* between physical *law* and lingual *norm* that we are in fact able to *distinguish* theoretically between the different ways in which laws and norms operate, since analytical distinction is only possible on the basis of some common property; (b) it is interesting to note, secondly, that the rules of grammar tell us only that a person will *understand* a sentence in a certain way. Chomsky is still focusing his attention strictly on a rational understanding and not on subjective lingual production or performance.

Chomsky's position on lingual norm and lingual fact is not, however, unequivocally rationalist: he does at times take notice of the inseparability of 'structures' and empirical 'data'. Take, for example, the cautious note he strikes in the following passage (1972a: 111-112):

> So far, the study of language has progressed on the basis of a certain abstraction ... (i.e.) the working hypothesis that we can proceed with the study of 'knowledge of language' — what is often called 'linguistic competence' — in abstraction from the problems of how language is used ... Still, caution is in order. It may be that the next great advance in the study of language will require the forging of new intellectual tools that permit us to bring into consideration a variety of questions that have been cast into the waste-bin of 'pragmatics' ...

Here Chomsky is at least attempting to remove the rougher edges of a dogmatic rationalism. Whether the advance that he foresees will in fact abandon the rationalist leanings inherent in the theory of transformational grammar is of course another question. The problem of the separability or inseparability of lingual competence or knowledge and lingual performance will be discussed again below when we deal with the elementary linguistic concepts of lingual process and lingual competence (see below, Chapters 9 and 13).

Chomsky and Kant

All post-Kantian thinkers are in a certain sense Kantian philosophers, or at least view the history of scientific thought from a Kantian perspective. When we pick up some of the Kantian overtones in Chomsky's thought, the theme of structures and facts that was discussed in the last section will therefore at once acquire some historical relief.

In linking his theory to that of Descartes, Chomsky has himself partially obscured his indebtedness to Kant, and this makes the investigation of the Kantian heritage in his theory all the more necessary and interesting.

There is little doubt that Chomsky's distinction between 'formal' and 'substantive' linguistic universals (1965: 28-29) relies on Kant's scheme of form and matter. Chomsky's indebtedness to Kant is also evident, furthermore, when he quotes Konrad Lorenz (with whom he is in agreement) to the effect that one can shed light on the a priori *forms* of human thought that, as innate forms, categorize the *data* of experience (Chomsky 1972a: 95), and when he speaks of the human mind being "innately endowed with the structures of the postulated constructional system and with a procedure for applying the primitive notions to the data of sense" (Chomsky 1978a: 35). The concepts of 'knowledge' and 'intuition' referred to in the previous section also have a distinctly Kantian flavor.

Typically Kantian too, it seems to me, is Chomsky's notion (1975: 12; cf. too 147-148, 154) that the "faculty of language ... provides a sensory system for the preliminary analysis of linguistic data, and a schematism that determines, quite narrowly, a certain class of grammars." Neither has Chomsky's theory of language learning departed radically from the Kantian form-matter scheme. To him, perception of the experiential data of language is determined by 'theory formation' about language through processing this data by means of the innate properties of universal grammar: therefore the so-called 'innateness hypothesis' "will consist of several elements: principles for the preliminary, pretheoretic analysis of data as experience, which serves as an input to LT (H,L) [i.e. learning theory for humans in the domain of language - AJW]; properties of UG [universal grammar] which determine the character of what is learned" (Chomsky 1975: 34).

The Kantian form-matter scheme is also evident in the initial distinction made by Chomsky between deep and surface structure. After remarking that the syntactic component consists of a base that generates deep structures and a transformational part that maps them into surface structures, he goes on to state that the deep structure of a sentence is submitted to the semantic component for semantic interpretation, and its surface structure enters the phonological component and undergoes phonetic interpretation (Chomsky 1965: 135), before he concludes: "One major function of the transformational rules is to convert an abstract deep structure that expresses the *content* of a sentence into a fairly concrete surface structure that indicates its *form*" (1965: 136; emphases added).

Schematically, the picture in *Aspects of the theory of syntax* (Chom-

Developing a linguistic methodology

sky 1965) looks like this:

Syntactic component

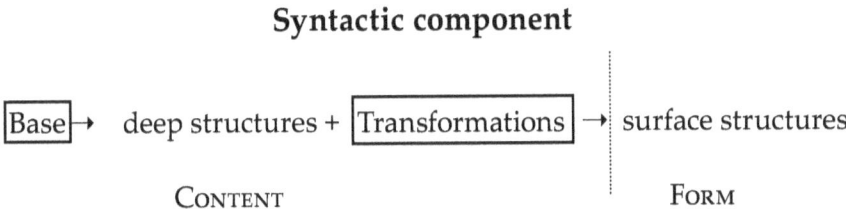

CONTENT FORM

For his own scheme, see Chomsky (1979: 137 and 1972a: 140; see also 1975: 80 ff. and, for the 'extended standard theory' version, especially 1975: 104-105). In his 'extended standard theory' (EST), Chomsky has modified his position to the extent that "perhaps all *semantic* information is determined by a somewhat enriched notion of surface structure" (Chomsky 1975: 82; emphasis added). The further explanation of this in *Language and responsibility* yields the alternative scheme (Chomsky 1979: 165; cf. too 150-152, 163 ff.):

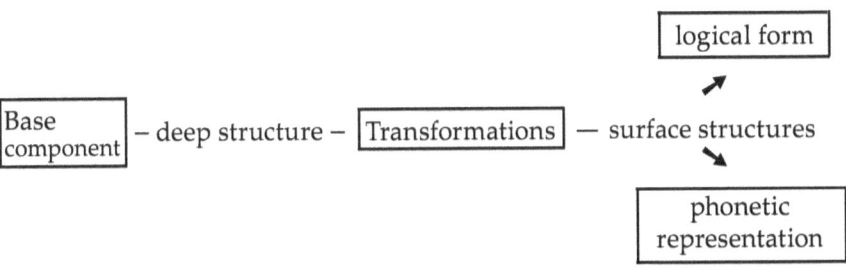

Here, "surface structures are associated by ... rules to representations of sound (phonetic representation) and meaning (logical form)," and by the phrase 'logical form' Chomsky means "that partial representation of meaning that is determined by grammatical structure" (Chomsky 1979: 165; cf. too 168). What is interesting to note, too, is that surface structure is something *quite abstract*, involving properties that do not appear in the physical form (Chomsky 1979: 175); more abstract even than the earlier concept of surface structures, since it now includes traces (1979: 177).

The shift in Chomsky's position on this point is already evident in some pronouncements in *Language and mind* (1972a: 31, 59, 60, 107-111, and also 126), and the modification raises a question of interpretation. If the thesis that Kant's influence on Chomsky has been undervalued up to now is correct, the question is whether this modification constitutes an abandonment of the Kantian form-matter scheme.

The answer would seem to be no. A possible reason for the modification is set out below (see p. 46); but it is to be noted here that in the very work by Chomsky that explains the modification of the standard theory in the EST, he still holds (and within same context) to the Kantian form-matter scheme as far as language learning is concerned (see above, and Chomsky 1979: 168). The more proper question to ask, then, is whether Chomsky has, in both the standard theory and the EST, merely given a transformationalist reinterpretation to the traditional distinction between form and content, or whether he has abandoned it entirely in favor of a radically different interpretation. The former seems to be more likely, and if so, Chomsky has in principle not abandoned the Kantian form-matter scheme that has been with language theorists since the days of Von Humboldt and De Saussure (1966).

One of the few references in Chomsky's work to Kant is in fact made within the scope of the form-matter scheme, and specifically concerns the question whether the schematism of human understanding enables us to speak, eventually, of scientific progress (Chomsky 1975: 156). Exactly the same passage from Kant is quoted in *Problems of knowledge and freedom*, Chomsky's Russell lectures at Cambridge (1972b: 17).

Sampson (1979: 120), too, has indicated that Chomsky's brand of rationalism is closer to that of Kant than it is to Cartesian rationalism. Sampson's observation in this regard is one of the few references in the linguistic literature to Kant's influence on transformational grammar, and deserves to be noted.

In the next section attention will be paid to yet another, even more fundamental reason for an investigation of the Kantian elements in Chomsky's thought.

Freedom and determinism

Freedom versus determinism has been a recurrent theme in the history of linguistics, and has assumed many shapes and forms in

Developing a linguistic methodology

language theory, masquerading either as the dialectic of freedom and constraint or as the duality of 'creativity' and mechanical device. As an example one might take the chapter on the "Creative aspect of language use" in *Cartesian linguistics*, where Chomsky (1966) summarizes the Cartesian view as one that regards language as being free from stimulus control and not serving a merely communicative function; language is rather an instrument for the free expression of thought and for appropriate response to new situations. Chomsky invokes the Cartesian distinction between human and animal, pointing out that to Descartes animal behavior is instinctive, and therefore explicable in 'mechanical' terms (Chomsky 1966: 13).

Throughout this chapter it is clear that Chomsky's concern is to illustrate the Cartesian opposition between freedom and determinism, as is evident from the following passage (Chomsky 1966: 6):

> In summary, it is the diversity of human behavior, its appropriateness to new situations, and man's capacity to innovate — the creative aspect of language use providing the princip(al?) indication of this — that leads Descartes to attribute possession of mind to other humans, since he regards this capacity as beyond the limitations of any imaginable mechanism. Thus a fully adequate psychology requires the postulation of a 'creative principle' alongside of the 'mechanical principle' ...

Essentially the same point is made in Language and mind (Chomsky 1972a: 11): "...the generative ability... is revealed in the normal human use of language as a free instrument of thought. If by experiment we convince ourselves that another organism gives evidence of the normal, creative use of language, we must suppose that it, like us, has a mind and that what it does lies beyond the bounds of mechanical explanation ...". That Chomsky intends to define his own position in terms of the Cartesian opposition that he describes, is at least a sub-theme of the chapter in Cartesian linguistics that was referred to above. This is why, for example, Chomsky is able to criticize Von Humboldt for not clearly distinguishing between rule-governed creativity and innovative grammatical modification (Chomsky 1966: 27-28).

The scales are tipped in favor of the freedom motive in Chomsky's theory, for, according to him, the normal, creative use of language lies outside the framework of stimulus-response psychology, i.e. it is free from being controlled by external (or internal) stimuli. This is why language can serve as an instrument of thought and self-expression (1972a: 12).

The conflict between freedom and determinism in Chomsky's linguistic theory derives mainly from the fact that the human's capacity for language learning is biologically *determined* (Chomsky 1975: 39; cf. too 4, 34.), whereas, simultaneously, the use of language reflects the human's *freedom* and creativeness, those qualities that set him apart from 'nonhuman organisms' (Chomsky 1975: 40). In essence, for Chomsky, humans have infinite capacities, but can nonetheless never escape from the limitations imposed by their biological nature (1975: 124; cf. too 125-134, for the historical concern of rationalism with human freedom). Sampson's disagreement with Chomsky over the use of the term 'creativity' revolves around the self-same opposition of freedom and constraint, for, remarks Sampson (1979: 108), when Chomsky calls humans creative, he is merely referring to the human ability to conform to certain fixed, rigorous rules. To Sampson this conformity to rule undermines the very nature of what we should understand by the human's (unpredictable) creative freedom.

That Chomsky has opted for the rationalist idea of freedom is clear. While empiricism has made a significant contribution to freedom, it is, in his view, the task of a libertarian social theory to

> refute Bertrand Russell's pessimistic speculation that man's 'passions and instincts' render him incapable of enjoying the benefits of the 'scientific civilization' that reason can create ..., at least if we understand 'passions and instincts' (as Russell sometimes did) to include the 'instincts' that provide the basis for the achievements of the creative intellect, as well as the 'instinct of revolt' against imposed authority — in some measure, a common human attribute. Rather, success in this endeavor might reveal that these passions and instincts may yet succeed in bringing to a close what Marx called the 'prehistory of human society'. No longer repressed and distorted by competitive and authoritarian social structures, these passions and instincts may set the stage for a new scientific civilization in which 'animal nature' is transcended and human nature can truly flourish (Chomsky 1975: 133-134).

Here the naked secularism of humanism, especially its freedom ideal, is linked to the 'instinct of revolt' against authority, and the radical doctrine of humans transcending their 'animal nature' in true human freedom. In the same way that the humanistic freedom motive immediately allied itself to the ideal of science upon its inception in the Renaissance, the ideal of the free human personality in Chomsky joins hands with, and sets the stage for a new scientific civilization. What makes the radical secularism of this passage all the more remarkable, especially in view of the age-old positivist dream of an 'objective' or neutral scientific analysis, is that it forms the conclusion to an essay entitled "Some general features of language". No-one can divorce Chomskyan linguistics from its humanistic roots, because its whole conception is based upon this. And it is exactly this root, with its intrinsic dualism between freedom and determinism, that is one of the *often neglected* implications of Chomsky's theory. Would one, on the basis of this duality, be able to hold, for example, that the human's biologically *determined* mechanisms of mind will themselves be altered to enable them to enjoy their newly found human freedom, after they have transcended the barrier of their animal nature?

That humanism, and not in the first place the rationalistic mould in which it is cast, is the true foundation for the dualism between creativity and rule, or between nature and freedom, is clear also from Chomsky's self-confessed humanistic starting point, one that he shares with Russell (even though the latter's thought retains a strong 'empiricist flavor'). For at the end of the first Russell lecture, he first states that an investigation of the most ordinary achievements of the human mind, such as the use of language, are characterized by free creation, before drawing this conclusion (Chomsky 1972b: 46):

> I think it is fair to say that it is the humanistic conception of man that is advanced and given substance as we discover the rich systems of invariant structures and principles that underlie the most ordinary and humble of human accomplishments.

If one is to believe Bruns (1975: 233-234), the dialectic of freedom and determinism in another way also defines the *conflict between structuralism and the phenomenology of language* in the history of linguistic thought, because the structuralist views the sign as a negative Entity:

its being lies in what it is not, i.e. in its systematic opposition to other objective lingual units: "Removed from the system, it ceases to be anything at all." Bruns continues: "For Heidegger, however, the sign must escape its bondage to system, for it is a mediation in a discourse whose subject is a presence that can never be reduced to the status of a signified."

Contrary to Hjelmslev's conclusion (1963: 127) at the end of his *Prolegomena*, that structuralism, after having established an immanent point of departure for linguistic theory, "to the apparent cost of fluctuation and nuance, life and concrete physical and phenomenological reality" may eventually "elicit from language itself its secret" and arrive at its true goal (*humanitas et universitas*), Bruns restricts the structuralist contribution to the dialectical opposite of freedom, viz. bondage to system, which must be escaped if language is viewed from the angle of the freedom motive. In a somewhat generalizing statement, Bruns (1975: 235) continues to elaborate this polarity:

> For the structuralists, the sign is a closed, empty form ... For Heidegger, however, the sign is open — or rather it is an opening through which the world of things is allowed to make its appearance.

Nevertheless, Bruns deplores this dialectical opposition, and proposes that we must seek to overcome it by adopting an interpretive, historical attitude (1975: 240 ff.; also see below, Chapter 14, where Bruns's distinctions are dealt with within the context of the distinction between linguistic concept and linguistic idea). But the pervasive influence of the theme of freedom versus constraint *in* the history of linguistic thought shows that the nature of this dualism is itself more than historical, and therefore cannot be overcome merely by adopting an historical attitude. If this dualism were a mere historical phenomenon, an interpretive, historical attitude would not be able to synthesize the polar opposition of freedom and determinism. This dialectic reflects, rather, the spiritual dialectic inherent in the basic motive of humanism — a dialectic that the structural-empirical method also seeks to overcome, but in a different way.

Linguistic ideas

Before we return below to an elaboration of the notion of linguistic ideas, as well as to the distinction between linguistic concepts and linguistic ideas, we should note that, like all other theories, linguistic theory is guided by theoretical, linguistic ideas, which in turn are shaped by a pre-theoretical, 'practical' idea of what language is. There can thus be no question of 'objective', neutral data which shape our theories of language. In fact, a theory of language can be drawn up in hypothetical form before empirical evidence is produced in support of the theoretical claims of such a theory; yet we know that theoretical investigation and collection and organization of data go hand in hand, being interdependent activities (Chomsky 1978a: 58). But one cannot describe a lingual system in any meaningful way, Chomsky says, without a conception of the nature of such a system, and he adds: "The development of a conceptually complete theory of linguistic structure may be an essential step toward obtaining evidence which will ultimately give this theory its empirical support" (Chomsky: 1978a: 58).

Chomsky has here formulated two fundamental truths of scientific, and therefore also linguistic analysis: (a) it is guided by a pre-theoretical idea of what is to be analyzed (i.e. it must have some conception of the nature of a lingual system) and (b) it is only in light of a theory, developed on the basis of the pre-theoretical idea, that one may discover *facts* that support the theory.

Lingual principles

This means that the human has, quite apart from scientific, theoretical analysis, an implicit or explicit knowledge of fundamental lingual principles that underlie the ordinary use of language. And because our pre-theoretical experience of language is much richer than the rational, scientific analysis of language, one can only discover upon analysis certain normative moments, the latter being reflections in the theory of the lingual principles that determine our day to day employment of language. Our language is always determined by these lingual principles, whether the scientist takes care to analyze them or not.

One of the basic assumptions of the reformational philosophy that has become known as the philosophy of the cosmonomic idea is that reality is orderly, and that in the experience of reality we may distinguish various modal aspects that follow one another in the order of time. One may distinguish, for instance, aspects of number and space, of kinematic movement and energy, and an organic (biotic) modus as well as a sensitive aspect of feeling. But there are also analytical, historical, lingual, social and economic functions in the order of time, and if the analysis of these transcendental modi is extended, one may also discover that reality contains aesthetic, juridical and ethical aspects, including a confessional aspect of belief.

In the case of the first six aspects mentioned here, the modal laws that determine how concrete objects function in these spheres have the character of natural laws, but from the logical sphere onwards the modal laws are given only as regulative principles which cannot be realized on the factual side without rational consideration or distinction (Dooyeweerd 1953 vol. 2: 237). Yet this rational consideration and distinction is of a pre-theoretical nature, and we must not confuse it with the abstracting methods of theory formation.

Since the lingual aspect has not only a post-logical (analytical) position in the order of time, but follows also after the historical (more accurately called the 'formative') aspect, the normative lingual principles that determine the factual use of language require a variable formation and formulation, by means of which "they become positive norms accommodated in a more or less adequate way to the course of cultural development" (Dooyeweerd 1953 vol. 2: 237).

Whereas in the pre-logical aspects of reality the modal laws are realized in the facts without human intervention, the opposite is true of post-logical modal principles, that only offer a rule of conduct to human judgment, since a principle requires human formation for its further specification and formulation (Dooyeweerd 1953 vol. 2: 237-238). The super-arbitrary normative content is given in principle only (1953 vol. 2: 238) and acquires a concrete sense through human positivizing of normative principles. This means that also in the case of the lingual aspect, the modal laws of which characterize the concretely factual language that we use, there is to be found a subjective moment in the form of the human formative will, operating on the norm-side in the human formation and formulation of lingual principles (Dooyeweerd 1953 vol. 2: 239). While one can therefore give a positive formulation to lingual principles in the concrete form of lingual norms, the structural lingual principles are nonetheless preserved and saved from human arbitrariness (Dooyeweerd 1953 vol. 2: 336). These principles remain the relatively constant starting-points for any normative formulation of their content.

Elementary and complex linguistic concepts

A distinction can now be drawn between the elementary and complex systematic concepts that are investigated in linguistic theory.

The investigation of elementary concepts in linguistics, to which this study is limited, comprises an enquiry into the structure of the lingual aspect of reality, and the way that this experiential mode coheres, by way of analogy, with other aspects in the order of time.

This analysis will not prove fruitful if the various complex systematic linguistic concepts that can be understood only in light of an analysis of the different analogical, elementary concepts are not also brought into play, for the one cannot do theoretically without the other, as will become clear subsequently. Since the main focus of this study is the different elementary linguistic concepts, a few preliminary remarks must first be made, therefore, about complex linguistic concepts.

The three major complex linguistic concepts that can be distinguished are (a) the categorial relation of lingual norm and lingual fact; (b) the categorial relation between lingual subject, i.e. the human being who produces language in response to lingual norms, and lingual object, which is the concrete language that is produced in this response; and (c) the categorial lingual relation between the origin, acquisition, growth, maturation and extinction of language.

To the first complex linguistic concept mentioned here a large section of this chapter was devoted, and it will receive further attention in the outline that I wish to give below of the elementary linguistic concepts. Since the complex linguistic concepts are totality-concepts in terms of the various elementary modal concepts, because they function in all aspects of reality, this holds for all three complex linguistic concepts mentioned above.

As regards the second complex linguistic concept, that of the relation between the human lingual subject and the lingual object of concrete language that is produced by this subject, it is to be noted here that the objective realization of signs inseparably coheres with subjective human signification, and is independent of a second person. A second person enters the picture of this complex linguistic concept only in the actualization of the lingually qualified structure of the objective lingual fact of something like an utterance, paragraph, chapter, speech or book. Bruns's discussion of Ricoeur's distinction between 'virtual' and 'actual' — a discussion of writing as an objective lingual fact that remains lingually virtual until it is actualized by reading or interpretation (Bruns 1975: 252) — deals with this complex linguistic concept.

The rise of semiotics has once again drawn attention to the existence of subjective and objective lingual facts that do not necessarily have a lingual qualification in their typical individuality structures, and have long been excluded from linguistic study in reductionist approaches. The lingual aspect of reality functions as an aspect of all concrete things, whether these things belong to the natural environment or to our cultural life. It is this function of the lingual aspect in every conceivable factual thing, process, event or concrete object or subject, that is the focus of Greimas's remarks about the 'semiotization of nature', and that leads him to conclude (1974: 78) that "semiotics ... explores the world in trying to extract from it all the *modi significandi.*" And it is also the objective lingual factuality of concrete events and processes that eventually leads Hjelmslev (1963: 127) to declare in the final pages of his *Prolegomena* that "all those entities which in the first instance ... had to be provisionally eliminated as non-semiotic elements, are reintroduced as necessary components into semiotic structures ... Accordingly," Hjelmslev concludes, "we find no non-semiotics that are not components of semiotics, and, in the final instance, no object that is not illuminated from the key position of linguistic theory. Semiotic structure is revealed as a stand from which all scientific objects may be viewed."

The third complex linguistic concept, especially in its concern with the acquisition of language, has acquired a richer significance in recent linguistic study due to the Chomskyan emphasis on a language acquisition device. Although this complex linguistic concept also falls outside the systematic purview of an investigation of the elementary linguistic concepts, some attention will be given to it below in so far as it is defined by the latter set of concepts.

Developing a linguistic methodology

Among the elementary linguistic concepts, a systematic distinction must also be made between linguistic concepts and linguistic ideas. The analogical reflections that the aspects which precede the lingual in the order of time have within the structure of the lingual modus of signification are called retrocipations, and the study of these analogical coherences is limited to restrictive, constitutive elementary concepts. On the other hand, the analogies within the structure of the lingual aspect which express the coherence between the lingual aspect and those that follow it in the time-order of experiential modi are true anticipations that can be formulated in a theory of language only in the form of (elementary) linguistic limiting concepts or ideas.

The material distinctions that can be made to distinguish the typically different lingual spheres, and that are discussed in detail in Chapter 4 below, are indeed *complicated* linguistic limiting concepts or ideas, but by definition belong systematically to the *elementary* linguistic ideas investigated by sociolinguistics. These material spheres in which our everyday uses of language are set are therefore not truly *complex* linguistic concepts. They will acquire further relief, after the initial discussion in Chapter 4, in the chapter dealing with social anticipations in the structure of the lingual aspect (see Chapter 14, below).

3 Sample of a previous attempt

The language philosopher today need make no apologies for an interest in the field of philosophical linguistics. One reason for this may be that, after Chomsky had written a study entitled *Cartesian linguistics* (Chomsky 1966), philosophy and the philosophical assumptions on which linguistics is based have once more become topical in linguistic studies. Another reason is that linguistics, if it is to assume a critical attitude, needs philosophical perspectives from which it can answer at least some of the perplexing questions raised by the history of linguistic thought. How is one to understand, from a purely linguistic perspective, the different approaches known as 'structuralism', 'transformationalism', 'behaviorism' and 'mentalism', for example? All claim to be purely 'linguistic' approaches, and most would call the empirical facts or some aspect of language as witness that theirs is the most objectively verifiable linguistic description; and yet it cannot be denied that all these approaches are either essentially, or at the very least in broad outline, different. This is the point where linguists need a consistent philosophical groundwork against which they can test and evaluate the theoretical perspectives upon which all linguistic descriptions are based.

The third reason why philosophical linguistics has once more become topical in our time is the academic disillusionment with all the linguistic studies that have claimed either to be or to have been founded upon purely linguistic perspectives. Today's linguist cannot in all honesty claim to have found this purely linguistic approach. It may be true that linguistics may have wrested itself free from the grip of 19th century positivism and from other philosophical or historical approaches to language, but the fact remains that this development away from certain philosophical assumptions in the study of language has been influenced by other, opposing philosophical theses. In fine: the claim that linguistics has freed itself from philosophy is, ironically, itself no purely linguistic statement, but a philosophical one. If linguistics is to comment theoretically on language, it cannot simultaneously be competent to comment on itself, because linguistic theory, although expressed in language, is not a lingually structured activity, and does not have as one of its aims an analytically qualified self-clarification. When linguists comment upon linguistics, such commentary not only needs, but is either implicitly or explicitly based upon a theoretical philosophical perspective. Comment in academic discourse upon the nature and field of one's study irrevocably enters the realm of the philosophical foundations of the discipline.

It is in light of these introductory remarks that an assessment of the linguistics of P.A. Verburg can be made in this chapter. The intention is to take his linguistic theory as a sample of a linguistic methodology founded upon reformational philosophy.

P.A. Verburg's linguistic theory is one of the most complex attempts to base a theoretical perspective of language on a consistent philosophy — in his case the philosophy of the cosmonomic idea — and although various other attempts have been made to achieve this, notably by De Jongste (1949, 1956), Strauss (1967) and Yallop (1978), Verburg has been chosen as an illustrative example of both the weak and the strong points of such an approach.

An analysis of the linguistic perspective upon which this approach is based will reveal that Verburg's views are on the one hand a linguistic development of the basic assumptions of the philosophy of the cosmonomic idea and on the other a rather radical modification of these ideas.

Let me mention first some of the points of agreement between Verburg and the philosophy of the cosmonomic idea.

In the first instance, one would have to note that Verburg's use of the terms 'clarify' and 'clarification' as definitive or descriptive of what characterizes language, is much closer than one would expect at first glance to the terms 'signify' and 'signification' that are consistently employed toward the same end by reformational philosophy. It is also clear that, in spite of his intention to describe language as 'clarification' (cf. Verburg 1965: 78; also 1971: 271), Verburg implicitly (and perhaps unwarily) acknowledges that language is to be characterized by the terms signification (Verburg 1971: 281) or 'revelation' (1965: 78, 85).

It would indeed appear that Verburg's notion of clarity serves better as an indication of a normative moment in the anticipatory structure of the lingual aspect than as a formulation of the modal meaning-kernel of the lingual aspect of reality, that qualifies all concrete uses of language. Verburg himself has to acknowledge this when he states that one's fellow human beings are the ones for whose sake one is normally bound to be as clear as possible. But this makes it perfectly obvious that communicativity lies in the anticipatory direction — it is indeed a social anticipation within the lingual aspect — and thus cannot be employed also to characterize the modal meaning-kernel of the lingual aspect, that stamps its restrictive, retrocipatory structure.

Furthermore: Verburg is himself an outspoken critic of the idea that language can be characterized by the term 'communication' (Verburg 1965: 97):

> We think nothing is gained by connecting the idea of language with or subsuming it under 'communication'. In our opinion communication is so much a universal concept that it contains no specificity whatever that could define language ... To demonstrate the universality of communication we point to the fact that it ranges from inter-molecular physical communication up to inter-human highly spiritual communication. For this reason a thesis as: 'Language is communication' is almost as insignificant as 'Language is something'.

It is puzzling that Verburg can, on the one hand, link up the idea of clarification (used by him to characterize language) with the communicative function, and on the other hand ardently oppose the notion that language is communication.

Secondly, one would have to give Verburg credit for including all human signs under the terms 'clarity' and 'language'. Cf. for example his observation (1965: 78): "Oral and gestural, auditory and visual language may both be regarded as *delotic* acts, as acts originating from the human desire for *clarification* (or revelation in the case of self-clarification)". This is also what Verburg (1951: 22) admires most in the thought of De Saussure. In view of this, it would be reasonable to presume that his 'delotic model' (1965: 93) can also be interpreted as an 'expressive model', but Verburg would not fully agree with this interpretation: "*In* de clarificatie ... speelt de significatie ... of *betekening* een ondergeschikte rol," he says (1971: 276). Therefore, as he remarks in a note (1971: 282), it is not to be recommended that we conceive of linguistics as the 'science of signs': such descriptions confuse the authentic and characteristic aspect of what he terms the delotic act with the sub-aspect of the lexico-semantic sign.

Two critical comments may shed light on this last remark. In the first instance, Verburg seems here to be identifying the human signaling action or subjective signification with the objective meaning of lingual facts. I think there is good reason to suppose that the meaning of a lingual fact is closely related to its objective lingual identity or distinctiveness, and that the meaning of a word is thus indeed in its turn related to the analytical element in the structure of the lingual aspect (Verburg calls it its 'lexico-semantic' element). But meaning simply is not signification, and vice versa. They are but the objective and subjective sides of the same lingual coin. In the second instance, when we examine Verburg's position on this point (1965: 98), we see that clarity is to be understood rather as norm for language than as a characterization of language. However, language is by its nature symbolic signification or expression; whether that expression is clear or obscure (cf. Verburg 1971: 282, note 5) is a matter of judging it in terms of norms.

We can wholeheartedly agree with Verburg (1965: 98) that the norms for language are criteria that we apply in everyday life and that the knowledge that we have of these criteria is of a pre-theoretical nature, but the fact remains that the notion of clarity is useful only in the anticipatory, transcendental direction of time as a norm-idea (Verburg 1965: 98, 99) that guides the opening-up of the structure of the lingual aspect and the concrete, factual language that is qualified by this aspect.

Verburg is also close to the philosophy of the cosmonomic idea in stressing the situation as "a necessary postulate in linguistics" (1965: 81-82; cf. too 1971: 271-273). Language without a theme, embedded in a situation, is pseudo-language, he claims. A specimen sentence like Chomsky's "Colorless green ideas sleep furiously" cannot merit serious linguistic attention any more than an artificial flower can require the attention of the botanist (Verburg 1971: 272).

Another bonus point of Verburg's linguistics is that it wishes to draw into the scope of theoretical linguistic analysis the results of both synchronic and diachronic information: "Delotics wants to be allergic neither for introspective, nor for *historical* information" he observes (1965: 97). This remark is aimed against De Saussure, who claims (1966: 83) that the "opposition between the two viewpoints, the synchronic and the diachronic, is absolute and allows no compromise". Verburg's position seems wholly compatible with the attitude taken by reformational approaches in linguistics, simply because a consistently worked out, philosophically founded approach has to confront, challenge or agree at almost every turn with the work of any linguist, from whatever school of thought. Both synchronic and diachronic approaches have made, and must make, contributions to linguistics.

Verburg's thought is, however, closest to that of the philosophy of the cosmonomic idea in the assumption that language, or more specifically the lingual aspect of reality that qualifies and structures language, is not self-sufficient and therefore does not have an unrelated, absolute existence. Fundamental to this perspective is the assumption that the lingual aspect of reality is indeed unique, but that this uniqueness is counterbalanced by the fact that it coheres with all other aspects of life. This coherence is expressed in the structure of the lingual aspect itself, because in its structural build-up the lingual aspect of experience contains an echo of (and thus has a relationship with) other temporal modalities.

In analyzing these structural relationships within the lingual aspect, Verburg has made a significant contribution towards formulating a reformational approach in linguistics. His analysis of the technical element in the structure of the lingual aspect (Verburg 1965: 85) covers much of the material that should systematically be surveyed there. An important statement that he makes at this juncture is that the study of grammar is related to this element. Since it reveals the grammatical-technical aspect of language to be only one aspect among others, this statement at once relativizes an approach that identifies linguistic theory with grammatical investigation or emphasizes only the study of grammar in linguistic studies, and simultaneously puts grammatical study in a proper over-all linguistic perspective. That Verburg (1965: 78) apparently restricts grammatical study to the investigation of the grammar of speech is regrettable, for it is inconsistent with his intention of including in linguistics the study of all human signs.

In identifying the analytical element in the lingual aspect Verburg also comes close to the target set by systematic linguistic analysis. By calling lexemes 'identifiers' and 'intellective discriminators' (Verburg 1965: 86; cf. too 87, note 19), Verburg tries to disclose the relationship between the lingual and logical aspects of reality. Unfortunately, however, this touches only the factual, objective meaning of a lexical item, and only casual reference is made to the subjective expressive activity of the human lingual act and the lingual norms that regulate factual lingual signification and identification.

By defining the lingual act as an act of personal volition, Verburg (1971: 270, 271) discloses the sensitive analogy in the structure of the lingual aspect (cf. also his criticism of Bloomfield, 1971: 268); similarly, the biotic analogy is approached theoretically by pointing out that the human personality can and does function as a living organism (Verburg 1971: 268). As far as the physical analogies are concerned, Verburg's notion (1965: 88) of periodicity is valuable. However, it needs both to be elaborated and corrected: in actual fact lingual periodicity can be analyzed as a kinematic analogy, but Verburg unfortunately identifies the physical aspect of energy operation with the aspect of kinematic movement.

Although Verburg discusses the contribution of what is called 'distributional' linguistics and the positional value of phonemes under the rubric of the spatial analogies, it appears that, for the greater part, he has seen only the external connection between language, as a concrete phenomenon, and space. This problematic conceptualization will be dealt with again below; it is sufficient at this stage to point out that there is a distinct difference between the *external* relation of language and space, that views language as *ex-*pression or *ut-*terance (Verburg 1971: 268; 1965: 89) on the one hand, and, on the other, the *internal* link between the lingual and spatial aspects.

It is this very distinction of external and internal relations between the lingual and other temporal aspects that leads us to discover the rather radical modification that Verburg makes to the theoretical groundwork of the philosophy on which he apparently bases his linguistic theory. By turning the *time* order of *aspects* into a *hierarchic* order of higher and lower *levels* or layers, Verburg makes a radical departure from the theoretical intentions of this philosophy. One of the numerous instances of this can be found in his essay "De mens in de taalkunde" (1971: 267); cf. for example too "Delosis and clarity" (1965: 81, 93), and "The idea of linguistic system in Leibniz" (1976: 612). Far from being concrete realms or entities, these aspects are functions of entities. The time order of temporal aspects, too, is an order of earlier and later aspects: the notion of higher and lower does not apply to it in Dooyeweerd's work.

Verburg thus seems to disregard the fundamental distinction between the modal and typical dimensions of experience, because he turns the various modal aspects into concrete levels that constitute language (1971: 266 ff.), whereas the philosophy of the cosmonomic idea proposes that all aspects (including the lingual) are merely functions of concrete things that each have their own typical structure of individuality. This view of Verburg is related to his identification of concrete language with function (1965: 84, 86, 94, 98).

It is a pity that Verburg limits the scope of his linguistic theory to speech (cf. e.g. 1965: 85, 98), locutional facts (1965: 91), and the study of *homo loquens* (1971: 266). Consequently, he considers the language of texts as indirect usage (*ibid.*) instead of as a materially different type of language (see below, Chapters 4 and 5). In all fairness, however, it must be stated that this view is at odds with his declared intention (Verburg 1965: 78) to bring all human acts of clarification (signification) into the linguistic perspective of delotic theory, and that at times he treats speech and writing as equally important manifestations of language (1971: 270, 279).

Another inconsistency is that Verburg does not escape the trap of the form/content (word/meaning; exterior/interior; language/thought) scheme (cf. the discussion above, in Chapter 2, of this concept in the thinking of Kant and Chomsky) that he criticizes in the theories of Von Humboldt (Verburg 1951: 18) and De Saussure (Verburg 1951: 22), for he says (1971: 275): "Deze signifitatieve of semantische ... intrazone ... bevat ... de in taaldaden geïnvesteerde gedachten, begrippen en noties." This criticism is in fact echoed in his praise of Reichling (1951: 27-28) and his own analysis of the relation between language and thought (1951: 28 ff.; cf. too 1971: 270, 281.)

But the major difficulty with Verburg's theory lies in his concept of language and situation. His paradoxical opposition of language that is both free and situationally restricted threatens to dissolve into a theoretical duality between freedom and restriction, which in turn corresponds closely to the dualism of freedom and determinism in current linguistics that was discussed in the previous chapter. This dualism is evident, for example, in the opposites limitation in form/ unlimited semantic applicability; perceptible, concrete and classifiable lingual facts/non-verifiable abstract meaning; rule/creativity; and form/content (meaning). This opposition in Verburg's conceptualization of linguistics, together with the fact that he considers the different aspects of language (in reality analogies of different aspects in the lingual) as concrete levels, explains why at one point he views the social anticipations within the structure of the lingual aspect as non-lingual additions to language. These additional aspects ('functional super-addita') do not condition the loquential clearness: "Whatever restraint there may be felt," he concludes (1965: 83), "it is not of a lingual nature". Here the almost complete freedom of the speech deed is in fact opposed to the (social) situation in which it occurs, and the situation becomes the source of any limitation there may be in speech: "In language," Verburg claims (1965: 83), "the restraint has to do with the situation."

This is an unfortunate stumbling block in Verburg's perspective, for it prevents him from calculating the effect that the various typically different social spheres, by way of intrinsically *lingual* norms, have upon the language used in various social contexts (see below, Chapter 4). The effect of a social context on language use is not something additional or an 'adherent functional goal', but an inherent, typical lingual norm that is part of the language used in such a sphere. These typical norms specify and complement the modal lingual principles that apply to all types of human language.

I believe that the radical alteration that Verburg's theory makes to the insights of reformational philosophy in the field of linguistics can best be explained by the fact that he maintains that his theory is a *functionalist* (1965: 97) or even *plurifunctionalist* (1971: 281) theory, and that he describes his own position as 'personalist-functionalist' (Abraham 1975: 12). While this does not cancel out the significant contribution that Verburg makes to clarify many of the issues surrounding the search for linguistic universals, his initial attempt as a whole needs modification and further elaboration.

4 Material lingual spheres

Introduction

Under what conditions would one be able to understand a remark like: "This is cute! 'Bosal wants to lift the world'"? Would it make any sense for someone to utter it if the person who is being addressed cannot see, or does not know, that the speaker is reading a newspaper at the time of the utterance, or, further, that she is commenting on the caption of a report in the newspaper she is reading? The sentence in question can only be fully interpreted and understood if we know that the caption 'Bosal wants to lift the world' headed a report in the business section of the newspaper, and, furthermore, that the report dealt with the success a motor vehicle component manufacturing company called Bosal had had in increasing its profits chiefly through the production of motor car jacks during the financial year that was under scrutiny in the report.

This example wants to say, simply, that an utterance cannot be taken out of its context, or even out of the situation in which it is used, if it is to make any sense. And this is the case because language 'an sich' — pure language — does not exist. In written or in spoken form, language is always used in context, and in a given situation.

Language does not exist in a void or vacuum, but in concrete situations. More specifically, there are various spheres in which language operates, and the concrete language used in these zones differs from one lingual sphere to the next.

If one compares the language of poetry to that of academic discourse, or the long-winded legal language of an insurance policy to the terseness of an army telex message, one soon discovers that there are distinct differences among the various brands of language used in these typically different contexts. Formally, one may try to come to an understanding of these differences by pointing out, for example, that they exist on both the lexical and syntactic levels. Thus, one would find words like 'Russellian', 'transcendental' and 'ontological' in academic discourse, but not the suggestive 'wilful-wavier mealdrift', 'wanwood', 'leafmeal', 'wind-wandering' and 'weed-winding' of Hopkins's poems. Likewise, the formulaic 'declared and agreed', 'shall notify to the Company' and 'the same shall come' that are so typical of the contractual legal language of the insurance policy, will not be found in the rather cryptic syntax of the army telex message, where combinations like 'G/TRG/6/37INF 7526' may occur side by side with highly specific abbreviations like 'ITO' and 'ATI' (meaning respectively 'in terms of' and 'Army Training Instructions'). In the latter case, the urgency and speed with which the message is sent may cause 'errors'; in the original message from which this example has been taken, for instance, we find 'AMNEDED' for 'amended', 'A COURSES' for 'a course', and so forth, errors that we would not expect in the careful wording of an insurance policy. All these differences are formal ones.

But the difference in content between these various types of language soon leads one to discover not only objective, formal differences, but also various *typical* norms and principles that give a different content to the factual language used within such a typical sphere.

The various lingual spheres may therefore be called typical if we wish to refer to the typically different social forms or relationships (such as that of the academic community, the army, club, home, school, business, church and so forth) that each requires typically different uses of language. On the other hand, these typically different spheres of language may be called material if we acknowledge that what Halliday (1979: 221, 223) calls the 'field of discourse' (as one of the features of the lingual sphere or context) to a large extent determines the content or subject matter of the concrete language used in such a sphere.

The various material lingual spheres are integrated with many typically different concrete situations that we encounter every day, and these different situations all have their own particular language register. Human beings, in their subjective lingual role as speakers, writers, hearers or readers, build up a whole repertoire of such lingual registers — a repertoire that enables them to make the delicate choices of how to speak in a given situation without crashing their lingual gears.

The linguistic idea of typically or materially distinct lingual spheres thus consists of a differentiated classification of language types that is inextricably bound up with the *subjective* human lingual capacity for producing *objective*, factual language in various social spheres. But the idea of differentiated lingual ranges is linked not only with this correlation of lingual subject and lingual object, but also with the complex linguistic concept of lingual norm and lingual fact.

This becomes clear as soon as one attempts to ascribe the typical differences between one material lingual sphere and another only to the different factual situations in which language may be used. The factual situation can never fully determine the type of language used, because the situation is itself regulated by normative principles of a logical, aesthetic, legal, technico-formative, economic, social, ethical or confessional nature. Language simply cannot be explained only in terms of the factual situation. Each different situation has different language requirements that act as lingual demands, conditions or norms. In view of the difference between lingual norm and lingual fact, one has to distinguish between the lingual requirements and conditions *for* the situation and the situation itself.

Formal and informal

Since the material differences among the various lingual spheres are related to typical differences among social structures such as the school, the university, the club, the business firm, the art studio, the family, the press, marriage, the state, the church and so forth, the traditional distinction between 'formal' and 'informal' language cannot account fully for them either. This distinction is evidently incapable of doing full justice to the diversity of material lingual spheres.

Both the scientific language of academic discourse, the stiff stylishness of a business letter and the inverted grammatical order ("Belts, waist, leather: 1 / Frogs, bayonet, leather: 1 / Helmets, steel, covers, camouflage: 1") of an army kit issue receipt may be described as 'formal' in a sense (cf. Weideman & Van Rensburg 1984), and yet there is a systematic, principled difference between the context of these examples of different types of language that cannot be accounted for wholly in terms of degrees of formality (or informality), because the difference is not a gradual but a typical one.

Furthermore, informal or formal types of language in their extreme forms (for example as slang and jargon) always seem to develop *within* the contours of a certain material lingual sphere. Thus we should perhaps reserve the distinctions of standard language, sub-standard language, cant, jargon, argot and slang to indicate *formal* differences within given *material* lingual spheres. Only in this formal sense there appears to be a possibility of a hierarchy of good and bad, or standard and sub-standard forms of language. This view would go some way towards providing a solution to the classicistic leveling of differences between various material spheres of language, as well as to the problem of arranging the language of these spheres in a hierarchy of more authoritative or less authoritative forms. The linguistic idea of a differentiated spectrum of material lingual spheres accords equal lingual (and theoretical linguistic) status to each of these spheres.

Neither can justice be done to these material differences if they are considered to be differences merely in lingual style. Lingual style refers to a formative analogy in the lingual aspect, as do the terms formal and informal. Although the normative, material differences among various typical lingual spheres are also evident in factual stylistic variations, this by no means exhausts such differences. Lingual style, moreover, is a term used quite appropriately to indicate the peculiarly factual historical or formative characteristics of the language of a given material sphere in a specific period of history or in the context of a typically specified situation.

Reduction of typical structures to general concepts of function

The term 'typical' that is employed in the previous two sections refers to the typical structural identity (or individuality structure) of things. One can form an idea of the individuality structure of a concrete, individual thing by finding, among the diversity of experiential aspects in which it functions as an individual whole, its two terminal modal functions, viz. its typical qualifying function and its typical foundational function, even though this theoretical idea does not exhaust the individuality of the thing in question. Besides the dimension of modal aspects, therefore, the horizon of human experience has another dimension that is of essential importance, Dooyeweerd remarks (1953, vol. 2: 557). This is the dimension of the structures of individuality, which manifests itself in concrete things and events, and also in the typical structural relations of human society. Both the dimension of modal aspects and the plastic dimension of typically different structures of individuality are founded in the cosmic temporal order. As groupings of modal functions, the "typical total structures of individuality in principle function at the same time in all the modal law-spheres. And it is really a question of structural *principles*, not one of the factual individuality of the things that are *determined* by these principles" (Dooyeweerd 1953 vol. 2: 557).

Dooyeweerd (1953 vol. 1: 98) also makes it quite clear that a consistent rationalistic point of view, which in linguistics would attempt to reduce lingual facts to lingual norms, can never tolerate the investigation or accept the existence of *typical* structural laws, since the normative idea emanating from a rationalist starting point remains *functionalistically* focused and applied only to the norms that operate in specific temporal aspects or functions. In light of this observation, it is evident that in Chomsky's rejection (1974: 51-52) of any attempt to determine the properties of language from its social, communicative function, we have an indication that his theoretical focus remains primarily on the constitutive structure of the lingual modality, whereas the mainline communication theorists or sociolinguists focus their attention on the deepened structure of the lingual aspect, especially its social anticipatory element, where the typical structures of individuality of human society come into play. Chomsky's position on this is that linguistics has no need of a social or sociological metatheory. While he has no objections to such projects, he has serious doubts about studying language in a social or cultural context (Chomsky 1974: 53).

It is clear, however, that Chomskyan linguistics and sociolinguistics represent complementary and not necessarily contradictory points of view (Halliday 1974: 81), both from Chomsky's position and from the side of the cosmological distinction between the constitutive and anticipatory analogies in the lingual aspect. As we shall see below, Chomsky's focus on the constitutive structure of the lingual aspect allows him to see the expressive character of language, while the intention of sociolinguistics is to venture beyond expression into an investigation of the realm of shared expression or communication.

In discussing Chomsky's rationalistic functionalism we have to distinguish between at least two senses of the term: (a) functionalism as an instrumentalist theory that holds that the 'object' of study, in this case language, can be explained in terms of its functions and goals, and (b) functionalism as a theory that surveys only the functional (modal) structure of an aspect (such as that of the lingual modality) and expresses its inability or general unwillingness to comment theoretically on the role of that function or aspect within the typical structures of individuality in human society. Of the first brand of functionalism, which may be called a *telic* functionalism, Chomsky is very critical (cf. Chomsky 1979: 85 ff.), but his own work could be said to fall within the *modal* functionalism, i.e. the second brand of functionalism as defined above.

The initial functionalistic reduction entertained by transformational grammar, in that it wished to consider only functional linguistic concepts without reference to the linguistic idea of language-in-communication or language-in-use, is evident in the way that the distinction between lingual *competence* and *performance* is utilized to differentiate between 'meaning' and 'interpretation'. Smith and Wilson (1979: 148) declare:

> The competence-performance distinction ... implies as a special case a distinction between the meaning of a sentence and the interpretation of an utterance. Sentence-meaning, dealt with by the semantic component of a competence grammar, is only one among the many factors involved in the interpretation of utterances in context. Others include the beliefs of speaker and hearer, the nature of the occasion, and the principles which underlie conversational exchanges themselves.

And, they conclude (1979: 150), the interpretation of an utterance is not always fully determined by the rules of a competence grammar alone. This is why communication theory must take over the task of building a more complete theoretical clarification of the interpretation of utterances.

If linguistic theory is guided by linguistic ideas, however, the question remains whether a theory that restricts its view to functional linguistic concepts without reference to the typical spheres in which language is used, can develop a balanced linguistic perspective. The question is thus simply whether one can omit reference to different typical lingual spheres even when one is dealing with fundamental (constitutive) linguistic concepts. It will be the purpose of this study to show that this is impossible, if the theory is informed by a balanced linguistic perspective. The formulation of constitutive linguistic concepts depends on regulative linguistic ideas, and the latter have to include an idea of the typically different material lingual spheres if the theory is not to result in an impoverished linguistic description.

The reduction of semantic data to entailment relations and the logical truth of a proposition — a reduction that can be made on the basis of the distinction between competence and performance quoted above (cf. Smith & Wilson 1979: 150 ff.) — leads to a level of theoretical abstraction that ultimately divorces theory from fact. Smith and Wilson (1979: 156-158) therefore proceed to discuss the difficulties encountered in this reduction and how it can be resolved (see below, Chapter 12), although they maintain the distinction between 'linguistic' and 'non-linguistic' knowledge (1979: 188-189, 194) that can of itself also involve a reduction of typical lingual structures to a general concept of the lingual function (see below, Chapter 14).

It does seem, however, that Chomsky is not entirely consistent in limiting the investigational field of linguistics to the constitutive structure of the lingual aspect, for he remarks in a footnote (1975: 232, note 4) that "the knowledge of language attained by an individual in a real speech community is far more complex than under the idealization that we are considering, involving many styles of speech and possibly a range of interacting grammars." This is a most significant statement, for varying 'styles of speech' and ranges of 'interacting grammars' are indeed the subject matter of serious studies in sociolinguistics, subject matter that does not come into focus when theoretical linguistic analysis insists upon investigating only the constitutive structure of the lingual function, and especially those elements or analogies that have a bearing on the functionalistically conceived, idealized lingual competence or knowledge of the language user. Serious linguistic investigation must be able to grasp theoretically both the constitutive lingual structure and the typical structures of human society in which language is used, and form some idea of the typically different varieties of speech styles and interacting ranges of grammar in respect of the language used in such structures or spheres.

In the exposition of his extended standard theory, especially, Chomsky at least in principle makes provision for other sets of rules beyond the rules of 'sentence grammar' that he has investigated; he says (1975: 104-105):

> What we have been calling 'grammar' ... is actually sentence grammar ... Given the logical forms generated by sentence grammar, further rules may apply ... These further rules of reference may involve discourse properties as well, in some manner; and they interact with considerations relating to situation, communicative intention, and the like ... As noted before, rules of sentence grammar obey quite different conditions from those that apply beyond ... [In the case of the latter] other semantic rules apply, interacting with rules belonging to other cognitive structures, to form fuller representations of meaning (in some sense).

It should be clear then that when Chomsky began to develop the extended standard theory, the unobscured functionalism of his rationalistic starting point was gradually being whittled away in favor of a broader, more inclusive perspective. This is the fundamental interpretation one should attach to the shift of emphasis that resulted in the extended standard theory, however numerous the technical reasons are that Chomsky himself cites. *The extended standard theory constitutes a turning away by Chomsky from a functionalistic reductionism,* because it allows — at least in principle — for a linguistic perspective that can account for the constitutive, general 'sentence grammar' as well as the regulative interaction of 'logical forms' (into which surface structures are converted by certain rules of semantic interpretation) with other 'cognitive structures' (Chomsky 1979: 105). In the later Chomsky an acknowledgement is to be found of the greater complexity of the sociolinguistic perspective (that concerns itself, in our terms, with the regulative idea of language and differs from the functional, constitutive lingual concept), for sociolinguistics has now become "part of linguistics. A linguistics that takes the idealization of ordinary linguistics one step closer to the complexity of reality" (Chomsky 1979: 54). Nevertheless, Chomsky does not hesitate to add (1979: 56), almost in the same breath, that the very existence of a discipline called 'sociolinguistics' remains to him an obscure matter.

Van den Berg (1979: 20) argues that De Saussure too is guilty of reducing typical lingual systems to a general concept of the sign function. He remarks that De Saussure had indeed with the distinction between 'langue' and 'parole' indicated the coherence of lingual norm and lingual fact, but that his concept of system had not penetrated to the true nature of lingual norms. According to Van den Berg, De Saussure did not manage to discover norms of a truly lingual (as opposed to historical) nature, i.e. norms that transcend historical relativity as modal and typical structural principles; De Saussure had thus in the course of his analysis found the general modal sign function, but at the same time had denied the existence of a variety of typical lingual systems.

Material lingual spheres

The material distinctions between typically different lingual spheres are particularly relevant to the field of sociolinguistics. De Jongste (1949) was the first among reformationally-inclined linguists to draw attention to the rich diversity of material lingual spheres that unfold upon investigating the analogical, anticipatory link between the lingual and social aspects, when he pointed out that in social life our lingual expression becomes deepened into the shared expression of communication: "... in de omgang wordt de expressie eveneens sociaal ontsloten ... Door de omgang ontplooit zich heel de rijke verscheidenheid van taal, waarin het intieme familieleven een ander 'idioom' eist dan het verkeer met vreemden, en andere 'toon' ook" (1949: 50).

The sociolinguistic idea that humans use language in typically or materially different spheres cuts across the boundaries of native and national languages like English, French, German, Afrikaans, and so forth. An extreme example of this "is provided by those communities in which different situations demand the use of different dialects, or even different languages," Smith and Wilson (1979: 195) remark: "An educated Indian, for instance, typically discusses his work in English but his family affairs in Hindi ..." Something similar also occurs in South Africa. A woman whose native language is Sesotho perhaps never speaks in any other language than Afrikaans at work; high-level political discussions are generally conducted in English by people whose home languages are not English, but Afrikaans, isiZulu or isiXhosa; and schoolboy jargon, which contains a mixed bag of expressions taken from various native and national languages will make way for another 'purified' form the instant a teacher appears.

It appears that material or typical differences are discernible too on almost every level of language: phonological, lexical, syntactic, semantic, and so forth. An example of a typical difference in the pronunciation of the same word in different lingual contexts is given by Smith and Wilson (1979: 196), who relate how, on the occasion of the Queen's Silver Jubilee, the BBC had first stressed the last syllable (jubi*lee*) as younger speakers were wont to do, before reverting to the older pronunciation of stressing the first syllable (*ju*bilee): in the end, at least some speakers acquired two variable pronunciations of the same word, the one used with older people or on more formal occasions, the other used with younger people, or on more informal occasions. Likewise, differences in tone may give formal indications of the material lingual spheres in which a sentence is used. Robinson (1975: 45-46) gives an example of when the abstract functional concepts of a transformationalist sentence grammar will not serve to indicate such various uses of what may seem to be the same sentence: "... take Browning's line 'Oh! to be in England, now that April's there.' The last time I heard that spoken was in tones of withering contempt by an old miner, climbing aboard a bus in Nottinghamshire as the grey light of dawn was breaking on All Fools' Day in the middle of a snowstorm. Do the circumstances not affect the sentence?" he asks. It should be obvious that one must acknowledge that they do.

An earlier view, put forward by Pike (1959: 51), was that the various lingual spheres or fields should be understood as memory reservoirs, or pools of common experience, "against which particular speech events at a particular moment stand out as figure on ground, and provide the structure which provides the potential for patterned events."

However, it is doubtful whether subjective human memory

or experience would have this structural potential if it is not itself responding to material principles. If language is indeed a mode of behavior, as Pike believes, and not merely a code, or set of symbolic forms, or a mathematical logical pattern (1959: 52), then it must, like all human behavior, respond to principles from which it derives its specific lingual character and content. My thesis is simply that these structural principles are given, and that they reside in a law order, and not in any subjective human capacity which is itself *subjected* to such a law order.

The term 'typical' that is employed to indicate the distinct differences among various lingual spheres is always qualified to mean lingually typical, and must therefore not be confused with Lyons's (1968) distinction of 'typical' situation. Lyons bases this distinction on the fact that every "language utterance is made in a particular place and at a particular time: it occurs in the same spatio-temporal situation" (Lyons 1968: 275). Thus, speaker and hearer "are *typically* in the same spatio-temporal situation". But it seems that the 'spatio-temporal' situation that Lyons refers to is not *lingually* typical, for there "are many common situations of utterance which are 'untypical' in these respects: ... if one is speaking on the telephone, the hearer will not be in the same spatio-temporal situation" (1968: 275). If the situation of speaker and hearer in a telephone conversation is characterized by the term 'typically lingual', however, the non-lingual criteria of spatiality and temporality become linguistically irrelevant, for there is no doubt that both participants in a telephone conversation find themselves in the same lingual (i.e. typical lingual) situation.

Register

The notion of 'register', introduced in the 1950's (Halliday 1979: 110) has affinities with the sociolinguistic idea of material lingual spheres. Registers may be defined as varieties of language which depend on the use of language (cf. Berry 1975: 2). Taken as a term referring to a type of language or a style appropriate to the occasion, 'register' roughly corresponds to what we have been calling material lingual spheres, although one could say that the term 'register' may be used more appropriately to indicate the lingual norms that hold For a given material lingual sphere, whereas the idea of context of situation may refer, broadly speaking, to the factual usage in such a sphere. Halliday (1979: 31-33; also 109-110), following Bernstein, makes a distinction between the factual lingual situation as "the environment in which the text comes to life" on the one hand, and the situation type, or social (i.e. normatively lingual) context on the other. The latter "consists of those general properties of the situation which collectively function as the *determinants* of text, in that they *specify* the semantic configurations that the speaker will *typically* fashion in contexts of the given type" (emphases added). This closely approximates what is meant by a material (or typical) lingual sphere: it is a set of specifying, typical properties determining the language used in a special context.

'Register' may otherwise be distinguished from the 'situation type' or typical lingual sphere as "the configuration of semantic resources" someone "typically associates with a situation type" (Halliday 1979: 111; cf. too 136), but from a *linguistic* point of view this 'association' can, it appears, be disregarded if the theory adequately recognizes the existence of typical lingual spheres, which already provide, *inter alia*, for the notions of semantic (i.e. *lingual*) resources or meaning potential, and situation type or social context (*typical sphere*). It seems an unnecessary complication to require two closely related concepts where one would allow linguistic theory to make the same distinctions. In any case, Halliday's definition (1979: 123) of register as a range of meaning potential seems to approximate closely the idea embodied in the term typical or material lingual sphere, for it is considered to be also an institutional variable of language (Halliday 1979: 183).

The only other legitimate use for the term 'register' is to indicate through it the subjective human lingual capacity for speaking or writing in typically different, materially distinct lingual zones. A distinction might in such a case be made between the typical lingual norms that apply in these spheres and the subjective lingual register as a normative human understanding of these norms.

Attempts at distinguishing between material lingual spheres

"When we talk about 'a language'," Crystal and Davy remark (1976: 3), "we must not be misled into thinking that the label should in some way refer to a readily identifiable object in reality, which we can isolate and examine ... There is no such object. The label 'the English language' is in fact only a shorthand way of referring to something which is not, as the name may seem to imply, a single homogeneous phenomenon at all, but rather a complex of many different 'varieties' of language ..." The problem for linguistic theory, however, is how to account for the intuitive knowledge that the user of language has of these varieties, and to give a theoretical explanation of how we as users of a language without any reflection come to recognize a dialogue between two academics and know that it is different in content from the transactional exchanges that take place between businesspersons and their clients, or from the friendly conversational chat between two neighbors.

Surely vocabulary alone is insufficient as a criterion to distinguish between two material lingual spheres, say for example between the written or spoken language of poetry and a variety of prose. Haddakin (1955: 155) is no doubt correct in thinking that poetic words viewed in isolation may justifiably be considered 'prose' words, while the *collocation* of words may yet be unprosaic. Sinnema (1975: 7) makes the same kind of observation in an essay on the language of faith. In spite of the fact that lexical considerations *on their own* cannot yield a criterion of distinguishing between different material lingual spheres, however, the typical differences between these spheres may often be in part suggested by certain words "which retain the coloring of a particular context," viz. "those which become specially stamped by frequent recurrence in sentences of a particular kind, the technical terms or jargon" (Sinnema 1975: 7).

This is the case because the material distinctions between typically different lingual spheres are especially relevant at the discourse level of language where all language is qualified by some aspect of experience. Thus courtroom discourse is qualified juridically, poetry is qualified aesthetically, conversation between husband and wife is ethical

> ... [T]he various areas of scientific discourse, ... historical writing, the language of social etiquette, the economic business talk of the marketplace, the many aesthetic genres of literature and also the various kinds of certitudinal discourse found in sacred writing, liturgy, creed, prayer, etc. all display the uniqueness of distinct spheres of discourse. We might say that every sphere of activity ... has its own language (Sinnema 1975: 6-7).

When one attempts to distinguish between the language of two lingual spheres, therefore, the material distinctions that obtain must enable one to state whether the language is qualified by the logical, aesthetic, juridical, ethical, confessional, economic or social aspect of experience, thereby giving an indication of the expected content of the type of language in question. Any further distinctions that can be made that are of linguistic relevance must rely in the first instance on the typical qualification of the social structure in which the language in question is used. Even if the linguistic analysis comes up with further criteria, these must of necessity rely on the primary, typical distinctions that refer to the qualifying function of the social relationship in which language is used.

Crystal and Davy's (1976: 8; cf. too 9-22) analysis of the material lingual spheres of conversation, cultic worship, newspaper reporting, law and so forth, is just such an attempt to point to further criteria, usually of a formal, stylistic kind, by which we may distinguish between typically different, material lingual spheres:

> The aim of a linguistically orientated, stylistic approach is clear: the varieties of a language need to be studied in as much detail as possible, so that we can point to the formal linguistic features which characterize them, and understand the restrictions on their use.

In the next few sub-sections some of the material and formal criteria employed to distinguish between typically different lingual spheres are surveyed.

The material lingual sphere of conversation

The socially qualified exchange of language between equals in conversation is characterized by various typical norms. Crystal and Davy's (1976: 102-109) provisional formulation of some of these norms included (a) the inexplicitness of the language (b) the (at that time apparent) randomness of the subject-matter and general lack of conscious planning coupled with (c) an optional unpredictability, the juxtaposition of normally distinct linguistic features, resulting in a high degree of flexibility, as well as (d) variation on several linguistic levels, and (e) the so-called 'normal non-fluency'.

A good example of how the first typical norm identified by Crystal and Davy for this kind of language, i.e. its inexplicitness, is complemented by its non-technicality, can be given when one compares the words used in this sphere with others that are used to express exactly the same objective state of affairs in spheres that possess a stricter, more highly formalized and technical vocabulary. Smith and Wilson (1979: 194) give an example of this: " ... in normal, non-medical speech, a woman who loses her baby prematurely has a *miscarriage* if the event is accidental, but an *abortion*, if the event is medically contrived. In medical language, however, the former occurrence is described as abortion, and the latter as termination of the pregnancy. That is, the word abortion ... has two separable, though largely overlapping senses, which are used by different groups of speakers, and may also be register variants for a single individual."

The typical characteristics of a lingual sphere may therefore be indicated on the lexical level (Smith & Wilson 1979: 194-195):

> Choice of vocabulary, then, is often a good indication of the register being used, and a potential signal of the degree of formality of the occasion as well as the area of specialization. Thus the use of compound forms including *there* and *where*, such as *thereof, whereat, thereby, wherein*, is typical of very formal styles, and the use of slang and colloquialisms of informal style.

As we shall note below, some of the typical norms for conversation between equals that Crystal and Davy provisionally identified, especially the supposed randomness of the subject matter and the apparent lack of conscious planning, have been challenged by work in conversation analysis (cf. e.g. Sachs, Schlegoff & Jefferson's groundbreaking study [1974] on the turn-taking organization of conversation). All seem to appeal, however, to our intuitive knowledge of this material lingual sphere. Take for example the typical norm for conversational language known as 'normal non-fluency', which also involves the discounting (Crystal & Davy 1976: 5) or toleration (1976: 104) of what may or be considered as errors in other modes of speech and writing. It does not necessarily mean that features that can be described by this norm are indeed errors. Or take another example, from an early linguistic analysis, where Gleason, in discussing the transformations of a statement into the question form, correctly observed (1961: 177) what we today take for granted: that in colloquial usage, including informal writing, *who* is much more likely to be used than *whom*, and that such 'errors' are not the result of 'loose grammar', but of very rigid and explicit patterns. What may be considered grammatically erroneous in one material lingual sphere, in other words, could be a rigid and acceptable norm for another. The material lingual sphere of literary English at a particular time in history, for example, could not tolerate what was acceptable in colloquial usage.

The typical characteristics of certitudinal discourse

Certitudinal discourse is the language of faith, of believing and simultaneously surrendering. The Bible, as a book written in human language, is qualified by the creaturely aspect of certainty. "I propose to talk of the Scriptures," remarks Olthuis (1979: 71), "as a book of certainty, as the Word of God in certitudinal focus. In other words, the Scriptures belong to that category or classification of books that have as their governing focus ultimates or end-questions. The overriding, pre-eminent concern of this type of literature is the terminal matter of certainty. It can deal with any subject-matter — and usually does — but its manner and mode of treatment evinces its overriding design to strengthen confession, to engender belief, and to promote hope."

Olthuis (1979: 70) makes it quite clear that the sacred/secular distinction, instead of helping our efforts at interpreting the Bible, is exactly what must be overcome if any headway is to be made in our hermeneutical efforts. The distinction is without any value to determine the typical certitudinal qualification of this type of language, which Olthuis calls its 'structural specificity'.

Some of the distinctions made by Sinnema (1975) in his essay on the uniqueness of this type of language appear to be inadequate. Sinnema (1975: 17) characterizes certitudinal discourse as "imaginative, fresh, fluid, connotative language. Unlike scientific (including theological) language it is not conceptual, univocal, precise, denotative language." The fact that scientific language is not necessarily unimaginative, stilted or archaic Sinnema would probably concede, but his characterization is interesting because it illustrates a particular problem in distinguishing between two material lingual spheres by means of formal criteria. The latter kind of criterion may apply to more than one material lingual sphere, as is evident when one applies the descriptive terms 'imaginative', 'fresh' and 'fluid' to the language of poetry. But the language of faith, even though it may assume a poetic form or perhaps even display distinctly poetic rhythms and tones, is by and large different from poetry in its structural focus. This typical distinction cannot be formulated with reference only to formal features, for even the well-worn and traditional distinction between denotation and connotation does not serve to distinguish properly between two material lingual spheres.

Scientific language

This last remark is especially pertinent in view of our traditional characterizations of scientific language. It is often heard that scientific language requires words to denote, to indicate or express with a high degree of accuracy and precision, and that the words used must have the bare minimum of connotations. Brooks and Warren (1960: 5) point out, however, that even though the language of science represents a high degree of "specialization of language in the direction of a certain kind of precision, ... literature in general — poetry in particular — also represents a specialization of language for the purpose of precision." The distinction between poetic language and scientific discourse, then, is not a question of formative purpose, *viz.* 'precision', which may apply to both lingual spheres in equal measure, but the typical kind of precision that is required for each. And this typifying qualification that must be attached to the characterizing term 'precision' in distinguishing poetry from scientific language is the terminally important, structure-specifying qualification of the logical aspect of experience that stamps scientific language and sets it apart from the aesthetically qualified features of the language of poetry. Moreover, even though scientific discourse may attempt to eliminate the lingual phenomenon of connotation by means of logical definition, the terms of a scientific definition more often than not reveal precisely not only what is being defined in clear and unambiguous terms, but also the scientific and pre-scientific bias of the theorist. It is part of the intuition and experience of the practising scientist and academic to hear positivist, structuralist, phenomenologist, transformationalist and other overtones upon reading a definition. It appears that even in attempting to distinguish between two obviously different kinds of language the distinction between denotation and connotation seems to let us down.

Perhaps another formal criterion for distinguishing scientific language from other lingual spheres would serve the linguist's purpose better in this case. Halliday (1979: 202) has observed that in certain scientific fields a high degree of nominalization obtains, and this appears to merit more serious consideration in view of the difficulties experienced with other formal criteria. However, although scientists probably agree that the language they use requires exact formulation, Halliday points out that the high degree of nominalization that obtains in scientific discourse actually at times may obscure ambiguities. It is strange that Halliday, with his notion of the social context of language, does not refer the resolution of these ambiguities to the knowledge that the language user has of the field as a whole. Ambiguities that may arise in a sentence marked by the frequent use of the noun can be resolved not only by rephrasing the statement in a non-nominalized form, but also by the scientists' knowledge of the language used in their special field of inquiry.

The language of art

Language of an aesthetically qualified nature is limited not only to literary language and the language of poetry, that has received some consideration above. One tends to forget that dancing, sculpture, painting, music and drama also move, like poetry and other literary genres, on various lingual or semiotic levels at the same time, We hesitate to call this function of the lingual aspect in other activities 'language' simply because our notion of language has come to mean merely verbal language. But this is surely an impoverished notion, for every aesthetically qualified activity has a readily recognizable expressive basis, without which it cannot communicate. Rookmaker (1974: 94-95) remarks:

> De beeldende kunst bedient zich van een taal, een beeldtaal, iconisch te noemen. Deze taal is middel tot visuele communicatie. Beeldende kunst is iconische poëzie of proza.

He then makes an interesting observation on the formal precision or clarity of this kind of language (1974: 95):

> De iconische taal is niet duidelijker maar ook niet minder duidelijk dan de gesproken of geschreven taal. De mogelijkheden zijn echter verschillend.

These differing possibilities are of course the result of giving different positive forms to the various typical aesthetic principles governing the function of the lingual aspect and the use of language in the different forms of art. It is the lingual function of a work of art that enables the art theorist to develop a theory of the interpretation of such works, and to speak of, for example, the hermeneutics of painting and sculpture.

The language of art moves on several lingual or symbolic levels simultaneously; it is in the subtle interplay between these levels that the qualifying aesthetic function plays its integrating and specifying role that enables us to understand what the artist wants to put across. This is what lies behind the distinction between connotation and denotation, behind Anthony Burgess's notion of the poet "not restricting his words" (1974: 7), Seerveld's idea (1968: 85) of the multidimensional, dense nature of poetic diction, and Bruns's view (1975: 2) that "in poetry ... language finds a form of discourse in which it need not hold itself back ..." In spite of the difficulties that may arise with these notions from a linguistic point of view (since other lingual spheres may have the same formal features), they all capture something of the typical difference between the language of poetry and language as it is used in other kinds of discourse.

The material lingual sphere of legal language

As is the case with the language of art, legal language also is not limited to verbal language: " ... niet alleen in woorden, ook in gebaren, tekens, seinen e.d. kan de juridische norm worden uitgedrukt," Hommes (1972: 376-377) observes; "Het rode stoplicht, het stopteken van een agent van politie etc. brengen een concrete rechtsnorm tot uiting".

The juridical qualification of the language of law is a *sine qua non* for its interpretation. The requirement that legal language be accurate, fixed and uniform does not guarantee its juridical clarity, but at least facilitates its interpretation (Hommes 1972: 381). On the factual side of juridical life the expressive function of the lingual aspect is operative in the legally registered name of a corporation and in the objective juridical meaning of initials inside a hat, a boundary fence, etc. (Hommes 1972: 399), as well as in the legal interpretation of a registered trade mark or the contractual meaning of handing over the keys of a building (1972: 400).

Application of material distinctions in language teaching

The present discussion of 'language and situation' has focused the attention of linguists and educators alike on the fact that the subjective human lingual act takes place within the so-called context of situation, which determines the kind of language that must be used. This insight into the materially different lingual spheres serves to oppose effectively, among other things, a prescriptive grammatical point of view in applied linguistics — especially prescriptive grammar in its rigorous, classicistic and conservative form. It is nonsense to hold, for example, that 'dilemma' should be taken to mean only 'a situation in which one has just two choices' and not 'a perplexing situation'. This prescriptive and inherently rationalistic point of view shows a lack of insight into (a) the multi-leveled character of language as revealed in the variety of spheres within which a given national language functions, and (b) the fact that language, both with regard to its factual side and its norm side, is dynamic and subject to change.

The word 'dilemma' might mean different things in different contexts, and the requirements of the formal academic essay, where — supposedly — it should preferably be used only to have the first meaning, may not necessarily be the same as those for conversational language, where it might legitimately have also the second meaning. This means, in other words, that there is no one correct form of English for all occasions, but many different forms of English that are all appropriate to different occasions. For a similar example in Afrikaans, one may refer to the article "Gewig bly gewig ... en massa bly massa" (Die Volksblad 1976). If the language teacher does not heed this, the consequences speak for themselves; the teacher has to give guidance to pupils who still have to build a whole repertoire of language registers for using language with skill and effect in various material lingual spheres. The idea of the material lingual spheres must therefore have relevance for language teaching curricula and textbooks:

> One test of a successful education is whether it has brought us to a position whereby we can communicate, on a range of subjects, with people in various walks of life, and gain their understanding as well as understand them. But to be in such a position requires a sharpened consciousness of the form and function of language, its place in society, and its power (Crystal & Davy 1976: 4-5).

Crystal and Davy point out (1976: 7) that this notion applies also to the student of English as a foreign language; they insist that it is important that the syllabus for foreign language teaching must include instruction in those varieties of English encountered most frequently.

It should immediately be evident that a linguistic theory that restricts itself to the study of one form of language, or to the theoretical analysis of speech only, is imposing limitations upon its application not only in language teaching but also in other areas. The classicistic, prescriptive grammar that has been with us so long has made the language teacher indifferent, as Lennox-Short (1977: 136-137) has indicated,

> to the relevance of a particular style to a particular occasion, an indifference to the individuality of, for instance, the English of the pulpit, the platform, the party, the microphone, and the professional interview, and, above all ... to the characteristic qualities of spoken as opposed to written English. Far too many students write much as they speak and so transfer to their written English characteristics of spoken English that are serious deficiencies anywhere else. The approach of the tutor should ... be ... the study of language in action rather than in isolation ... there is a need to extend this application to the world about us. Précis can be related to the problems of the editor; punctuation to the reading of a radio script; syntax to the exactitude of law or the duplicities of diplomacy.

5 The expressive character of language

Communication versus expression

The dictum *quot homines tot sententiae* seems to apply to questions on the nature of language. Thus Reichling (1962: 7ff.) is sharply critical of Zellig Harris's positivistic view of language as an analytical ordering of lingual facts by the scientist. Language cannot be equated with science or its scientific study, since it has an autonomous system, with laws of its own (cf. too Van Heerden 1972: 7). Nor is language history, or reducible to a merely historical phenomenon, since language can only signify the meaning of history (Dooyeweerd 1953 vol. 2: 221 ff.). It cannot simultaneously signify and be the same thing.

Neither can the objective fact of concrete language be only communication, as some linguists wrongly assume. Communication as such, as Verburg (1965: 97) points out, is so much an undefined, "universal concept that it contains no specificity whatever that could define language." Verburg demonstrates that 'communication' could range from inter-molecular physical communication to inter-human, 'spiritual' communication.

What characterizes the objective fact of language is its *expressive, signifying* character, and not the fact that it is a set of sounds, that it is arbitrary, that it is systematic and that it is relatively complete (as defined, for example, by Hill 1969: 38-42). This does not mean, of course, that language does not have these characteristics, but merely that they are not defining, typical characteristics, setting language apart from what is not language.

Language denotes, signifies and expresses by means of lingual signs and symbols. Language can be spoken or written, or formed by the human hand, face or other parts of the bodily musculature in disclosing its qualifying expressive or signifying aspect, and is thus not restricted to speech only.

This applies to language as something concrete and individual. A distinction must be made, however, between language in its concrete form and the lingual aspect of symbolic signification. The objectively factual language used by humans has a terminal qualifying or characterizing aspect which in this study has been termed the *lingual* modality of expression by means of signs.

Every concrete thing, as has been observed, has a lingual aspect: the mere fact that we have names to denote and signify concrete things, states and events like books, chair, coal, trees, animals, meetings, states, churches, clubs, sport, art, etc., illustrates this point.

Viewed from the angle of human subjectivity and the differentiated material lingual spheres, language requires a juridical, certitudinal, aesthetic, logical, economic, social, technical or ethical qualification, and thus can be said to have a socially differentiated function of communication. This was the topic of discussion in the previous chapter. But viewed from the objective, factual side, only language of all individual concrete things is qualified by its lingual aspect. The objective lingual qualification of language sets it apart from non-language, but at the same time enables it to be enkaptically linked (Dooyeweerd 1953 vol. 3: 627 ff.) and of service in another, non-lingually qualified whole.

Chomsky's emphasis on the expressive function of language (Chomsky 1974: 52-53; 1979: 55-73) as compared with the communicative uses to which language can be put shows clearly that (a) communication is one of the functions of language, but certainly not the only one; and (b) the communicative need not necessarily be opposed to the expressive function of language. In *Language and responsibility*, Chomsky criticizes at length the view that language can be defined in terms of its ends and purposes (of which communication is one). He notes (Chomsky 1979: 88):

> Language is used in many different ways. Language can be used to transmit information, but it also serves many other purposes: to establish relations among people, to express or clarify thought, for play, for creative mental activity, to gain understanding, and so on. In my opinion, there is no reason to accord privileged status to one or the other of these modes. Forced to choose, I would have to say something quite classical and rather empty: language serves essentially for the expression of thought.

The distinction that Chomsky makes between communication and expression is done within the framework of 'Cartesian' linguistic theory and what he calls the 'creative aspect of language use.' The contribution of Cartesian linguistics as defined by Chomsky is, firstly, the insight that the normal use of language is free from the control of external or internal stimuli, and, secondly, is not restricted to communication. Lingual creativity entails that the language is free to express; it has infinite expressive possibilities constrained only by rules of concept formation and sentence formation (Chomsky 1966: 29). The distinction that Chomsky makes between expression and communication thus fits into a fairly well-developed anthropological perspective; a perspective that defines human existence in terms of *mechanically* explicable bodily functions that are transcended by human *freedom* of thought and the expression of that thought in language, the one human faculty that Descartes claimed exhibits the essential difference between humans and animal most clearly (Chomsky 1966: 3), and it is a perspective that is undoubtedly influenced by the humanistic ground motive of freedom and determinism (cf. above, Chapter 2).

Lingual subjects, i.e. the human beings who, in response to norms, produce language, do not merely transmit effectively or communicate: they also produce or create that transmission or communication. Whereas the question for information/communication theory thus may be "What is communication/transmission?" the question for linguistics is "What is language, by means of which we communicate?"

or "*What* is it that is produced in the process of communication, and how is it created?"

Other arguments against the view that language is communication come from those belonging to the transformationalist school who point out that, though language is necessarily rule-governed, the rules of language formation are not with equal necessity shared rules, i.e. rules of lingual habit, convention or custom. This is especially true of child language and dialects, which use rules that may seem strange to adults or speakers of other dialects (and consequently jar or impede the communicative process), but that nevertheless are undoubtedly rules governing language in its qualifying expressive character (cf. Smith & Wilson 1979: 14-21). Once these rules become shared or conventionalized, expression becomes deepened into shared expression or communication, but it is not until this social disclosure of expression occurs that we can see the communicative dimensions of language. It is in this venturing beyond expression (see Chapters 4 and 14) that the constitutive structure of the lingual aspect of our experience is deepened and disclosed, and this is the subject matter of sociolinguistic study. Viewed from the restrictive structure of the lingual aspect, however, the characteristic feature of language is expression.

The field of investigation of linguistics

If language is not exhausted in verbal language (Dooyeweerd 1953 vol. 2: 137), then the field of study of linguistics cannot be restricted to the language of words either. What is more, linguistic study can be delimited only with reference to the lingual aspect of experience, and not by the empirical phenomenon of language (Dooyeweerd 1953 vol. 1: 565; vol. 2: 55, 226) which may be studied from various modal angles such as the certitudinal, numerical, sensitive, juridical, etc. — modalities that delimit the fields of study of branches of academic inquiry (*viz.* theology, mathematics, psychology, jurisprudence and so on) other than linguistics. As Wells (1971: 15) asks in his interpretation of De Saussure: "... the phenomena of language can be studied from different points of view. Dozens of sciences can study linguistic phenomena ... from as many points of view — each one putting these phenomena into relation with phenomena of some other sort. What aspect of the phenomena, if any, is left to linguistics as its exclusive property?" The answer that a systematic approach must give to this is clear: linguistics has as its legitimate field the lingual aspect of experience.

The modal identity or structure of this aspect that defines the theoretical field of linguistics has as a guarantee of its uniqueness among the variety of other aspects a distinct nuclear moment or modal meaning kernel that may be defined as expression that is related to the understanding of signs (Dooyeweerd 1953 vol. 2: 222, 223).

If Hjelmslev (1963: 127) is correct in saying that ultimately there is no object that is not illuminated from the position of linguistic theory, then there is no single reason for defining the field of linguistic study as the objective phenomenon of language. Linguistics, then, must eventually be able to account for the lingual function of objects and subjects that are of themselves not lingually structured in the sense of being characterized by the lingual aspect. It is true, of course, that not all objects are lingually qualified; but it is just as true that there is no single phenomenon, thing, event or process that does not have a lingual (semiotic) dimension. And if this is the case, it follows that the field of study covered by linguistic theory can never be the concrete fact of language — which may be studied from the vantage points of many different disciplines — but is of necessity the lingual aspect of experience, in its function either of leading structural principle or non-characterizing aspect of a concrete, individual thing. Not the concrete object of language, therefore, but the experiential lingual modality that functions as an aspect *of* concrete things although in itself it is never concrete, defines the field of linguistic enquiry.

The lingual aspect of symbolic signification that determines the field of study of linguistics should be distinguished theoretically from other aspects of our experiential horizon, *viz.* the aspects of number, space, movement, energy-operation, organic life and sensitivity, as well as the logical, formative, social, economic, aesthetic, juridical, moral and certitudinal aspects, to which it cannot be reduced without inner antinomy. Of course, linguistics should also investigate the objective structure of concrete language, pointing out that language necessarily rests upon a physical basis (i.e. the physical sounds of spoken language, or the chemical structure of written and printed symbols on paper and other material) or that it has a biotic basis in the muscular structure of the human body in the case of gestural signs, all of which do not qualify or function as language without the leading expressive function from which it derives its meaning.

A typological linguistic classification

A linguistic typology will aim at classifying factual lingual objects, whereas the diversity of distinguishable material lingual spheres will be related to the subjective lingual function in various social spheres. In so far as linguistics is in need of a typological classification of lingual objects to counter an historicist elimination of objective lingual structures (cf. Dooyeweerd 1953 vol. 3: 94), the distinctions that Dooyeweerd (1953 vol. 3: 80 ff.) introduces between radical types, geno-types, sub-types and variability types may prove useful for a preliminary outline.

As a radical type factual, concrete language has two terminal functions: a leading or *qualifying* objective lingual function and a *foundational* formative one. It thus "belongs to the kingdom of historically founded and symbolically qualified things" with "letters, scores, signs, banners ... and so on" (Dooyeweerd 1953 vol. 3: 150).

The different materials that are used in the foundational structure through enkaptic interlacement of their natural structures are of importance to distinguish between the geno-types of spoken, written and gestural language. The latter types of objective language are geno-types of the same radical type of formatively founded and lingually qualified things, and may be divided into further sub-types which in turn may be classified into the different variability types. Schematically, a linguistic typology such as this may be represented as in figure 5.1 below.

The objective lingual types in the last column are closely related to the various material lingual spheres, since as variability types they point to the enkaptic interwovenness of objective lingually qualified structures with other structural principles (Dooyeweerd 1953 vol. 3: 127) in the horizon of the typical structures of human society. The variability types are objective types of language that, while retaining their objective lingual character, assume a qualification that is other than lingual in a relation of enkaptic interlacement.

Radical type	Geno-types	Materials bound enkaptically into the foundational structures of genotypes	Sub-types	Variability types
Lingually qualified objects	Speech	The physically qualified structure of sound	The different native and national languages, such as English, French, German, Afrikaans, etc., including sign language, and artificial languages such as Esperanto.	Scientific language and terminology
				The technico-formative language of engineering, medicine, monuments and other historical or formative objects and events
	Writing	The enkaptic interlacement between physically qualified things, for example ink and paper, paint and metal, etc.		Colloquial, Conversational language
				Business language and signs such as trade marks, price tags, etc.
				The language and symbols of art
				The juridical language of laws, and the tokens of property
	Gesture	The organic structure of the human body and musculature		The language and symbols of love, including rings and presents
				The language of faith, including the sacramental symbols of bread, wine and water, and the cultic symbols of blood, the cross, etc.

Figure 5.1: A linguistic typology

The various language genealogies drawn up by historical linguistic studies of the past only make sense as distinct languages in different stages of development within one or more of the sub-types in the third column. The same is true for a distinction between 'primitive' and 'civilized', or synthetic and analytic languages.

The schematic representation in Fig. 5.1 gives in broad outline the linguistic scope of lingual objects, but by no means exhausts the wealth of objective lingual facts. Furthermore, the scheme is useful in coming to an understanding of the sub-disciplines within the scope of linguistic study. Thus the lingual qualifying function of language is the field of investigation of the branch of linguistics called semantics, while the formative foundational function of lingual objects is investigated by morphology and syntax. The physical sounds of the objective facts of speech constitute the field of phonology.

Speech as object of inquiry

In light of the conclusions reached in the previous two sections of this chapter, it is hard to find a reason for the traditional, self-imposed restriction of linguistics to the investigation of speech. For most linguistic theories claim to be limiting their theoretical inquiry to this one objective, geno-typical variety of language; many indeed express disdain at studying written language or the 'pseudo-language' of gestures. One wonders if Robinson (1975: 174) is not correct in noting the almost dogmatic nature of this linguistic attitude, and in finding it hard to understand, since even when they are reporting speech, the examples in linguists' arguments always happen to be written down and not spoken. He remarks (1975: 175: "The familiarity of linguists with two millennia of the Greek/Alexandrian tradition of literacy has bred a most misleading contempt."

Hjelmslev (1963: 101) had already in 1943 foreseen that "precisely when we restrict ourselves to the pure consideration of 'natural' language" the excluded lingually qualified structures "obtrude themselves with inevitable logical consequence." Thus:

> If the linguist wishes to make clear to himself the object of his own science he sees himself forced into spheres which according to the traditional view are not his (Hjelmslev 1963: 101-102).

Hjelmslev (1963: 102) reminds us that in his own linguistic theory aspects of literary science, general philosophy of science, epistemology and formal logic have all played their part.

The traditional restriction of modern linguistic study to the spoken form of language Hjelmslev persuasively ascribes to the illegitimate supremacy of the study of language sounds. Thus, he points out (1963: 103), "the fact has been overlooked that speech is accompanied by, and that certain components of speech can be replaced by, gesture, and that in reality, as the Zwirners say, not only the so-called organs of speech (throat, mouth, and nose), but very nearly all the striate musculature, cooperate in the exercise of 'natural' language." Furthermore, Hjelmslev explains, "it is possible to replace the usual sound and gesture with any other that offers itself as appropriate under changed external circumstances." This not only reinforces the distinction between the various kinds of materials used in a foundational role in the different geno-types of language outlined in the last section, but emphasizes the replacement function between genotypical varieties of language. Hjelmslev (1963: 104, 106) for his part provides not only for the replacement of one lingual 'substance' by another, as when writing, a naval flag code or sign language is (supposedly) derived from speech, but for substantial individual differences that may be discovered among speech, writing and code.

The net result is that the linguist is obliged "to consider as his subject not merely 'natural', everyday language, but any semiotic — any structure that is analogous to a language ... A language (in the ordinary sense) may be viewed as a special case of this more general object ..." (Hjelmslev 1963: 106-107). From the angle of lingual objectivity, the topic of linguistic inquiry includes everything that belongs to the radical type of lingually qualified and formatively founded objects. It is not so much the analogy between language (as speech) and other semiotic structures that obliges linguistic theory to pay attention to the latter, as Hjelmslev believes, but the nature of the analogy, which on both counts is of a lingually expressive character. All structures 'analogous to language' belong to the same radical type of lingually qualified objects. This is the real reason why "the linguist cannot with impunity study language without the wider horizon that ensures his proper orientation towards these analogous structures" (Hjelmslev 1963: 107). To the extent that linguistic theory therefore restricts itself to the study of speech alone, it will be unable to produce the 'general encyclopedia of sign structures' envisaged by Hjelmslev (1963: 109).

Speech and writing

The spoken and written forms of language are distinguishable as two different geno-typical varieties of lingually qualified objects, and as such have equal theoretical status in linguistic theory. This is why linguists must be hesitant to categorize them as 'primary' and 'secondary' forms of language, or even to produce arguments to demonstrate that the one may be derived in some way from the other. The very relation between speech and writing is highly problematic, Robinson (1975: 175; cf. too Bruns 1975: 258 ff.) points out, for "even with the most meticulous phonetic script, the transition from discrete written characters to the flow of language read aloud (not at all the same as speech) is deeply mysterious. No script gives more than hints and guesses about what one can call here its interpretation as sound." Crystal and Davy (1976: 69; cf. too 70), with characteristic meticulous attention to formal details, make the same point in distinguishing writing from speech. Indeed, the very problematic character of the relation between spoken and written language, even the relation between the sounds of reading a text aloud and 'ordinary', unscripted speech, points to the distinct difference between speech and writing.

Apart from the phonic/graphic material of which the different foundational structures of these two geno-types are made up, a crucial feature that distinguishes speech from writing is, according to Halliday (1979: 224), the 'lexical density' of the latter, its "packing more content words into each phrase or clause or sentence." At the same time, too, written language is grammatically less complex than speech, since "especially informal speech such as casual conversation, displays complexities of sentence structure that would be intolerable (because they would be unintelligible) in writing" (Halliday 1979: 224; cf. too Weideman & Van Rensburg 1984).

Although one must, in view of the geno-typical variation of spoken and written language, agree with Bruns (1975: 261) that speech and writing are two different types of lingual performance, each requiring a different order of skills, but both grounded finally upon human lingual competence, it is not necessary to relate this difference to the supposed duality of 'world' and 'word' or the 'priority of being' as opposed to the 'priority of form'. Writing is no less real than speech, and need never be a withdrawal from the natural intimacy of life if it is to remain language. If we take the written text of a love letter, we discover in it some of the most intimate, real-life language. Some of the most poignantly real lingual utterances can be effectively expressed only in the written form. The geno-typical distinction between speech and writing can only undergo a mystification if we wish to explain it by referring the difference to a duality and dialectic that — ultimately — springs from the humanistic dualism of freedom and determinism (see above, Chapter 2).

Verbal language

In defining its field of study, linguistics has encountered difficulties similar to those in other scientific disciplines. Like jurisprudence, that has traditionally limited its view to the legal sphere of constitutional law to the exclusion of the spheres of ecclesiastical law, internal family law, and so forth, linguistics has held that its field of study concerns only speech, or at best both speech and writing. The gestures that accompany the use of most forms of speech (even telephone conversations!) have not received the serious attention of linguists, nor is much said in linguistic theories about the expressive value of typography in the case of written language.

Nevertheless, one must ask of linguistic theory to do exactly this, because the complex linguistic concept 'lingual object' is broader than the words of any concrete language. If we were unable to make any sense of the objective lingual factuality (the so-called semiotic structure) that surrounds the 'wording', to use Halliday's term (1979: 189), we would simply be unable to understand one another, for the correlation of lingual subject and object would be short-circuited. The meaningful objective elements in any situation or event are simply not reducible to the words that are spoken. Everything in reality, also the circumstances that constitute a situation or event in which language is used, has an objective lingual factuality that must be interpreted in the dynamic flow of events through the human's subjective lingual capacities.

Saying, therefore, is only one way of meaning (Halliday 1979:

192), and a linguistic theory that does not recognize this fact will be the poorer for it.

Some remarks on terminology

The typological distinctions made in this chapter, as well as some of the systematic terms introduced earlier, require some further terminological clarification.

First, the terms 'lingual' and 'linguistic' must be used in such a way that they echo the distinction between what is theoretical and pre-theoretical. The lingual aspect is indeed a fundamental experiential mode that is discovered only through theoretical analysis and reflection, but is simultaneously independent in its functioning from its analytical discovery. To the extent that linguistics has traditionally refused to honor the distinction between theoretical (linguistic) and pre-theoretical (lingual) fact, the difference between an irreducible expressive modus and its theoretical explanations has been denied and lost sight of.

Similarly, there is a terminological vacuum whenever one wishes to distinguish between a person with a flair for languages (which need not necessarily constitute a theoretical knowledge of such languages) and a language theorist; due to the traditional combination of both meanings in one word it is doubtful whether any coined term, say 'linguistician' to refer to the theorist, will gain acceptance. The distinction has to be introduced, however, for it signals the same reality as that which can be indicated through the terms 'lingual' and 'linguistic'. Since a newly coined term is not crucial for what follows, a statement of the ambiguity inherent in the term 'linguist' will suffice at this juncture.

Secondly, renewed interest in semiotics in recent years has raised the terminological question whether the term 'lingual' should not be scrapped in favor of 'semiotic' to indicate the irreducible temporal mode of expression by means of signs. There seems to be some validity in the argument, but it is doubtful if much can be achieved in opting for such a change. Traditional distinctions take a long time to die, and are forever being revived in terminological squabbles. The traditional terms used to refer to the lingual modality probably appealed to either the norm-side of this aspect ('semiotic' as the norm for signifying) or to that which is signified factually in an objective form ('meaning'), while the indication of this aspect as the modality of 'symbolic signification' ('betekening') latched on to the subjective lingual activities of human creatures (cf. Strauss, Van den Berg & Weideman 1979: 3). As long as the term 'lingual' is employed in a carefully defined context to be applicable to more than verbal signs, it seems, for the moment at least, to be preferable; it is certainly not perfect as a term, but it can perhaps help to avoid getting involved in an academic routine of terminological in-fighting about the true meaning of 'semiotic' and the 'real' position of linguistics as opposed to semiology.

Anthropological foundations of linguistics

Not only the objective fact of language, but also the subjective human capacity for producing language must be accounted for in linguistic theory. Verburg's assumption (1971: 262 ff.) that a view of the person is necessary for linguistics is echoed — although now from a mentalistic bias — by Chomsky (1974: 54), who hopes to demonstrate that a theory of the human mind allows the postulation of a unique human lingual faculty that interacts with other faculties. On various occasions, Chomsky insists that "the ability to acquire and use language is a species-specific human capacity, that there are very deep and restrictive principles that determine the nature of human language and are rooted in the specific character of the human mind" (Chomsky 1972a: 102).

It is one of the significant contributions of transformational grammar that it has drawn the attention of linguists anew to the human capacity for language, i.e. to the subjective human ability to form language. It is, according to Chomsky (1972a: 27), this subjective lingual capacity that must therefore be studied in a general linguistic theory:

> The study of universal grammar ... is a study of the nature of human intellectual capacities. It tries to formulate the necessary and sufficient conditions that a system must meet to qualify as a potential human language, conditions that are not accidentally true of the existing human languages, but that are rather rooted in the human 'language capacity' ...

The expressive character of language

Though from a different philosophical perspective than the rationalistic and mentalistic one that undergirds Chomsky's linguistics, this is exactly what the purpose of this study is, namely to formulate the necessary and sufficient conditions that a system must meet to qualify as a potential human language. These conditions can only be formulated with reference first to the complex linguistic distinctions between lingual norm and lingual fact, and, second, to the subjective human ability to produce the objective facts of language in obedience to normative lingual principles.

In broad outline, the conditions that are to be analyzed in the following chapters are that a human language, if it is to be called such, must (1) have an ordered system of rules that unify the facts of such a language; (2) have a normative dimensionality that guides the factual extensions of the language; (3) have a consistent regularity of pattern that guarantees the constancy of lingual facts; (4) have a dynamic normative operation that has factual effects on the language; (5) be relatable to the necessary subjective organs that specify the factual organization of language; (6) exhibit through these organs a normative sensitivity to the rules of the formation of language, the facts of which must be perceptible; (7) be capable of being related or imputed to responsible human beings who have the competence of identifying the facts of language; (8) be used by human beings capable of exercising control over the facts of language for the sake of expressing themselves.

The conditions mentioned are related to the architectonic structure of the lingual aspect of experience (an aspect which finds expression not only in the objective fact of language but also in the subjective human capacity for producing language), since the constitutive structure of the lingual aspect is related to and linked with (1) the numerical, (2) spatial, (3) kinematic, (4) physical, (5) organic, (6) sensitive, (7) analytical and (8) formative aspects of our temporal experience.

The inter-relations between these eight aspects and the lingual aspect guarantee our insight into the conditions that constitute language, and the conditions formulated above are merely provisional formulations of the analogical aspectual coherence between the lingual modality and the aspects that precede it in the order of time.

Once we venture beyond these constitutive moments, the modal meaning of the lingual dimension of experience as expression, which characterizes its retrocipatory structure, deepens and unfolds into the shared expression of human communication. We return to this in the final chapters after first analyzing the constitutive structure of the lingual aspect below.

6 The elementary linguistic concept of lingual unity and multiplicity

Introductory remarks

The lingual aspect of reality reflects the other aspects of experience by way of analogy, and these analogies constitute the structural basis, i.e. the transcendental conditions for language. The scientific investigation of these analogies is guided by a theoretical idea of language. In light of this theoretical idea the structural conditions for the existence of language and the factual lingual expressions that are regulated by these conditions will be analyzed systematically in the following chapters.

The numerical analogies in the lingual aspect provide a systematic starting point for such an analysis, although it is not the only or even the most important place to begin, since the numerical analogies already presuppose, as will become clear, many other implicit and explicit analogical modal distinctions.

No matter where a start is made in a systematic linguistic analysis, the following complications will always arise:
- The lingual aspect in its retrocipatory reflection of the numerical cannot analogously bypass the spheres lying between the numerical and the lingual in the modal order of time. This means that a discussion of the numerical analogies must also take into consideration the spatial, dynamic, historical and other analogies, although these may not be its specific analytical focus at this stage.
- One aspect does not analogously reflect another only in one

specific way. More than one numerical analogy in the lingual aspect will therefore present itself in the analysis that is to follow.
• No analogical modal concept can be formed of the structure of the lingual aspect apart from the typical structures of individuality of human society.

Apart from these systematic complications, there is also the historically important requirement that no attempt at forming a systematic linguistic concept may ignore the work of earlier and contemporary linguists who, although they do not follow every contour of the structural-empirical method, have also discovered and discussed what may be called elementary linguistic concepts.

The first constitutive structural element to be investigated is that of lingual unity and diversity. The investigation must try to clarify theoretically the internal coherence between the lingual aspect and the numerical, and therefore the external quantitative relationship between mathematics and language is not considered.

Lingual system and its formal and material aspects

On the norm-side of the lingual aspect the numerical analogies function as a lingual unity within a diversity of lingual norms. If it is assumed that the lingual norms within a given social sphere form a lingual unity within the diversity of such lingual norms, then it means that these norms constitute an ordered unity that may be called a lingual system. The distinction between the norm-side and the factual side of language is probably what De Saussure has in mind with the distinction between 'langue' and 'parole', between the system and the fact of language; for Chomsky, as for De Saussure, it is the "system that underlies the *actual* use" of language (1979: 113; emphasis added).

This system has a formal lingual and material lingual side.

The formal lingual unity of a given lingual system is derived from the formal validity of the various sources of lingual norms within a lingual sphere. A good example of such a competent and valid source of lingual norms within a lingual sphere is the manual that binds all service writing in an army into a unity, so that all military correspondence follows the same patterns and rules. The formal competence to enforce the rules of such a manual is in this instance derived from a hierarchical unity of higher and lower-ranking formers of military language. The manual for service writing is, however, only one of several sources of lingual norms within this sphere. Even spoken language in the army has to follow the formalities laid down in various other rule books and manuals, directives and operational orders. There are, for example, directives for the form of spoken verbal orders, manuals for drill commands and rules relating to voice procedure on the military radio.

But the formal lingual unity within the diversity of lingual norms within any sphere is not the ultimate guarantee of the individuality, of the relative autonomy that, say, the military lingual sphere possesses in respect of other fields in which language is used, since in various other lingual spheres there are manuals, instructions and directives that regulate language. In the field of medicine, for example, we find a system of lingual norms regulating the written form of medicinal prescriptions, and these formal instructions have to be adhered to just as meticulously.

What is indeed the ultimate guarantee of the lingual unity of differing lingual systems are the material differences between various lingual spheres, and these differences are closely related to the typical structural differences among the respective social spheres. These material differences do not depend on the forms, such as manuals and directives, in which lingual norms come into being and are unified, but on the typical structures of various spheres of social relationships in which different systems of lingual norms apply. Halliday, for example, is concerned with the material side of a lingual system when he remarks (1979: 192):

> With the notion of system we can represent language as a resource, in terms of the choices that are available, the interconnection of these choices, and the conditions affecting their access. We can then relate these choices to recognizable and significant social contexts, using sociosemantic networks ...

These typically different systems of lingual norms reveal their distinct character best when we examine the different consequences that may follow their transgression. A transgression of a lingual norm in the sphere of the system of military writing may lead to a court martial. The most disastrous consequence of not adhering to the rules for medicinal prescriptions may result in the death of a human being. Transgressing the system of lingual norms that applies to conversational language may result in being ignored or ostracized; a loving reprimand may follow if the normative system of lingual rules operative in the intimate sphere of the family is ignored. One must therefore agree with Searle (1969: 41) that not all constitutive rules have penalties when violated; however, this lack does not do away with the truly normative character of such rules.

In these examples the third complication mentioned above is very much in evidence. A lack of insight into the different typical social spheres in which different material systems of lingual norms obtain will result in a linguistic perspective that disregards the systematic pluriformity of language.

From every analogical moment on the norm-side of the lingual aspect that is discovered in a systematic analysis, there will emanate a normative appeal that applies to all users of language. Any lingual system entails a certain *uniformity* of norms. We cannot imagine a medical practitioner having one system of writing out a prescription, and the pharmacist who has to execute this written order, another. Uniformity in the lingual system in a particular sphere may be a matter of life and death; civil engineer and foreman have to be on the same lingual wavelength if roads are to be safe and bridges to stand, and one of the guarantees for this is the uniform system of lingual norms that the one applies to formulate and the other uses to interpret and execute the written order for erecting them. International organizations like the UN and its subsidiaries have contributed much to impose a measure of uniformity on certain types of lingual systems. In this regard one may also refer to the uniform signs and symbols of the International Phonetic Alphabet, and the immense impact made on written language by the introduction of a standard alphabet.

The lingual unity and diversity of lingual subjects and objects

The lingual unity and diversity of lingual subjects and objects functioning on the factual side of the lingual aspect are subject to and determined by the lingual unity of materially different systems of lingual norms. The systematic unity of order on the norm-side is therefore correlated with the factual unity of lingual subjects and objects.

The elementary linguistic concept of lingual unity

The factual users of any lingual system are called lingual subjects, who, in order to form a language, have to be lingually competent and responsible. In this sense every human being, in their lingual subject function, is a lingual unity within a diversity of lingual possibilities of expression within the various material lingual spheres. This observation may correspond in certain respects to De Saussure's 'langage'. Because these lingual subjects also form a lingual unity with the social organizations within which they use a language, both of these can be termed lingual subjects.

Nevertheless, lingual subjectivity remains a complex linguistic concept, and the factual lingual unity of this subjectivity is but one aspect, one of the many elementary linguistic concepts from which the complex concept 'lingual subject' can be approached.

The same applies to the complex linguistic concept 'lingual object'. By lingual object may be understood any factual expression by means of a sign. The lingual objectivity of something is made patent in the form of a sign.

There has been much discussion in linguistics on the possibility of isolating the word as a factual unity of objective lingual parts from the stream of lingual sounds in speech (cf. Pike 1959: 45 ff.; Palmer 1976: 37-42; Strauss 1967: 58 f.). Of course, the existence of dictionaries points to a positive answer to this. Nevertheless, it has been difficult, if not impossible, to separate words from the stream of sound even with the help of sophisticated technical means.

The factual lingual unity of objective lingual facts or lingual signs is, according to De Saussure (1966: 66 ff.; also 102 f.), a unity not of a thing and a name, but of concept and sound-image, a signified ('signifie') and signifier ('signifiant'). Much has been said by way of criticism of De Saussure's psychologistic point of view in this regard. One possible way out of the problems that linguists have encountered with De Saussure's view is the suggestion that concrete entities have a latent, objective lingual function that can be made patent in a name; thus the latent objective lingual function of a concrete thing like a chair can be made patent in the name /chair/, the latter being a second kind of entity in distinction from the signified chair, and having "its own latent, objective sign function which can be made patent in its turn by synonymous names like /stool/ or /seat/, or by a diagrammatic representation of a chair" (Strauss, Van den Berg & Weideman 1979: 4).

The concept of the factual unity of lingual objects also concerns the relationship between geno-typical varieties of language such as speech and gesture, or speech, gesture and writing, that were distinguished and discussed in the previous chapter. The 'language' of many situations embodies an intimate unity of two or more of these geno-typical varieties of language. An academic lecture, for example, may from a lingual point of view depend upon a closely-knit unity of gesture, speech and writing. In spite of geno-typical differences, the factual unity of spoken and gestural forms of the language is guaranteed by their unity of lingual function: "... bodily and facial gestures and expressions add meaning to spoken words. We stamp a foot, wiggle a finger, raise an eyebrow, clasp hands, bend forward or backward, shrug a shoulder, grin or grimace, nod or shake the head ... meaning in talk is also affected by pauses and halts that are often as significant as words themselves" (Shaw 1970: 361).

The *multidimensionality* of the meanings of an objective lingual unit like the word can best be examined when the second systematic linguistic concept, namely lingual *extension*, is analyzed, yet it is quite appropriate to remark here that the number of different meaningful dimensions of a word has a numerical basis; this is evident when we speak of a word as a unity in a multiplicity of lingually significant possibilities. "Multiplicity of meaning is a very general characteristic of language," writes Palmer (1976: 71), for it cannot be confined only to the lexical level, but extends to the objective lingual meaning of grammatical elements and syntactical ambiguity.

The lingual unity of lingual subject and lingual object speaks for itself. When human beings speak, they are revealing their subjective lingual ability to express themselves, and also their responsibility for the lingual objects that they produce out of their free human lingual will and intention. Words, sentences and other lingual utterances, in spoken or in written form, are always the words of lingual subjects. This is known in speech theory, a branch of linguistic study, as the relation between speaker and speech, or the act of signification and the signifier; sometimes a third element is added: that which is signified. This relation can be formulated as follows: the lingual subject-object relation is the relation which exists between the lingual subject-function of the totality of the human personality and the lingual objectification, in various means of expression (speech, writing or gesturing) of the lingual object-function of a concrete thing (that which is signified).

Other objective lingual units that function on the factual side of the numerical analogy in the lingual aspect include, in the case of spoken language, phonemes, morphemes and what Pike (1959 40 ff.), following Bloomfield's terminology, calls a tagmeme.

Pike (1959: 43), interestingly, also wants linguistic theory to provide for the study of larger units, such as the (long disregarded) syllable (as a larger phonological unit that has as its parts the minimal units of sounds or phonemes), the stress group, the pause group and the rhetorical period. As far as the lexical level is concerned, Pike draws our attention to the objective lingual unity of idioms, and ultimately even sonnets or limericks, as units larger than the morpheme.

Expanding on this, one may add to the list the objective lingual unity of a sentence, or of the noun phrase or verb phrase that is part of the sentence, or, broader still, if we consider the factual units of the written language, the objective lingual units of paragraph, chapter and book. For each of these objective entities linguistics must attempt to give a formal, explicit definition. Pike's three diverging viewpoints of language as particle, wave and field are of systematic interest in that they echo the numerical, spatial, kinematic and physical analogies in the lingual aspect. These viewpoints are not exclusive but complementary theoretical angles from which the total descriptive linguistic statement can be derived (Pike 1959: 52-53).

The lingual unity and diversity of lingual facts

Another numerical analogy on the factual side of the lingual aspect concerns the lingual unity and diversity of lingual facts.

A distinction should be made between subjective and objective lingual facts. The former are human acts, or conditions called into being by humans with respect to their lingual function, while the latter are events, things and conditions that come into being and exist without the intervention of the human lingual will, i.e. natural facts, events and conditions, also with respect only to their lingual function. Both subjective and objective lingual facts can be meaningful or meaningless, in so far as they are brought or not brought together into a *factual lingual unity* by and in subjection to a system of lingual norms.

Subjective lingual facts like human actions in respect of the state and church may function as symbols within a literary work of art (cf. Bloom's avoidance of the representatives of state and church in Chapter 10 of Joyce's *Ulysses*) as may objective lingual facts like light and darkness, as in the work of Joseph Conrad. This explains why, within one material lingual sphere such as that of literary art, there may exist different formally devised *symbolic systems* from one form to the next. Gestures and gesticulating may also be qualified respectively as objective and subjective lingual facts. The polite nod or bow, the lifting of a hat or the hand and the act of standing back to enable another to pass first are all subjective lingual facts, since they *signify* social conventions.

Both subjective and objective lingual facts require *interpretation*, and this interpretation rests upon an understanding of the lingual norms or systems that bring them into a factual *symbolic unity*. In Joseph Conrad's works, for example, the symbolic system revolves around light and darkness, perfumes and dirt, butterfly and beetle, sinner and saint, and so forth. To take a second example: objective lingual facts like disease symptoms have to be interpreted as a coherent whole by the physician making an interpretative diagnosis. And as a final example, consider the act of forecasting the weather in a naive or even in a more technical way, which depends upon interpreting the factual objective lingual features of natural states and events as a *unified* whole.

To subjective lingual facts also belongs the erection of visible signs of cultural and historical development such as monuments. These monuments, as objective lingual signs, are the objects of subjective human lingual activity, and in this we note again how the existence of subjective and objective lingual facts depends on the lingual subject-object relation. Observe also the lingual subject-object relation in the following examples of correlated subjective and objective lingual facts: the *building* of *marks* of juridical property in the form of fences; the *wearing* of external *signs* — like clothes in their various fashions — of a particular social status; the *marking* of a product by a *sign* of economic goodwill in the form of a trademark or brand name; the act of *supplying* a *token* of economic and contractual security as in a written guarantee; the *use* of the *symbols* of faith, like the cross, the bread and the wine in Christianity; the *giving* of *tokens* of troth in the

The elementary linguistic concept of lingual unity 83

form of rings and other presents, and the *wearing* of *badges* of rank in the army. Their factual lingual unity is important, and it is ruled and regulated by unified symbolic systems, such as the regulations applying to military insignia, the uniform prescriptions pertaining to written guarantees, etc.

The unity within the diversity of objective and subjective lingual facts can never be grasped apart from the factual lingual *position* and *place* these facts occupy within the different material lingual spheres, and this fact makes clear the irresistibly dynamic character of this kind of analysis, that has to progress from the one systematic concept, in this case the numerical analogies in the lingual modality, to the next, i.e. the set of spatial analogies.

Thus the adopted method cannot be accused of imposing a preconceived static linguistic-analytical form upon the dynamic facts of language, for already in this sample of such an analysis the following analogical concepts apart from the numerical have had their proper place: we have spoken of

- the validity of lingual norms, which refers to the physical analogy where the analytical focus is on the concept of lingual energy or power, since the dynamic process from lingual cause to lingual effect is implied;
- the typically different lingual spheres, which refers to both the spatial and social analogies;
- lingual users, formers and producers, which are formative, historical analogies;
- lingual competence and responsibility (formative and analytical analogies);
- lingual dimensionality, which is another spatial analogy;
- lingual meanings, which give us echoes of the analytical, in that they concern the lingual identity and distinctiveness in the meanings of words, and
- the lingual will or volition to produce language, which has an emotional or sensitive foundation.

7 Spatial analogies in the lingual aspect

External and internal coherence

As regards the spatial analogies in the lingual aspect, the inner connection between the spatial and lingual modalities should form the basis of a systematic investigation. Thus the theoretical interest is not in the first place focused here on the external, concrete relationship between language and space, studied by linguistic geography, but on lingual extension on both the norm-side and the factual side of the lingual aspect. A linguistic methodology must constantly guard against selecting, in Hjelmslev's words (1963: 4), only disconnected, external facets of language for study. De Saussure (1966: 20 f., 191 ff.; cf. also Wells 1971: 10-11), too, holds the view that dialect geography, for example, is 'external linguistics.'

The kind of lingual extension to be considered in this chapter figures on the norm-side as the *lingual sphere* or *range* in which lingual systems are accepted as valid norms for the language used in such a sphere, and on the factual side of the lingual modality as the *lingual position* occupied by lingual facts in a *continuous succession* of objective lingual facts:

> Even a short speech is continuous: it consists of an unbroken succession of movements and sound-waves. No matter into how many successive parts we break up our record for purposes of minute study, an even finer analysis is always conceivable. A speech-utterance is what mathematicians call a *continuum*; it can be viewed as consisting of any desired number of successive parts (Bloomfield 1958: 76).

At this stage of a systematic linguistic analysis the dimensions of lingual systems and facts must also be investigated. Accordingly, the fact that the lingual act, as *ex*-pression[3] (Afrikaans: *uit*-ing) needs space, or even the acoustic, three-dimensional extension of lingual sounds into space (Verburg 1965: 89) does not concern linguists.

What do concern linguists are the normative lingual possibilities of arrangement that determine the position of objective lingual facts. The factual lingual position of objective lingual forms or constituents depends on their successive ordering or arrangement through the mediation of lingual norms, which arrangement constitutes grammar (Bloomfield 1958: 163). It is significant that Bloomfield, while trying to relegate the description of meaning outside the scope of linguistics, nonetheless defines grammar (1958: 163; emphasis added) as the "*meaningful* arrangement of forms in a language ..." Robinson (1975: 139) has this to say about "the wild goose chase of meaning out of language":

> Meaning is not a *component* of language, but a characterization. When language is itself it is meaningful, and the meaning is whatever makes language language. Hence grammar is indeed the study of meaning.

Bloomfield, however, tries to emphasize that in linguistic study no accurate (in his terms 'scientific') description of meaning is possible: linguistics merely has to accept the relatively constant[4] meaning of a linguistic form (Bloomfield 1958: 145, 158) and proceed from there.

---

3. Cf. Verburg (1971:268), where the spatial substratum of language is considered to be the 'spatio-quantitative' space outside the speaker into which he or she 'forces out' a certain volume of language.
4. The lingual constancy of lingual forms is a kinematic analogy on the factual side of the lingual aspect which will be discussed in the next chapter.

In defining the different possibilities of arrangement that determine the factual positioning of lingual forms, Bloomfield is acknowledging the unbreakable correlation between lingual law (norm) and lingual fact, as it presents itself in the sphere of the spatial analogies in the lingual aspect. It is this correlation that Hjelmslev (1963: 39) initially calls 'process' and 'system', and later specifies in the analogical spatial terms 'syntagmatic' and 'paradigmatic' as applied to semiotic process and system, or simply as 'text' and 'language' in the case of 'natural' (verbal) language.

The lingual sphere of applicability of a lingual system

The spatial analogies on the norm-side of the structure of the lingual aspect may be disclosed theoretically as the field in which a certain lingual system is valid, i.e. the area in which a set of lingual norms is applied.

Various material lingual spheres may co-exist in the forms in which concrete languages are called into being and the subsequent forms in which they exist. The same applies to geno-types and sub-types of lingually qualified objects. Thus one may find in the area of military language certain forms of the languages (e.g. English and another language) that people use in other spheres too. The co-existence of different kinds of language within certain fields does not, however, do away with the material distinctions between one lingual sphere and the next, or with geno-typical and other variations. Such co-existing languages are unified in such a way that these differences remain intact.

This of course invokes the complex question concerning the relationship between different material lingual spheres. The typical characteristics of the different spheres are closely connected with the question whether the social structure in which language is used possesses an authority-relationship between people who are in authority over others, who are subjected to such authority.

In the military sphere, for instance, such an authority-relationship creates the possibility of exercising formal control over language usage by prescribing certain sets of rules. But since there are not only people with higher or lower ranks in any army, but also many who are of equal rank, we find intertwined in the sphere of military language conversational forms of languages such as English, which lack such an authority-relationship in that particular form.

Just how the relationship between two lingual spheres combined in such a way may eventually be determined is a problem that can be approached systematically only when the linguistic analysis has progressed to the social analogies in the lingual aspect, where the different social spheres are discussed in terms of their institutional, communal, inter-communal and inter-personal relationships. One may, however, at this stage of a systematic analysis take note of the difficulties that arise when the spoken form of conversational language, which usually lacks such an authority-relationship, is subjected to the regulations of an academy that tries to prescribe lingual rules. It soon becomes apparent that such an attempt at regulating the language of conversation amounts to nothing more than a recognition of certain conventions of speech (and, very often, also conventions governing the written forms of the language) that have not yet received formal recognition in the form of such a regulation, or of conventions that have changed in spite of regulations to the contrary. The sometimes ineffectual efforts made by the compilers of technical dictionaries to have their work accepted as authoritative fall into the same category.

Every set of analogies on the norm-side of the lingual aspect discloses a normative moment to which concrete, everyday language is subjected. As regards the spatial analogies this lingual principle may be formulated as the need to recognize the limits and limitations of lingual systems. Purists may strive to purge conversational language of what, in their opinion, are gross errors, but the attempt usually fails. In spite of numerous arguments to the contrary, agreements are still 'finalized' and people persist in trying to 'contact' each other by telephone. Ignoring the limits of one's lingual authority produces only negative results.

Linguists have in the past attempted to formulate the normative scope or range of systematic lingual patterns by pointing out formal lingual features (cf. Crystal & Davy 1976: 8). McIntosh (1961: 337), for example, introduces (by way of definition) a distinction between grammatical pattern and lexical range; 'range' specifically, "has to do with the specific collocations we make in a series of particular instances." His view is that, quite apart from considerations of pattern in the grammatical sense, and yet wholly within the dictates of pattern, the objective, factual collocations that a language allows are regulated by a normative potential of collocability (1961: 327 ff.) that may be specified in 'tolerated ranges of collocability.'

One may observe that both of these terms, pattern and range, are of an analogical spatial nature, and that McIntosh attains the desired distinction between them (which is, within the context of his argument, both necessary and realistic) only by definition.

What is also interesting about McIntosh's view is that he provides for the extension of patterns and ranges (1961: 331 and 335) as well as for their restriction, both of which again are terms operative within the sphere of spatial analogies in the lingual aspect. More specifically, one has here an analogy functioning on the norm-side of the structure of the lingual aspect, and McIntosh also makes it clear in a footnote (1961: 335; cf. too 337) that what he has to say about the extension and restriction of normative ranges of collocability, applies equally to (normative) grammatical patterns.

In so far as the concepts of normative extension and restriction embody a certain consistent lingual *mobility*, they actually belong to the sphere of kinematic analogies operating on the norm-side of the lingual aspect, and will again be dealt with below when this set of analogies is systematically discussed. A study of the period of appeal to authority will lead us to essentially the same conclusion as McIntosh, namely that in light of the analogical relation between the lingual and kinematic aspects, one must admit that there "are ... pattern-extending tendencies also, which amounts to saying that grammar does not remain fixed ..." (McIntosh 1961: 331, footnote 15).

In order to distinguish between the various material lingual spheres, McIntosh makes use of yet another analogical spatial term, namely dimension. This time, however, the term indicates a factual state of affairs that one may evaluate in terms of the general lingual norm of avoiding both triteness and obscurity (McIntosh 1961: 332):

> It is important to stress the word 'dimension'. For different users of language (and indeed different traditional styles of language) vary as to the point where they kick off into the void; below a certain dimension their collocations may be very 'ordinary', but the collocation of these collocations may be much more daring and unusual. At whatever point we kick off, if we depart too far from some sort of tolerated range, we run the risk of being obscure. The balance we have to strike is therefore between triteness and obscurity.

Incidentally, these remarks reinforce McIntosh's distinction between collocational range and grammatical pattern, because in poetry, for example, we may find highly 'normal' grammatical patterns contrasted, in the same text, with unusual collocations.

The question, then, is this: are we compelled, in view of McIntosh's distinction between pattern and range, to abandon the concept of the *normative* range of a lingual pattern? The answer seems to be no. McIntosh's distinction is a necessary one, employing analogical spatial terms to differentiate terminologically between two different normative lingual phenomena. For both of these phenomena one may specify a normative *scope* or range of applicability. The concept 'normative range of a lingual pattern', however, is just as necessary a distinction in linguistic theory as the phenomena described by McIntosh. As long as it is clear terminologically what is meant by these terms, there should be no confusion, and one need not consider exchanging one analogical spatial term (e.g. 'range') for another (say, 'scope').

The crucial importance of the concept of the normative range of a lingual pattern becomes clear when one reviews the sad history of prescriptivist grammar in languages like English and Afrikaans, a history that was at times characterized by efforts to purge all varieties of language of what were considered to be errors. In certain material lingual spheres, this constitutes an overstepping of normative lingual principles and limits, a denial thus of the norm that is disclosed theoretically in an analysis of the spatial analogy on the norm-side of the lingual aspect; it must be countered by an appeal to the need to recognize the restricted and limited range of any lingual pattern. The analogical spatial term 'range' is a useful one in this regard, because it can evoke the immensely rich scope of possibilities of language while at the same time indicating the limits of that scope.

The constitutive linguistic concept of normative lingual range applies also to other levels of language. Crystal and Davy (1976: 18) mention, for example, the patterned range of alphabetical shapes in the written form of the language, that, together with the sounds of the spoken language have a "predictable and limited number of combinations to build up larger units, such as words and sentences. The sounds and letters of English have a clearly definable form and function, and their systematicness may be formalised in rules (of pronunciation and spelling respectively)."

Even though this correlation between normative range of possible combination and the factual units and forms that are described by it is a constitutive linguistic concept, it may be used to distinguish or to assist in distinguishing between the various material lingual spheres that function as anticipatory moments in the *regulative* idea of language. The constitutive moment of normative lingual range is a necessary prerequisite for the formulation of regulative linguistic ideas.

On the musical or tonal level of spoken language there are further conventionalized normative ranges of meaning (cf. Crystal & Davy 1976: 33), and as regards the rules for the combination of morphs "their scope can be left open" in the case of regular forms, whereas "irregular words are handled by special rules of restricted scope" (Lyons 1968: 187).

The lingual dimensionality of a lingual system

The lingual dimensionality of a lingual system is another spatial analogy on the norm-side of the lingual aspect that requires theoretical consideration. The original modal meaning of space, as Dooyeweerd points out, is dimensional continuous extension; dimensionality, "however, is an element of the spatial modality of meaning (viewed from its law-side) which cannot exist without its coherence with the numerical aspect. As space may have two, three or more dimensions, it always refers to the arithmetical aspect as its substratum" (1953 vol. 2: 86 f.; cf. too 163).

Van Heerden (1972: 8-10) discusses the fundamental difference between a formally conceived code, which has a one-dimensional sign system, and the spoken form of conversational language, that possesses a multidimensional lingual system which enables it to symbolize more dynamically. In a similar vein, Chomsky has (1965: 136), on the basis of his distinction between phrase structure and transformational grammars, asserted that the grammars of the artificial languages of logic and the theory of programming are apparently without exception simple phrase structure grammars.

This means that only by an additional, transformational dimension which transforms the simple phrase structure grammar with its simple rewrite rules (e.g. 0074 → the pension scheme number of C.J. Smith in the computer printout "0074: C.J. Smith") into a more complex language mechanism, can one get an approximation of the complexity of human language. This complexity of human language cannot adequately be described merely by means of a phrase structure grammar; and in this lies the distinction between language and code.

Even if one doubts the validity of the concept of linguistic transformation as developed by transformational grammar, it is possible to distinguish between language and code by means of the concept of normative lingual dimensionality. A language simply has more systematic (and therefore normative) dimensions than a code: "Most coding systems are on two levels: a *content*, and an *expression*: for example, traffic signals, with content 'stop/go' coded into expression 'red/green'," says Halliday (1979: 187); "But language has evolved a third, abstract level of *form* intermediate between the two: it consists of content, form and expression, or, in linguistic terms, of semantics, lexicogrammar and phonology".

It is also clear that the normative *possibility* of *systematically* combining and positioning lingual facts in codes and in other types of language regulates the factual lingual position of lingual objects, and that different codes and languages have two or more systematic dimensions. In this way a language may, with extremely limited phonemic possibilities, be able to yield an infinite number of new and original lingual utterances. The phonemes that form the constituent sound-forms of a language possess a limited number of possibilities for systematic combination, and are thus adapted to the limitations of the physical, organic, emotional and act-structures of the human personality (cf. Van Heerden 1972: 4; also his 1965: 128). The systematically determined sequence of speech sounds as lingual parts within a lingual whole such as the word is studied by the linguistic sub-discipline known as phonology.

The lingual position of lingual facts

The lingual position of lingual facts functioning on the factual side of the lingual aspect is in the first instance related to the lingual system to which such facts are subject. The factual position of any lingual object is always determined by historically variable syntactic systems that control and are valid for lingual positioning and combination.

The lingual positioning of lingual objects was, according to Reichling (1969: 76), for the first time studied seriously and explicitly by language theorists of the 'distributionalist' school (including Zellig Harris). Objective lingual distribution is a characteristic of every objective lingual fact smaller than the sentence; whether it be of a distributionally equivalent, complementary, inclusive or overlapping type, it is always distribution over a *range* of *contexts* (Lyons 1968: 70 f.). The spatially conceived terminology is obvious in the notion of lingual distribution; Lyons not only presents these different kinds of distribution schematically, but also, significantly, uses the term 'mathematical linguistics' in this respect (1968: 71). The numerical and spatial aspects define the field of study of mathematics proper. Harris's (1966: 15-16) initial definition of the lingual distribution of objective lingual facts, namely that it is "the total of all environments" in which the element "occurs, i.e. the sum of all the (different) positions" of such an object, relies heavily on analogical spatial terms.

The factual position of a lingual object becomes interesting from a linguistic point of view when one considers that word order in itself is a significant expressive factor, especially in certain fields such as poetic language. The objective lingual position of the formal, grammatical subject of a sentence in various types of discourse is ruled by considerations of what is being spoken or written about, and may explain why active forms are preferred, in some stretches of a text, rather than passives, and vice versa (Hendricks 1973: 52 f.).

Structuralism as relationism

Structuralist linguistics seems to concentrate especially on the mathematical-spatial analogies in the lingual aspect. Of this the concepts of lingual relation, correlation, cohesion, sequence, linearity, combination, co-ordination, dependence, whole, parts, totality, constellation and so forth, encountered often in structuralist theories of whatever brand, supply ample evidence. Wells's (1971: 6) characterization of De Saussure's thought is significant:

> The crux of De Saussure's theory ... is the role of relations in a system: Signs are constituted partly, and phonemes wholly, by their relations, that is by belonging to a system ... For them, to be is to be related.

Spatial analogies in the lingual aspect

Similarly, Greimas (1974: 55) defines structure as a relation between terms, and claims:

> 'Being a structuralist' should mean not to consider as objects of thought the phenomena, but the relations between phenomena ... 'Structure' means first a coherent set of relations, the elements being the termini of those relations (Greimas 1974: 56-57).

In much the same vein, Hjelmslev (1963: 83) remarks that the aim of science is to investigate cohesions.

Bruns is correct in ascribing the relationist starting-point of structuralism to an absolutization of the spatial analogy of lingual opposition when he says (1975: 233):

> From the structuralist point of view ... [the being of the sign] lies in ... the systematic way in which it signifies its opposition to other words in the language. Removed from the system, it ceases to be anything at all.

It is the particular factual spatial position of a given lingual object that places it in opposition to other lingual objects; in structuralist theory this opposition is both a defining mark of a lingual object and a means of conceiving the 'being' of a sign as its systematic, relational link with other signs. In structuralist linguistics 'opposition' as term appears always to include both of these meanings, namely definition or determination of the identity of a lingual object as well as relational or correlational position regulated by a lingual system.

The absolutization of the spatial analogy of relation within the lingual aspect is also the ground for De Saussure's (1966: 91) distinction between synchronic and diachronic linguistics:

> The synchronic and diachronic 'phenomenon' ... have nothing in common. One is a relation between simultaneous elements, the other a substitution of one element for another in time, an event.

We should note that 'simultaneity' is of course the expression of time in the spatial modality (cf. also De Saussure 1966: 100). The absolutization of the spatial analogy within the lingual mode of experience is also the basis of De Saussure's distinction between diachronic and synchronic law. Synchronic law, says De Saussure (1966: 93), is a law of arrangement.

Hjelmslev's theoretical stance is also thoroughly structuralist. Note, for example, the pivotal position of analogical spatial terms in the following passage (1963: 22-23; emphases added):

> It soon becomes apparent that the important thing is not the division of an object into parts, but the conduct of the analysis so that it conforms to the *mutual dependences* between these parts ... both the object and its parts have existence only by virtue of these dependences; the *whole* of the object ... can be defined only by the dependences joining it to other *co-ordinated* parts, to the whole, and to its parts of the next *degree*, and by the sum of the dependences that these parts of the next degree *contract* with each other ... the 'objects' ... are ... nothing but *intersections* of bundles of such dependences. That is to say, objects can be described only with their help and can be defined and grasped scientifically only in this way. The dependences, which naive realism regards as secondary, presupposing the objects, become from this point of view primary, presupposed by their intersections.

In this rather lengthy passage it becomes clear that Hjelmslev's position depends on a hypostatization of analogical spatial moments within the structure of the lingual aspect. Parts have existence *only* by virtue of dependences, he claims. It is significant to note how often the word 'only' is used in connection with spatial retrocipations in this passage. In fine, remarks Hjelmslev (1963: 23), linguistic theory must recognize "that a totality does not consist of things but of relationships, and that not substance but only its internal and external relationships have scientific existence ...." He thus finds himself close to the structuralist position of De Saussure, whom he admires for having recognized the priority of dependences within language. In saying, for example, that De Saussure "asserted that a language is a form, not a substance" (*ibid.*), Hjelmslev is contributing to the justifiable criticism of what he calls 'metaphysical' hypotheses, ostensibly that of the autonomous 'Ding an sich'; what "from one point of view is 'substance'," he remarks (1963: 81), "is from another point of view 'form', this being connected with the fact that functives denote only terminals or points of intersection for functions, and that only the functional net of dependences has knowability and scientific existence, while 'substance' in an ontological sense, remains a metaphysical concept."

Hjelmslev reinforces his structuralist starting point by distinguishing between three different kinds of lingual dependence, namely interdependence, determination and constellation. Significant too is the fact that he uses different terms to account for the operation of these different kinds of dependence on the normative and factual side of the lingual aspect, terms that are intended to describe how the different kinds of lingual dependence may function upon entering into a lingual process or into a lingual system (Hjelmslev 1963: 24). Thus interdependence on the factual side (i.e. in the lingual process) is called *solidarity*, and on the norm-side *complementarity*. Likewise, determination is distinguished as *selection* on the factual side and as *specification* on the norm-side, and in the case of the third kind of lingual dependence, namely constellation, he asks us to distinguish between factual lingual *combinations* and systematic *autonomies* (1963: 24-25).

Furthermore, a lingual hierarchy (as a class of classes) is termed a *chain* (composed of parts) if it belongs to the factual lingual process, and a *paradigm* (composed, in its turn, of members) if it forms a class within the normative lingual system (1963: 29-30). Hjelmslev (1963: 35) also proposes a common name for interdependence and determination, namely *cohesion*; interdependence and constellation he subsumes under the term *reciprocity*. Both terms again contain an echo of the spatial aspect. We should note, too, that the very terms that Hjelmslev uses to indicate the distinction between the complex linguistic concepts of lingual fact and lingual norm may, from his structuralist starting point, themselves be defined in terms of the spatial analogical concepts of correlation and relation; he states (1963: 38-39), for example, that "we can define a *system* as a correlational hierarchy, and a *process* as a relational hierarchy".

In fact, Hjelmslev's detailed proposals at every turn echo his reliance upon the structuralist emphasis on spatial analogies: syllables, for example, may under certain structural conditions be divided into central and marginal parts, since a marginal part presupposes textual co-existence of a central part (1963: 27); similarly we must conceive of parts as nothing but intersection points of bundles of lines of dependence (1963: 28), and our linguistic analysis consists of "registering certain dependences between certain terminals, which we may call ... the parts of the text, and which have existence precisely by virtue of these dependences and only by virtue of them" (*ibid*.).

Hjelmslev's structuralism also explicitly establishes that the spatial analogies depend on the numerical retrocipations in the structure of the lingual aspect, because

> The peculiar factor that characterizes the whole and the parts, that makes it different from a dependence between the whole and other wholes, ... seems to be the *uniformity* of the dependence: co-ordinate parts ... depend in a uniform fashion on that whole (Hjelmslev 1963: 28; for lingual uniformity, see above, Chapter 6).

Indeed, both *dependence* and *uniformity* are posited as indefinables (1963: 29) by Hjelmslev. There is no escape in the end for linguistic theory from the *indefinable modal aspects and their retrocipations and anticipatory analogical relations*, however much theorists wish to restrict their presuppositions. Structuralism presents us with a peculiar view of these analogical relations, because it proposes to survey objective lingual phenomena from the restricted vantage point of only the mathematical-spatial set of retrocipations in the structure of the lingual aspect. Even the original organic analogy of function, for example, is reduced by Hjelmslev to a spatial analogy, since for him it has a sense "that lies midway between the logico-mathematical and the etymological sense ... in formal respect nearer to the first but not identical with it" (1963: 33-34). Thus, when an entity has certain functions, it means, firstly, that it "has dependences with other entities" and, secondly, that it "fulfils a definite role, assumes a definite 'position' in the chain" (1963: 34). Both meanings, therefore, rely explicitly on the mathematical-spatial notions of relation and position.

Lingual extension on the factual side of the lingual aspect

Morphemes, as lingual parts that cannot express meaning independently, rely on the lingual whole of the word for their symbolically expressive existence. With a cautionary remark that in fact no lingual object has any meaning in absolute isolation, Hjelmslev (1963: 45) observes that none of the so-called minimal entities, nor the roots, have such an 'independent' existence that they can be assigned a lexical meaning. Together with flexemes, morphemes constitute the lingually economic means by which the expressive *area* of a language may be *extended* in the formation of new words.

The symbolic field of expression of a lingual object has a lingually determinable size, as the semantic field theory in linguistics has justifiably pointed out. The area of expression of a word does not comprise a merely static quantity of semantic possibilities, but undergoes lingual (i.e. expressive) *changes* from one *historical* period to the next, The constitutive linguistic concept of the magnitude of the area of signification of a lingual fact can therefore not be grasped apart from the analogical meaning of other retrocipatory moments within the structure of the lingual aspect, in this case the *physical* (lingual change) and *formative* (historical) ones; the spatial analogies in the lingual aspect are heavily charged with additional analogical meaning, because their coherence with the lingual aspect is mediated through a series of successively intervening law-spheres in the intermodal order of time.

The lingually identifiable distinctions in the meaning of a word may be subject to expansion or restriction, and the lingual possibilities of broadening or limiting such an expressive area are closely connected with the material lingual sphere in which the word is used. Anthony Burgess writes (1974: 7):

> The writer of literature, especially the poet, differs from the scientist or lawyer in *not restricting* his words. The scientist has to make his word mean one thing and one thing only, so does the lawyer. But once the word — like our note on the piano — is allowed to vibrate freely, it not only calls up associations but also, at times, suggests other completely different meanings and perhaps even other words.

Secondly, one must note that in the case of the word as objective lingual unit a restriction or extension of its field of meaning (cf. De Jongste 1956: 162 ff.) may be specified still further by its immediate lingual surroundings, for the lingual context in which a word is used also determines that the irrelevant connotations should be excluded and the relevant meanings included in its interpretation.

The factual lingual moment of context has been explored by the so-called 'context-theory of meaning'. This theory is characterized by its heavy emphasis on this spatial analogy on the factual side of the lingual aspect. The meaning of a word is determined by the context in which it is used. Verburg, however, puts semantic contextualism in its proper perspective when he remarks (1951: 31) that we should not lose sight of the fact that the reverse is also true: words, especially imperatives, always determine the situation. Lingual *context* may be defined as the *objective lingual vicinity* or *neighborhood* of an objective lingual fact, while the broader lingual *situation* or social context refers to the factual lingual usage within a material lingual sphere. Lingual context defined as the lingual vicinity or objective lingual surroundings of lingual facts concerns what De Saussure calls syntagmatic solidarities, the fact that almost all lingual units depend on what surrounds them in the speech chain or on their successive objective lingual parts (1966: 127), and what Harris (1966: 15) terms the 'environment' of an objective lingual fact.

Both syntagmatic and paradigmatic relations between objective lingual facts (cf. Lyons 1968: 73-74) are fundamental linguistic concepts that depend on the spatial analogies in the lingual aspect, since the lingual context of an objective lingual fact is specifiable in terms of these relations.

According to Reichling (1947: 41), extension or limitation of the meaning of a word may be noted particularly when we recognize and interpret the applicable and inapplicable distinctions of meaning that a word may possess in metaphorical speech. Bloomfield (1958: 149), too, links the phenomenon of metaphor to the spatial analogies of central and marginal meanings of objective lingual facts, and uses this distinction to account for factual changes of meaning, viewed then as expansion or extension of the lingual area of signification; the present multiplicity of meanings of a word like 'charge', for example, "is evidently due to expansion into marginal spheres followed by obsolescence of intermediate meanings" (Bloomfield 1958: 432; cf. too 431, 433, 435, 441). The exclusion or inclusion of certain distinctions of meaning does not, however, mean that the lingual sense of metaphorical utterances is difficult to determine, as is indeed the case with dream-images, whose symbolic fields are almost completely fluid (cf. De Jongste 1956: 169). Very often, in fact, the metaphor enhances the meaning of what is signified, and makes its signification more, and not less, accurate. This is also the case with academic discourse, where, contrary to what one may intuitively think, the use of metaphor is not only widespread, but desirable, in that it enhances the accuracy of the language, which is considered to be one of the hallmarks of such discourse.

It also appears that when the meaning of a word is extended, such objective expansion has a relatively longer or shorter lingual *duration* depending on the lingual system determining this. A metaphorical phrase such as 'the foot of the mountain' may in time lose its exceptional symbolic power and may eventually be included in the normal expressive range of a word, even to the extent of deteriorating into a cliché that will die of sheer lingual age (cf. too McIntosh 1961: 336). The lingual duration of an expression is a general indication of the part played by time on the factual side of the lingual aspect.

The originally spatial order of time, namely simultaneity, also enables us to define the phenomenon of ambiguity as a lingually simultaneous *co-ordination* and *localization* of contrasting meanings. Although transformationalist approaches were criticized initially for disregarding the semantic 'level' of objective lingual facts, it is significant to note Zellig Harris's expectation of what is to be achieved by transformational analysis: "Such an analysis," he says (1966: vii), "produces a more compact yet more detailed description of language and brings out the more subtle formal and semantic relations among sentences. For example, sentences which contain ambiguities turn out to be derivable from more than one transformational source." The concept of lingual correspondence or synonymy is also given a new dimension, from Chomsky's initial point of view, in respect of the grammatical level of the sentence: thus, the sentences "That Bill dreamt annoyed John" and "It annoyed John that Bill dreamt" were considered to be synonymous or in factual lingual correspondence because they have the same deep structure (Chomsky 1972a: 149).

As regards the constitutive linguistic concept of objective lingual co-ordination, structuralist theories have emphasized the mutual dependences that exist between syntagmatic groupings that reciprocally condition each other: "In fact, spatial co-ordinations help to create associative co-ordinations," says De Saussure (1966: 218). Spatial co-ordination that is not qualified by an associative, lingual function is of no interest linguistically.

Viewed from the spatial analogies on the factual side of the lingual aspect, the phenomenon of synonymy may also receive some theoretical clarification, since it entails an overlapping of the expressive areas of words, as has been pointed out by semantic field theory. The factual lingual ranges of antonyms are of course entirely disjunctive, though they are at the same time linked in a relation of contrast. Homonyms seem to possess completely different fields, and can in most cases be considered as totally different words (cf. also Lyons 1968: 90-91 for the resolution of homonymic conflict).

It is the analogical relation between the lingual and spatial aspects of our experiential horizon that enables us to conceptualize the objective semantic field of factual lingual units like words, or the objective domain of substitutes (cf. Bloomfield 1958: 247, 250). Because the symbolic field of a word places it in opposition to everything in the language it does not express (Van Heerden 1965: 137), it helps to define further the identifiable distinctions in the meaning of a word. Without a symbolic field meaning would cease to exist, and *vice versa*; by systematic lingual opposition the word as objective lingual unit receives its further delimitation and determination as a unit of meaning in its narrower context, where it is not the same as its fellows. The objective lingual factuality of a word is a lingual *unity* if we view it from the angle of the numerical analogies on the factual side of the lingual aspect; and it is this objective unity which is defined further in terms of the spatial analogy of *delimitation*. It is in this light that one should interpret De Saussure's (1966: 103) view that a linguistic unit is not defined accurately until it is delimited, separated and opposed to everything that surrounds it in the chain of sound.

The opposition of objective lingual units thus shows the systematic interdependence or analogical interplay between the numerical and spatial analogies in the structure of the lingual modality. This analogical interplay also forms the basis of one of De Saussure's definitions of language: "... just as the game of chess is entirely in the combination of the different chesspieces," he remarks (De Saussure 1966: 107), "language is characterized as a system based entirely on the opposition of its concrete units." We notice again, in this observation, the typically structuralist conceptual reduction in the use of 'entirely'. Objective lingual combination and contrast[5] is a fundamental principle (cf. Lyons 1968: 67) in modern linguistic theory because it constitutes one of the elementary linguistic concepts that is disclosed when the analogical relation between the spatial and lingual modalities is investigated. The fundamental linguistic concept of the objective *linearity* of lingual facts, as the second principle put forward by De Saussure (1966: 70) for the study of the objective lingual sign, likewise proceeds from this analogical relation.

On the supra-sentential level, the analogical spatial concept of objective lingual *cohesion* has also drawn the attention of linguists (cf. the groundbreaking work done by Halliday & Hasan 1976; also De Beaugrande & Dressler 1981, Brown & Yule 1983). Some of the formal lingual features of the objective lingual cohesion of texts —defined by some as 'sequences of sentences' — are, inter alia, juxtaposition, as well as dependency in the form of anaphora, ellipsis and so forth (Hendricks 1973: 48 f., 53), although these are by no means exhaustive explanations of the phenomenon (cf. Hendricks 1973: 56, 57).

A particularly interesting spatial analogy on the factual side of the lingual aspect concerns the limitations to objective lingual extension and variation in the case of the so-called 'ready-made' utterances. In contrast to these expressions, which permit no objective lingual extension on the grammatical level, there are partially structured, productive 'schemata' such as "What's the use of ...-ing ...?" which allow the creation of an indefinitely large number of sentences (Lyons 1968: 177-178).

Almost every analogical spatial concept discussed above is applicable also on the phonemic level of objective lingual facts. In the ascendancy of phonology over phonetics, for example, the application of the systematic linguistic principle of lingually significant phonemic opposition was of crucial importance (see Verburg 1951: 24). Objective ranges of sound such as [b] and [p] are phonetically relative, i.e. subject to continuous variation, but grammatically and semantically distinct as discrete units (Lyons 1968: 68). Another example of analogical spatial concepts in this regard is to be found in De Saussure's

---

5. Cf. also Crystal & Davy (1976: 19): " ... vocabulary contrasts are relatively discrete, finite and localised; semantic contrasts tend to be less systematic and definable, and are all-inclusive."

explanations (1966: 51 ff.) concerning the sequential limitations to the combinations of phonemes, and Bloomfield's discussion (1958: 181) of permissible phonemic clusters that are restricted as to position and combination of different sounds in most languages.

As is the case with all other analogies functioning on the factual side of the lingual aspect, it can be demonstrated that the factual phonemic environment is determined by rules. For example, the normatively permissible plural affixes for a large objective range of English nouns are /z/, /s/ or /iz/, depending on the features (voiced, voiceless or strident) of the preceding consonant, as in *legs*, *pets* and *courses*. The rule thus takes into account the objective phonemic environment of the facts that it regulates: " ... the form /-iz/ occurs in all and only those cases where a strident consonant /z/ or /s/ would otherwise be immediately *adjacent* to another strident consonant ... — i.e. in the *environment* 'after any phoneme marked [+strident]'. The form /s/ occurs after all other voiceless phonemes ... i.e. in the *environment* 'after a phoneme marked [-voiced]'; and /z/ occurs everywhere else" (Smith & Wilson 1979: 138; emphases added).

The environment in question is an objective *lingual* environment, because it is an environment within which the sounds of *language* occur, and it is regulated by a rule or norm such as the one formulated here by Smith and Wilson. Furthermore, the rule is a *limited* one, because it does not operate over the whole range of permissible plural forms in English. It does not say anything, for example, about such 'irregular' plural forms as *men, children, mice*, etc.

This is another illustration of the fact that spatial analogies can be discovered on both the objective factual side of the lingual aspect and on the normative side, as rules. The concepts lingual *environment, adjacency, sequence, cluster, position* and *combination* are all related to the factual side of the lingual modality, because we can describe phonemic facts — i.e. facts related to the objective sounds of the spoken language — in terms of them, and such a description is only possible because of the analogical link between the lingual and spatial aspects of our experience. The terms *environment, adjacency*, etc. are all original spatial concepts.

Moreover, the fact that the rule formulated above is *limited* in its application is evidence of the analogical link between the lingual and spatial aspects on the normative level, for a *restriction* that applies to the operation of a rule is a concept that utilizes the originally spatial datum of *limitation*. Because it is the scope of a *rule* that is in question here, the limitation is a *normative* one.

This is not the only example of how lingual factuality and normativity interact as regards the spatial analogies within the constitutive structure of the lingual dimension of our experience. Other systems of rules governing the objective sounds that are produced in the spoken language, for example the rules of assimilation, can also be described in terms of these spatial analogies on the normative and factual sides of the lingual aspect. Here, too, there are severe *restrictions* on the normative applicability of the rule that determines what the permissible assimilations may be within a given objective lingual environment.

8 Lingual constancy as an elementary linguistic concept

The theoretical problem

A concept of the kinematic analogies in the lingual aspect can only be formed on the basis of the elementary linguistic concepts of lingual unity and diversity on the one hand and the lingual sphere of validity and factual position of lingual facts on the other. How can one envisage the continuous regulating movement of lingual norms, in their application, by competent users of the language, from one lingual utterance to the next in a succession of lingual utterances, without continually bearing in mind the specific material lingual sphere in which these norms operate? And as regards the factual side, it is clear that one is able to speak of the enduring and constant expressive possibilities of a lingual object only on the foundation of its symbolic field.

Several complications are, however, involved in the formulation of the kinematic analogies in the lingual aspect. Systematically speaking, one must keep in mind that a formulation of these analogies must exclude an explicit consideration of the physical analogies in the lingual aspect, since the latter set of analogies does not form part of one's immediate field of investigation. The influences that cause changes in lingual norms and lingual facts must therefore be excluded from the discussion at this stage, although one will not be able to make any progress in the analysis without implicit reference to these physical analogies. The reason for this has already been dealt with above, but may briefly be repeated here for the sake of the argument: when one tries to comprehend the analogical relationship between one aspect and another, one's analysis cannot bypass the intervening modalities, and such an analysis is therefore modified by analogical overtones of all the intervening aspects, so that one cannot directly grasp the analogical relationship between two modalities. The investigator will have to carry with him or her the analogical burden of the mediating spheres, because they will be viewing the analogical moment under consideration in terms of the spheres occupying a position between the one aspect and the other in the order of time.

Applied to this specific problem, it would mean that when we try to come to grips with the analogical relationship between the kinematic modality, which is an earlier aspect in the order of time, and the lingual aspect, which is a later one, one will be viewing these analogies in terms of the physical, logical and formative modalities, to name but a few. Thus the provisional formulation given above already contains an echo of the sphere of energy-effect or energy operation in mentioning the applicability of lingual norms. Nevertheless, the theoretical requirement remains unchanged, and one will have to bear in mind all the time that such a reference should not become the topic: what is thus to be considered is the continuous movement of lingual norms recurrently regulating diverse series of lingual facts without specifically focusing on the dynamic force these norms display in their operation and application.

However, this is easier said than done. A serious difficulty seems to be the terminology one wishes to employ. For if one does not succeed in using terms that satisfy one's lingual intuition in that they echo the kinematic sphere, one will have to define accurately and at every turn the sense of what one is trying to put across. For example, the term 'dynamic lingual process' almost inevitably calls up the connotation of an input of energy that sustains the process. It is especially at this juncture that one is confronted with a fundamental truth of this kind of methodological analysis, namely that one is describing the same thing in terms of a different analogy; for what may in kinematic terms be called a continuous flow may be described in physical terminology as a process. The question may arise whether it has any sense to continue such an analysis if it is indeed the same complex state of affairs that is being described in different analogical terms. The answer is yes, because every different set of analogies, by approaching the complex material of the analysis from a different elementary modal angle, gives a closer specification to the meaning of what has to he analyzed. And this specification is not done merely in terms of a new metaphor: the new analogical angle that is discovered upon analysis is as real a condition as any other theoretical concept. We should, in other words, not interpret the theoretical disclosure of new sets of analogies merely as the discovery of successive new metaphors. Analogical relations within the structure of a modal aspect reveal themselves, as should be clear from the analysis so far, as very real theoretical conditions for the conceptualization of the basic, foundational distinctions in the field being analyzed, in this case the elementary concepts of linguistics as they are revealed in an analysis of the constitutive structure of the lingual aspect.

All this serves to underline, nevertheless, the fact that the methodological analysis proposed by the philosophy of the cosmonomic idea is and must always be a *dynamic* method of *successive* analyses. In such a succession of analyses we discover the conceptual variety and richness of the field under investigation.

In summary, one can thus say that an investigation of the kinematic analogies in the structural edifice of the lingual aspect must reveal how lingual norms exhibit a relative consistency in their persistent regulation of successive sets of lingual facts — a mode of regulating that remains relatively constant in its uniform movement (cf. McIntosh 1961: 331, 335) from one factual lingual utterance to the next, from one lingual context to the next, and from one lingual situation to the next, but always remaining within the boundaries of the specific material lingual sphere in which those lingual norms operate. On the factual side the analysis must disclose how the expressive field of discrete lingual facts exhibits a certain symbolic constancy in its lingual extension.

Lingual constancy is an inescapable reality that must be investigated if linguistics is to be called a science, according to Hjelmslev (1963: 8):

> A linguistic theory ... must, while continually taking account of the fluctuations and changes of speech, necessarily refuse to grant exclusive significance to those changes; it must see

> a constancy which is not anchored in some 'reality' outside language — a constancy that makes a language a language, whatever language it may be, and that makes a language identical with itself in all its various manifestations.

Hjelmslev's views at this point are concerned primarily with an opposition of the method prescribed for the humanities by what he calls the 'humanistic' tradition, a method of 'mere description', to a scientific analysis of the process of language, but the significance of the statement resides in the fact that it *clarifies the difference between the kinematic and physical analogies* within the structure of the lingual aspect. Harris (1966: 9), too, regards lingual constancy and consistency as one of the prerequisites for descriptive linguistic investigation.

Lingual constancy is not the direct result of human memory, for "rote recall is a factor of minute importance in ordinary use of language ..." (Chomsky 1970: 8); rather, lingual constancy is the result of internal regularity on both the norm and the factual side of the lingual aspect that qualifies language. Chomsky's claim (1970: 22) that Paul makes no distinction "between the 'creativity' that leaves the language entirely unchanged (as in the production — and understanding — of new sentences, an activity in which the adult is constantly engaged) and the kind that actually changes the set of grammatical rules ..." concerns the fundamental distinction between the kinematic and physical analogies in the structure of the lingual aspect. "In fact," Chomsky says (*ibid.*), "the technical tools for dealing with 'rule-governed creativity', as distinct from 'rule-changing creativity', have become readily available only during the past few decades ..."

The constancy in lingual norm and lingual fact that constitutes the kinematic analogies in the lingual aspect has indeed received particular attention in transformational grammar, and is in fact the basic presupposition, the theoretical cornerstone of this type of linguistic analysis.[6] And this, it seems, must apply to any linguistic description that calls itself 'synchronic'.

---

6. Cf. De Haan, Koefoed & Des Tombe (1975: 4-5): " ... we moeten ervan uitgaan dat zinnen worden uitgesproken en begrepen door het voortdurend in wisselende kombinaties, op een regelmatige manier, gebruiken van een aantal principes."

The consistency of lingual norms

Lingual norms call for uniformly constant application by competent users of the language in various material lingual spheres, and in their recurrent regulating flow exhibit a certain lingual consistency.

To Van Heerden (1965: 16 f.; also 1972: 3) the symbolic freedom of language resides in its capacity for symbolic mobility that is provided by a recurrent symbolic system, and he immediately correlates this systematic mobility with the regulative constancy of the lingual system. When he states that the infiniteness of language on the level of factual usage has, as its antipode and basis on the systematic lingual level, the finite character of the regulating means of the language, one can with certain reservations voice one's agreement. The problem arises, however, when we come across statements like the following in the same context: "Met die taal kom alles ... in beweging" (1965: 16).

The systematic mobility of language then, as also happens subsequently (Van Heerden 1965: 22 f.), becomes something that gives freedom from the static, non-communicable state of affairs (which Van Heerden also calls the 'world-before-us') that constitutes an immobile lump which is freed for communication by means of language. Apart from the objections that can be raised against the division between a static world and that which sets one free from the state of affairs in that world, this linguistic perspective also separates the lingual subject from its correlated lingual object by refusing to recognize the objective lingual factuality of things ('sake is nie-kommunikeerbaar'). According to Van Heerden an object that can be named does not itself possess a lingual object-side, but attains what he calls an 'objective and general form' or knowledge, that ultimately becomes language through sound-formation, but only after a process of abstraction.

An analysis of the kinematic retrocipations on the norm-side of the lingual aspect must also disclose the abiding qualities that are contained in the rules for the formation of language. As an example of this one may take the lingual phenomenon that De Saussure calls 'analogy', and that has in the analogical leveling process, according to Palmer (1968: 247), led to the formation of the Latin noun *honor* from *honos*. De Saussure (1966: 162 ff.) denies that analogical derivation necessarily results in factual changes in usage, since it often does not exclude older forms that are supplanted by newer ones (often both forms exist side by side for a considerable length of time), but is rather a 'conserving force' because it favors normative lingual regularity.

The normative appeal that the kinematic analogies exert on the competent users of the language is that they must continually *conform* to the norms that apply within the various material lingual spheres.

It is immediately evident, however, that this fundamental lingual principle can never be realized in isolation, without simultaneously bringing the other lingual principles into play; for such compliance with lingual norms within a material lingual sphere should never become a licence for stultifying language, but must provide also for adaptability and innovation. This means that one cannot succeed in attempts to fossilize something which has an essentially inescapable vitality. This modification of the principle of lingual compliance in terms of physical and biotic analogies results in the requirement to stimulate dynamic developments in language through a flexible application of norms, so that the language that we use can adequately meet new lingual demands. In light of this modification of the principle of lingual compliance or conformity, the linguist must endeavor to grasp the essential variations of this compliance that are required by the typical norms governing factual, concrete language in different material lingual spheres.

An example of an attempt to fix a language permanently by means of grammatical rules is to be found in the works of English grammarians of the 18th century. It goes without saying that this linguistic perspective, in which the kinematic and physical analogies on the norm-side of the lingual aspect are rationalistically distorted, cannot do justice to the lingual principle that calls upon the users of a language to uphold, maintain and conform to lingual norms in the sense that it has been formulated above. In the next section we take a closer look at the time in the history of the English language when grammar had a capital 'G'.

The period of appeal to authority

Perhaps to a greater measure than in any other earlier or later period, grammarians of the late 17th and early 18th century have focused linguistic attention on the norm-side of the lingual aspect. This period in fact presents us with a peculiarly 18th century view of the relation between lingual norm and lingual fact.

18th century reverence for rules and order does not dismiss the existence of facts as such, since it is, as historical studies seem to suggest, at least partly the result of a reaction against corruptions in the factual use of language. So one finds no denial of the relation between lingual norms and lingual facts, but rather a characterization of this relation as one of continual conflict — a conflict that had to be resolved, in the opinion of those involved, by means of an appeal to authority.

The reason for an appeal to a lingual authority during this period is to be found, amongst other things, in the antiquarian attitude that English would go bankrupt through excessive borrowing (Bolton 1972: 38 ff.), and this attitude was carried over into the latter half of the 17th century. Every change in the language is a gradual corruption thereof, Wilkins claimed (Jones 1953: 268, note 72; cf. too 269). John Davies insisted that the curse of Babel was responsible for lingual change (Jones 1953: 269, note 73), and these views are echoed in the works of his contemporaries. Conservative opinion lamented 'corruption' and instability, and added strength to Caxton's earlier complaint that English is like the waxing and waning, unstable and varying moon (Bolton 1972: 17, 38); it also reinforced the idea that the constancy and integrity of English was being threatened.

It is interesting to note, in passing, that the sentiments expressed by some of these scholars some 400 years ago are echoed in many of the laments of spokespersons for languages that are currently under threat. It is salutary, perhaps, to note that those most concerned, who were bewailing the imminent death of English so many centuries ago, would have found it difficult to believe the current global dominance of English.

Yet these views do not appear to be entirely irrational. The users of the English language seem to have experienced a genuine need at this time for some authoritative guidelines with regard to vocabulary and grammar. Mulcaster had stipulated among the requirements for an authoritative dictionary that it should be a spelling guide and that it must impose order in word usage (Bolton 1972: 43), and it is undoubtedly true that at this stage in the development of the English language these were still heartfelt needs for those who wanted to write polished and refined English. The way that Dryden, for lack of consistently formulated lingual norms in dictionaries and grammar books, tried to solve the problems he encountered in writing English by translating his efforts to see if they made sense, cannot simply be shrugged off as a mere historical whim (cf. Bolton 1972: 43 f.). Rather, the need for order and regularity seems to be one that is characteristic of any language that has not undergone a process of complete standardization.

Notwithstanding the score of English dictionaries and glossaries that were attached to books, the greatest need in the latter half of the 17th century seems to have been for a comprehensive, authoritative dictionary (cf. Jones 1953: 272, 274). Snell wanted such a dictionary to contain not only hard words, but every kind and assortment of word in order to make the English language a 'settled, certain and corrected' language (Jones 1953: 295). The reason for this need probably lay in the fact that the existing dictionaries covered smaller, particular areas of the language, or took the form of glossaries that explained, as supplements, the lexical matter of a certain book (cf. Jones 1953: 274, 275).

Nonetheless, one should not underestimate the attitude of the age in the pleas for stabilizing and regularizing English through some form of authority. Upon investigating this attitude, one should again take notice of its earlier roots that are, for example, to be found in Bullokar, Mulcaster and Palsgrave's opinions that English had reached perfection and was ready for a normative fixation (Jones 1953: 265, 266). Snell, and also the contemporaries of Dryden and Pope, follow closely in their footsteps (Jones 1953: 297 ff.; cf. too Hulbert 1955: 20) during the latter half of the 17th century.

The period 1650-1800 saw sentiments growing to make English a ruled language: this age has not without cause been called the Age of Reason, and, as Sheard (1954: 302) observes, there "can be no doubt that one of its chief characteristics was a strong tendency towards order and regulation, and a healthy respect for authority".

Perfect order and consistent regularity could only be obtained by the dictates of authority (Sheard 1954: 302; cf. too Bolton 1972: 46), and by the middle of the 18th century interest in 'correct' English had risen to fever pitch (cf. Hulbert 1955: 19). The prevailing linguistic attitude is manifested in pleas for a regularized lingual system, which in turn gave rise to what has been called the doctrine of correctness, the "worshipping of correctness for its own sake" (Sheard 1954: 302).

Closely allied to this idea is the line of thought that English should be founded also on rational principles, as the classical languages were supposed to have been (Jones 1953: 289, 296). Thus the aim of Wharton's *A New English-Grammar* of 1655 is to convince foreigners that the English language "is not barbarous, confused, and irregular," but orderly (Jones 1953: 287).

This trend gave birth to a rampant and rigorous rationalism, that even ruled out Ben Jonson's earlier formulation of the authoritative lingual norm as 'the consent of the learned' (Bolton 1972: 42, 49), owing to the 'imperfections' found in the prose of the best writers; it made provision for an ultimate norm, as is found in an 'analogy of languages' and an absolute standard above usage, as in Addison's idea of 'universal grammar' (cf. Potter 1953: 121): "the best Authorities and Rules drawn from the Analogy of Languages shall settle all Controversies between Grammar and Idiom," Addison confidently claimed in *The Spectator* of 4 August 1711 (cf. Tucker 1961: 68).

This was the rationalistic backdrop against which proposals for correcting and consistently regulating the English tongue were made. It was one thing to have regularizing intentions, however, but quite another to carry out such a regularizing project. Some practical proposals that were made during this time, and how they were implemented, therefore deserve a closer look.

A popular notion among the linguists of this period was that English could be given a polished, rational and authoritative form by appealing to the authority of Latin, which was regarded as a perfectly regular and constant language (Sheard 1954: 302, 303). Other suggestions imply making use of an act of parliament or a royal edict from which the authority to ratify grammar and vocabulary might be derived (Jones 1953: 296). Since the Italian and French academies had by then published authoritative dictionaries to bear out their aim of purifying language, proposals of this kind were heard in England too (Hulbert 1955: 20).

The three main proposals to provide a basis for appeal in matters concerning lingual inconsistencies were thus the foundation of an English academy, the compilation of an authoritative dictionary and the writing of a standard grammar.

Since foreign academies in Italy and France had already set the example (cf. Bolton 1972: 47; cf. too Potter 1953: 117 ff.) by which the first of these proposals could be realized, some saw in the English Royal Society a possible forum from which such an enterprise could be launched. In 1664 Dryden, amongst others, was appointed to a committee for improving the language (Bolton 1972: 48, and Potter 1953: 120 f.). This committee, however, soon disappeared from the scene, so that Defoe, in 1702, still lamented the fact that England had not followed the example of Paris, and that this venture by a sub-committee of the Royal Society had run aground because of "the Greatness of the Work, and the Modesty of the Gentlemen concern'd ..." In his "Essay upon Several Projects" (Tucker 1961: 58-59), Defoe again proposed the establishment of an authoritative society whose task would be

> to encourage Polite Learning, to polish and refine the English Tongue, and advance the so much neglected Faculty of Correct Language, to establish Purity and Propriety of Stile, and to purge it from all the irregular Additions that Ignorance and Affectation have introduc'd; and all those Innovations in Speech, if I may call them such, which some Dogmatic Writers have the Confidence to foster upon their Native Language, as if their Authority were sufficient to make their own Fancy legitimate.

To Defoe's appeals were added those of Swift, Addison and Pope (cf. Potter 1953: 120 f.; Bolton 1972: 48 f.). Language controversies should be settled by appeals to the authority of an academy, which would first purge the English tongue of its imperfections, and then fix it in a final, perfect and thus immutable form (Potter 1953: 121; Bolton 1972: 49; Sheard 1954: 303).

Addison also wanted to undertake the much discussed compilation of an authoritative dictionary himself (Potter 1953: 121), thus fulfilling the need for a standard, 'tolerable dictionary' which Dryden had earlier spoken of (Bolton 1972: 43).

The first step towards such a standard dictionary was the publication of Nathaniel Bailey's *Universal Etymological English Dictionary* in 1721 (Hulbert 1955: 19). This probably strengthened the idea that such a register of the language might provide a reasonable alternative for an academy, for in 1754 Lord Chesterfield (in Tucker 1961: 90), introducing Dr Johnson's dictionary, wrote in a letter to *The World*:

> ... I have as long wished that either some one person of
> distinguished abilities would undertake the work singly,
> or that a certain number of gentlemen would form them-
> selves, or be formed by the government, into a society for
> that purpose.

Dr Johnson's effort had taken eight years to complete, and included a lengthy preface and a short grammar (Bolton 1972: 50 f.). The aims of the purists had been realized at least in part, for one of the inevitable consequences of Johnson's work was that the *forms* of words were now authoritatively fixed (Sheard 1954: 309).

By including a grammar, Johnson also added impetus to the third way that the proposals for perfecting and systematizing the English language could be implemented. A few years later Priestley, Lowth and Murray published their *Grammars*. Although they were wary of forcing English into the pattern of Latin, one cannot overlook their rationalistic starting point, which provided for the *reduction* of lingual facts to lingual norms. This is evident when Lowth views grammar as a set of rules that exists *outside* the pattern of language (Bolton 1972: 55), or when he denies in his 1785 work *A Short Introduction to English Grammar* (Tucker 1961: 97) that English is so irregular and capricious that it is neither "subject, nor easily reducible, to a System of rules."

The rationalistic trend continued beyond the 18th century in a purist attitude towards vocabulary (Sheard 1954: 312) and a classicist adherence to 'correct' grammar, and its influence can be discerned in dictionaries and grammars up to the present day.

Arguments against

Even in the 18th century it was realized that language could not be fixed, and that the factual lingual flux could not be brought to a halt by normative fixation. Evidence of this is to be found in Johnson's admission that he had flattered himself to think he could accomplish this (Sheard 1954: 308; Potter 1953: 122) and also in his criticism of Swift's "Proposal for Correcting, Improving and Ascertaining the English Tongue" (Bolton 1972: 49).

In fine, linguists came to realize that a language, on account of its mutability, could not be embalmed (Sheard 1954: 308). Similarly, authors of modern dictionaries deny the authority of their work, and claim to be merely descriptive (Hulbert 1955: 99 ff.), and not prescriptive in their method and aim. A notable exception in this regard is Beeton and Dorner's (1975) *Dictionary of English usage in Southern Africa* (cf. their "General introduction", p. v). Hulbert (1955: 101) quotes Barnhart as stating: "It is not the function of the dictionary-maker to tell you how to speak, any more than it is the function of the map-maker to move rivers or rearrange mountains or fill in lakes".

Ironically enough, the reputable handbook or the reliable dictionary is accepted today as the authority more than ever before (Potter 1953: 129; cf. too 127 ff., and the influence of the Oxford, Longmans and Cambridge English dictionaries and Daniel Jones's [1975] *Everyman's English pronouncing dictionary*). Yet one can to a certain extent understand the modern dictionary-maker's point of view. A language most certainly admits of authority, since we always find an unbreakable coherence between lingual norms and lingual facts in any given language. These norms, in being correlated with lingual facts, do indeed exhibit a relative constancy in exercising their validity as norms. But the authority of a lingual norm is not always of the compulsory type that allows for retribution and redress in case of transgressions; it will possess or lack compulsion to lingual compliance with it by lingual subjects, depending on whether the social relationship in which such a lingual norm applies is of an institutional, communal, consociational, inter-communal or inter-personal type. On account of the irreducibility of language and legal action we cannot expect every socially differentiated language community to yield to a type of institutionalization by governmental edict, as the Period of Appeal to Authority would have preferred.

One cannot, however, as an alternative to a rationalistic reduction of lingual norms to lingual facts, establish lingual authority by making language subject only to social conventions. Often irrationalistic reactions against inflexible grammar rules pose 'social acceptability' as the only norm for usage. This is in itself a significant insight, since it opens up our linguistic perspective to the truth that lingual norms display a certain social diversity in various typically different lingual spheres[7], but it is guilty of a certain brand of reductionism too, for any

---

7. Lingual principles may be divided roughly into functional-modal and typical principles; see below.

attempt to subject language only to social norms in its turn denies the mutual irreducibility of the lingual mode of experience and the social.

Neither should one agree with Sweet's statement (Potter 1953: 123) that language is partly rational, partly irrational, if this should be taken to mean that the lingual requirements or norms are rational and fixed, and that only the factual lingual situation is inconstant and irrational.

What should be acknowledged is that language is in a constant state of flux with respect to both the norm-side and the factual side of the lingual modality by which it is qualified. Not only do we encounter changes in the factual situation throughout the history of a language, but we also meet periodic variations in grammar (Barber 1979: 271 ff.). Both the norm-side and the factual side of the lingual aspect are thoroughly and persistently dynamic.

The flowing, recurrent nature of lingual norms receives a specification in terms of the physical, organic and historical analogies in the lingual aspect. The continuous flux of lingual norms becomes dynamic, accelerates and gains momentum when a language develops from a more or less primitive beginning (usually called its 'synthetic' stage) to a more differentiated, civilized ('analytic') means of expression. For as soon as a language starts differentiating into various typical, materially distinct lingual spheres, these spheres immediately create new lingual requirements and demands. These demands are subsequently met by the formulation and reformulation of lingual norms that regulate the factual lingual situation each newly differentiated material lingual sphere requires, and these lingual norms will, of course, differ from one sphere to the next. Thus, for example, the language of poetry will be materially different in rule and in fact from the language of scientific enterprise.

But if lingual norms are also in a state of flux, what then provides the stability of a language (cf. Barber 1979: 275)? The answer is that the content of any lingual expression is determined by material lingual principles that are in their turn founded upon norms governing the lingual aspect. The material principles of language include both typical and modal principles. The typical principles are the sounding board for the formulated typical norms of each material lingual sphere, and will vary from one lingual situation to the next. The modal principles are the general, universal conditions for the existence of all concrete languages. Therefore the various lingual norms to which lingual facts are subject should always appeal to these principles if they are to require lingual subjects to conform to them and thus to exercise their validity as norms. That the lingual validity of grammar rules is persistently being challenged does not have to be argued or documented here. An example of a grammar rule which has been in a state of flux for some time — because its validity is being challenged increasingly — is the one for the formation of the possessive case in English. For the classicist formulation of the rule, cf. Strunk (1972: 1). For a similar case, the 'shall'/'will' choice, cf. Quirk and Greenbaum (1978: 47, 54). Although the material lingual principles are also dynamic to the extent that they are opened up and altered, for example, in the movement and progress of a language from a 'synthetic' to an 'analytic' stage, they provide the relatively stable basis to which appeals to alter the positive lingual norms of a language should be lodged.

In light of this analysis the kinematic analogies on the norm-side of the lingual aspect should never be taken up as a licence to conceive of lingual norms as static. The persistence of certain lingual conventions that encourage a continuation of affected pronunciation and accent is also a negation of the true meaning of the principle of lingual compliance.

The 'mechanical' elements of language

Chomsky himself (1966: 72) views transformational grammar as an elaboration of the theories of universal grammar that were put forward in the 17th and 18th centuries. This is not surprising when one takes into account that the systematic focal points of both these approaches in linguistics are the kinematic and physical analogies in the structure of the lingual aspect. It is also interesting to note that Chomsky, in reviewing later developments in linguistic theory, formulates the following Humboldtian statement in terms of the kinematic moment of lingual constancy: "The form of language," Chomsky observes (1970: 17), "is that constant and unvarying factor that underlies and gives life and significance to each particular new linguistic act." This constancy Chomsky relates to the 'fixed generative rules' that determine the manner of formation of individual objective lingual elements, as their underlying form.

It is this insight into what transformational grammarians themselves call the 'mechanical' elements of language[8] that requires systematic attention at this stage of the linguistic analysis. One may define the field of study of transformational grammar as an investigation of the recurrent and enduring rules that constitute the inherently systematic aspects or internally regulated mobility of language, and the relatively constant way in which these rules continuously extend to enable us to create uniquely new sentences from one utterance to the next. Its investigation covers those aspects of language that ensure its continual and persistent flow.

This theme concerns also the recurrent features of lingual norms:

> Since a language is infinite, it follows that the grammar that specifies and generates it, being necessarily finite, has recursive devices (Chomsky 1974: 28).

That the maintenance of lingual norms, which is a physical analogy, depends on the recurrent features of such norms, is evident in the following pronouncement of Greimas (1974: 59):

> From a syntactical point of view I would say that the fundamental problem is to know how we manage to sustain the communicative process ... Only if syntax is interpreted as recurrent, as a support for the content to be transmitted ... can the fact of communication be accounted for, in part at least. This syntactic recurrence, in my eyes, is founding the discourse.

In his discussion of Chomsky's theory, Verburg (1971: 280) notes on this point that normative recursiveness must be built into the formulations according to which the mechanisms of language operate, since that is the only way that the factual infiniteness of language can be considered by Chomsky as theoretically comprehensible.

---

8. For Chomsky's use of the term 'mechanism' as in the phrase "mechanisms that underlie the creative aspect of language use", cf. e.g. 1972: 22, 26. Verburg (1971: 264) makes the following observation: "Chomsky (wil) de toegepaste mechanismen *(devices)* universeel formuleren als geldend voor taal-in-het-algemeen ..."

The concept of lingual rules as recursive devices had already, according to Chomsky (1966: 41 f.), been discovered by 17th century grammarians, especially in the theory of deep and surface structure of the Port-Royal grammarians. Chomsky himself apparently uses the term 'recursive' in a twofold sense; firstly, as a highly technical term applying only to a specific group of rules; secondly, in a broader sense, to include all the rules of the generative grammar of a language: "In general, a set of rules that recursively define an infinite set of objects may be said to generate this set," he remarks (1972a: 126, note 12).

The contribution of transformational grammar is that it is an attempt to come to an understanding of the analogical kinematic concept of lingual regularity or consistency. It is this normative lingual consistency that forms one of the guarantees for the acquisition of language by children who are predisposed to search for certain types of regularity (Chomsky 1965: 44). This explains to a certain extent the wide-ranging impact of the transformationalist approach: in more than one aspect of language study it confronts and seeks to explain the realities of language.

The relative constancy of lingual facts in their lingual extension

The relative constancy of lingual facts is subject to and regulated by lingual norms. The unified symbolic area of a lingual object, which can be defined as its continuous, extensive and coherent semantic range, contains a variety of lingually identifiable distinctions of meaning. As Uhlenbeck (1968: 21) notes: "Binnen de betekeniseenheid zijn een van geval tot geval variërend aantal onderscheidingen te onderkennen." One or more of these identifiable distinctions in the meaning of a word is continually being applied from one factual use of the word to the next, without in any way detracting from its lingual constancy, which, according to Van Heerden (1965: 25), constitutes one of the most important qualities of the word. "Deze betekenis", remarks Uhlenbeck (1968: 21; cf. too Van Heerden 1965: 25), "is wel een eenheid ... — maar zij is als zodanig allerminst star, integendeel: zij is beweeglijk en vloeiend." And Uhlenbeck (1968: 22) gives an excellent illustration of this thesis: one can, for example, say to someone sitting on a table: "Nice chair, that!" without, through this actualization of the distinction 'a piece of furniture used as a seat,' in any way detracting from its lingual constancy. Uhlenbeck displays an acute insight into the mutual correlation of lingual norm and lingual fact when he remarks (1968: 41) that, apart from the situational frame of reference in which language is used (and to which, in our opinion, the typical lingual norms belong), the symbolic fluidity of words is also regulated by modal norms, which he calls "het universeel aanwezige middel der syntactische verbinding (volgens per taal variërende regels)." The relative constancy of lingual objects therefore depends not only on the material lingual sphere in which these objects are used, but also on the recognizable internal structure of objective lingual constituents (Aranoff 1976: 20 ff.) of such objects, so that, for example, we have difficulty in retaining the meaning of acronyms.

In this respect the relative constancy of morphemes and phonemes also merits attention. Not only is the constant nature of the morpheme distinguishable in the variety of objective lingual elements with which it may combine, but the alteration it effects in the meaning of such objective elements is usually also constant (cf. Van Heerden 1965: 39; Aranoff 1976: 7 ff., however, sets out to prove that morphemes do not have constancy in the traditional sense). Uhlenbeck (1968: 26) calls the sound form of a word a variable constant, and defines this durability in terms of the lingual position of phonemes in their regulatively determined sequence in the word. This again serves to illustrate the thesis that the kinematic analogies on the factual side of the lingual aspect can never be grasped unless it is done on the basis of the spatial analogies. It is the objective lingual succession of the sounds of the language that enables us to discover the relative constancy of recurrent sounds, which in turn makes it possible to distinguish between different phonemes (cf. Bloomfield 1958: 79).

As regards the constancy and mutability of lingual objects, one finds several interesting extremes in the views of De Saussure. This is how he puts it (1966: 71): "The signifier, though to all appearances freely chosen with respect to the idea that it represents, is fixed, not free, with respect to the linguistic community that uses it ... We say, to language: 'Choose!' but we add: 'It must be this sign and no other.'"

De Saussure's arguments at this point refer to word choice, but he immediately extends his discussion to language as a whole when he remarks (1966: 71) that language is always a heritage of a preceding period, and that no society has ever known and accepted it otherwise. Cf. too Uhlenbeck's observation (1968: 53): "Van taalverandering zijn de sprekers van een taal zich niet bewust; nooit blijken sprekers van verschillende generaties elkaar niet meer te kunnen verstaan; steeds is er continuïteit." De Saussure formulates the so-called paradox in his thought as follows (1966: 74; emphases added):

> Time, which insures the continuity of language, wields another influence apparently contradictory to the first: the more or less rapid change of linguistic signs. In a certain sense, therefore, we can speak of both the immutability and the mutability of the sign. In the last analysis, the two facts are interdependent: the sign is exposed to alteration because it perpetuates itself. What predominates in all change is the persistence of the old substance; disregard for the past is only relative. That is why the principle of change is based on the principle of continuity.

Or, as he puts it elsewhere (1966: 172): "Language is a garment covered with patches cut from its own cloth." However much one may try to give a more favorable[9] interpretation to some aspects of De Saussure's point of view, it seems that the typically humanistic division between the ever-present freedom of choice in language and the continuity and continuation that excludes such a free choice, is still, in certain instances at least, deceiving him.

The kinematic analogies on the factual side of the lingual aspect also enable us to speak of the positional mobility of an objective lingual unit. This factual mobility determines its so-called internal cohesion — which in turn serves as a stronger criterion for the identification (and identifiability) of the word than the criteria 'potential pause' or Bloomfield's 'minimal free form' — and is ably demonstrated as crite-

---

9. Which is quite possible: cf. e.g. De Saussure (1966: 72): " ... we must ask why the historical factor of transmission dominates it entirely and prohibits any sudden widespread change." Pike also remarks (1959: 50), in explaining the 'wave view' of language, that in "historical change one system does not cease and another one begin with a gap between them. Rather," he continues, "there are transition states. And yet all is not transition in a single 'flat' sense. Rather there are periods and peaks when certain items or certain phases of systems are prominent."

rion by Lyons (1968: 199-204). When transformations are understood, as for example in Chomsky's Revised Extended Standard Theory (REST), as rules for movement (Radford 1981: 146; Weideman 1988: 13-21), they are rules that regulate the positional mobility of objective lingual units. Cf. the following example that is given in Weideman (1988: 20 f.) of a transformational explanation for the ungrammaticality of

[1] * the books which he's on the shelf

compared with the grammaticality of

[2] the books which he has on the shelf

The argument that can be presented utilizes these two instances of normatively possible or grammatical [2] versus impossible or ungrammatical [1] objective lingual units as follows: if we assume that before a lingual constituent that is 'missing' at the S-level as a result of a transformational rule on the output of structures at a deeper level, no contraction is possible, then we have one possible explanation (there are others as well) for the ungrammaticality of [1], since the S-structure of the phrase may include a 'gap' to show that an element has been removed, as in

[3] the books which he has [_] on the shelf

It seems that, after the space left by the operation of a transformational rule (to move a Noun Phrase to another position), no contraction of *he has* to *he's* is possible. In this case, the transformational rule creates a condition that can explain a grammatical phenomenon. The general rule of *wh*-movement in Chomsky's REST in fact applies not only to Noun Phrases, but also to Prepositional, Adjectival and Adverbial phrases; cf.

[4] *To whom* has he given the books PP[e]?
[5] *How strong* is it AP[e]?
[6] *How quickly* did you say he read it AdvP[e]?

where the initial italicized lingual constituent is the part that has, by the application of the transformational rule, been moved out of the position marked as empty [*e*]. And the account appears to be more general still: Waher (1984: 17 f.) has shown that this rule applies not only to *wh*-elements, as the italicized lingual objects in [4]-[6] above, but can extend also to non-*wh* elements in, for example, the formation of the passive.

In conclusion, let us try to demonstrate how the analysis of the kinematic analogies on the factual side of the structure of the lingual aspect sheds light on the lingual phenomenon that we know as 'slang'. All slang expressions begin to exist, as it were, on the periphery of a material lingual sphere. But their lingual life, as slang expressions, is of short duration because they either vanish on account of their unabiding fashionability or they are rapidly absorbed into the constant vocabulary of such a lingual sphere. Hall (1950: 127 f.) remarks that today we are surprised to find that terms such as *jazz* and *jeep* had started their lingual life as slang expressions. All neologisms enter the language as slang terms, he says, except in those material lingual spheres where we find an existing tradition of re-definition or of coining new terms, as in scientific discourse. The relative constancy in the employment of an imported term is thus determined also by the lingual sphere in which it is taken up. In the sphere of theoretical discourse a new term can almost immediately obtain a measure of lingual constancy or currency, depending for the greater part on the acceptability of the terms in which it is defined, while a slang expression in the sphere of friendly social discourse will take much longer to begin to express what it was initially designed to convey with any measure of consistency and acceptability.

9 The operation of lingual norms in factual lingual processes

Physical analogies in the structure of the lingual aspect

The dynamic lingual *momentum* of the factual lingual process and normative lingual procedure is based on and presupposes the consistency of lingual fact and lingual rule or norm that was discussed in the previous chapter. This is a physical analogy in the structure of the lingual aspect, together with the concepts that one can form of the *operation* of lingual norms, the structural *changes* that these norms may undergo in the *procedure* of normative operation, the normative *power* of grammars as a lingual *force* or normative *energy* operative in the application of norms, and also the fact of language conservation and *renovation*. These various analogical physical concepts in linguistic theory reflect the internal modal coherence between the lingual aspect of experience and the aspect of energy-operation, and constitute the systematic focal point of this chapter.

Factual lingual process and normative lingual procedure

Factual lingual processes are subjected to normative lingual procedures. Lingual process, as a physical analogy on the factual side of the lingual aspect, presupposes, among other things, the normative numerical analogy of system, as well as the spatial analogy on the norm-side of the lingual aspect that specifies the possibility of combinations among objective lingual elements, and the kinematic analogy of recurrence on the factual side of the lingual aspect. Hjelmslev (1963: 9) remarks:

> ... it would seem to be a generally valid thesis that for every process there is a corresponding system by which the process can be analysed and described by means of a limited number of premises. It must be assumed that any process can be analysed into a limited number of elements recurring in various combinations. Then, on the basis of this analysis, it should be possible to order these elements into classes according to their possibilities of combination.

If linguistics is to be a truly scientific theory, says Hjelmslev (1963: 10), it must test the "thesis that a process has an underlying system — a fluctuation an underlying constancy". In an analogical physical sense the underlying systematic constancy on the norm-side of the lingual aspect must be understood as the *normative procedure in the operation of lingual norms*.

Although Chomsky (1965: 9, 139 f.; 1972a: 117) claims that his approach is not a study of actual lingual performance, i.e. a model of speech production, but a study purely of lingual competence, the fact remains that much of what he conceives depends upon the physical analogies on both the norm and factual sides of the lingual aspect, especially when he speaks of the subjection of utterances to generative procedures in order to understand them (1970: 10), or of the generative (1970: 27) or grammatical processes that underlie the richness of the structure of language and that "we use in producing and interpreting sentences" (1972a: 107).

What may from another perspective perhaps seem an apparently irrelevant remark, gains in significance when one considers that, according to our theory, Chomsky has contributed significantly to a systematic understanding of the kinematic and physical analogies in the structure of the lingual aspect; consider, for example, the statement by Chomsky (1975: 248, note 17) that "the relation between my pressing the accelerator and the car's moving is explicable in terms of known physical laws, and there seems no reason to doubt that attainment of knowledge of language is within the potential range of that part of natural science that is well understood."

This is certainly not intended to he read purely metaphorically;

on the contrary, the analogy must be understood quite literally, in much the same way that the term 'analogy' is understood in its defined technical and theoretical sense in our theory. An analogy, be it a retrocipation or anticipation, is, as we have remarked above, never a metaphor or the metaphorical expression of a relationship: it expresses in a very real sense the temporal relationship between one aspect and another in the sequence of aspects. The almost casual remark of Mitsou Ronat (in Chomsky 1979: 106), namely that in the first period in the history of generative grammar Chomsky sought to make linguistics a science, and that physics seemed to be the model of reference, is also relevant in this regard.

In our terminology, the terms lingual procedure and lingual process would indicate the normative and factual sides of the physical analogy within the structural edifice of the lingual aspect. In all fairness to Chomsky, however, one must add that his use of these terms, and also his intentions with regard to them, are not explicitly defined in the first chapter of *Current issues in linguistic theory* (Chomsky 1970), from which some of these remarks have been taken. It is, in fact, not wholly within the scope of the issues raised there. But, as we have indicated above (Chapter 2), it does seem that Chomsky, too, has tried to express the *unbreakable coherence* between norm and fact — procedure and process in analogical physical terms — within the theoretical framework that he employs.

In fact, whenever one does encounter a point where Chomsky apparently does not conform to the rigid distinction between competence, defined as a normative lingual command of the language, and factual performance, it is almost without fail done in the context of his explaining something else. It is in such instances that statements like the following produce specific problems of theoretical interpretation (Chomsky 1972a: 106; emphases added; cf. too 107): "A person who has acquired knowledge of English has internalized ... rules and *makes use* of them when he understands or *produces* the sentences just given as examples, and an indefinite range of others."

The problem of interpreting statements such as these arises only when they are read against the background of other statements, such as are found in *Aspects of the theory of syntax* (cf. Chomsky 1965: 9, 139 f.). Several suggestions can be made to circumvent the problems of interpretation raised in this connection. First, one may ask whether the immediate context makes any provision for a consistent systematic statement on the relation of 'competence' and 'performance.' Second, the question may arise whether the broader context, i.e. the careful choice of terminology in a theoretical study, or the somewhat looser choice of terms employed in an edited transcription of a public lecture, permits significant comparison between these two sets of statements. If both these questions can be answered in the affirmative, then a third possible question arises before one can conclude that we have a logical inconsistency, namely whether the statement in the one context is not in apparent conflict with its counterpart in the next because of a development or modification in the theory, which might have brought about a significant change in the initial formulation.

At this stage it seems to me that one must conclude that, in answer to the first question, the context of *Language and mind* (Chomsky 1972a) does not provide for a systematic pronouncement on the relation between competence and performance. And as regards the second question, one is obliged to note that the broader contexts of *Aspects of the theory of syntax* (1965) and *Language and mind* also differ significantly, and thus do not allow comparison, or allow comparison only within certain limits. As far as the third question is concerned, it is also difficult to say whether the slight shift that is evident in *Language and mind* as regards the determination of the meaning of a sentence by certain aspects of the surface structure (cf. Chomsky 1972a: 31, 59 f., 107 ff., 126) allows us to come to any conclusion regarding the relation of lingual procedure and process, or competence and performance.

The problem of interpretation remains a pertinent one, however, for a conclusive answer will enable us to determine whether Chomsky is in this respect a consistent rationalist by our definition, i.e. insisting on a consistent separation of competence and performance. This issue will be raised again below, and it will also be viewed from another systematic angle.

Transformations as normative lingual operations

'Transformation' as an elementary linguistic concept may in analogical physical terms be defined as a lingual operation of lingual norms. As a linguistic term, 'transformation' was used already by Hjelmslev in connection with the analytical procedure followed by textual analysis. If, according to Hjelmslev (1963: 96; emphases added), we are led to recognize the linguistic form behind the substance of language, it will be clear that the essence of the procedure "is a catalysis through which the form is encatalyzed to the substance ..." and that the procedure "is purely formal in this sense that it considers the units of the language as consisting of a number of figurae for which certain *rules of transformation hold.*" He adds that one must not expect from this deductive procedure any semantics or any phonetics, but only a *'linguistic algebra,'* which provides the formal basis for an ordering of deductions.

Hjelmslev's theoretical expectations anticipate and foreshadow the intended formalization of natural language in transformational grammar, and drive home the point frequently made by Chomsky (cf. 1979: 114, 115, 177) that his theory takes structuralism a step further by redefining it; or, at the very least, it illustrates that transformational grammar is in essence still a structuralist theory, as some of its detractors would have it. The latter view, however, is untenable in light of a systematic linguistic analysis of elementary linguistic concepts, since Chomskyan grammar, with its theoretical focus on the kinematic and physical analogies in the structure of the lingual aspect, does indeed take linguistic theory a step further than the spatially-oriented structuralist theories discussed above in Chapter 7.

Hjelmslev's adoption of the term 'transformation' enables him to note in De Saussure's thought the "conception of language as an abstract transformation structure" (Hjelmslev 1963: 108), in the sense that a sign system may be an abstract transformation system of a game system, and vice versa. The traditional use of the term also includes Carnap (1957) and Hilbert (cf. Hjelmslev 1963: 110). Bruns (1975: 247 f.) also traces a link between Chomskyan grammar and Husserl's thought.

Of more recent interest to linguistic theory is Harris's use of transformation as term, but it differs from Chomsky's concept of transformation in that it expresses a relation of "equal acceptability under systematic substitution" between what Chomsky in his early work (1979: 120-124, esp. 122 f.) would call 'surface structures'.

It is Chomsky's concept of transformation as an operational level of language (Chomsky 1978a: 72 f.) that is of systematic interest at this point. Chomsky (1975: 4) has defined language itself as "a product of human intelligence, created anew in each individual by operations that lie far beyond the reach of will or consciousness."

Chomsky has frequently claimed to have been misunderstood as to how linguistic competence is realized in actual performance, since the former is a necessary idealization and the latter inevitably degenerate, yet, in describing earlier rationalist theories, he does not hesitate to state that "the transformational operations relating deep and surface structure are *actual* mental *operations, performed* by the mind when a sentence is produced or understood." It follows, then, "that there must be represented in the mind, a fixed system of generative principles that characterize and associate deep and surface structures in some definite way — a grammar, in other words, that is used in some fashion as discourse is *produced* or interpreted" (Chomsky 1972a: 18; emphases added). The stock transformationalist answer to the problem of the relationship between competence and performance is that one must not confuse it with the relation between deep and surface structure. But it should be noted that in the statement by Chomsky quoted above nothing is said about the abstract character that even surface structures may have: the words that are emphasized refer to the actuality with which mental *operations* are *performed* as well as the *actual use* of a grammar in the *factual production* of discourse. To Chomsky the normative grammatical command of the language is very often "that system that underlies the *actual* use of language" (Chomsky 1979: 113; emphasis added).

It is clear that Chomsky indeed believes that earlier rationalist theories discovered the *actuality* of normative lingual operations. He criticizes the studies of language carried out under the influence of Cartesian rationalism merely because they do not fully appreciate "the length and complexity of the chain of operations that relate the mental structures expressing the semantic content of the utterance to the physical realization" (Chomsky 1972a: 25). Chomsky's own theory attempts to analyze the mental operations that provide insight into the understanding of a sentence not given by surface structure (1972a: 36 f.).

If, however, these operations are *actual* 'grammatical operations' (Chomsky 1972a: 28), then they do indeed tell us something of the relation between the normative devices of language and actual performance. It is with this in mind that one can analyze Chomsky's 'grammatical transformations' as the operation of lingual norms and the factual effects of this operation. This characterization of the contribution to linguistics by transformational grammar is an articulation of the truth that language theorists will be able to discover normative lingual operations and their factual lingual effects only if they have found the link between what we have been calling the lingual aspect of experience and the physical aspect of energy-operation and effect.

The physical analogies operating on the norm-side of the lingual aspect also enable us to speak of normative lingual transformations as structural changes. In one of the earliest comments on transformational grammar, Gleason (1961: 172) remarks:

> Clearly, not all operations of altering sentences to related sentences have the same linguistic interest. The ones involving structural changes stand apart from all the others. They will be called transformations ... A transformation is a statement of the structural *relation* of a pair of constructions which treats that relation as though it were a *process*.

Although *Syntactic structures* (Chomsky 1957) is, understandably, the only work by Chomsky referred to by Gleason in his bibliography, it is beside the point, and irrelevant to the systematic interpretation that can be given to this formulation of the concept of lingual transformation, that Gleason makes use only of the very early Chomsky, or that the formulation may be inconsistent with Chomsky's subsequent intentions. What seems to be important in a systematic interpretation of Gleason's definition is that it captures the constitutive lingual elements of operation, change, process and relation. It views the analogical physical moments of lingual change, process and operation on the one hand, and the analogical spatial moment of lingual relation on the other, as being interrelated, at least by definition. For it is certainly valid from a systematic point of view to point out that the lingual process of structural change through transformational operations presupposes and depends on the fact that there is a definite lingual relation between different 'constructions,' because the physical analogies in the structure of the lingual aspect presuppose the spatial analogies.

It is indeed so that transformational grammar constitutes a significant step forward in linguistic analysis, and that the theory continues, as Gleason (1961: 194) predicted, "to play a significant role in the development of linguistics by virtue of having raised some important, previously overlooked issues, and perhaps by contributing to their solution." It would, from a systematic point of view, also mean that some of the earlier linguistic theories, especially structuralism (in the sense of 'relationism') and the applications of phrase-structure grammars, that took account only of the lingual relations that hold between lingual units and lingual utterances, had indeed to be complemented by other elementary concepts. These theories had to be carried further or stimulated by lingual concepts that went beyond the almost exclusive examination of spatial analogies within the lingual aspect, i.e. beyond problems of lingual relation: they had, in fact, to be carried further by lingual concepts such as operation, process and change, concepts that express the indissoluble link between the lingual and physical aspects of our experiential horizon, for any significant 'advance' to be made. Viewed thus, transformational grammar has indeed made a systematic contribution in that it has broadened the scope of our theoretical linguistic framework to include not only lingual concepts concerned primarily with spatial analogies, but others too, especially those lingual concepts that concern the analogical link between the lingual and the physical modalities.

Chomsky himself gives an indication that the concept of lingual transformations (as normative lingual operations that serve as causes for objective lingual effects) presupposes the analogical spatial notion of dependence, by pointing out (1972b: 30) that operations such as the question transformation are structure-dependent and not structure-independent:

> ... all known formal operations in the grammar of English, or of any other language, are structure-dependent. This is a very simple example of an invariant principle of language, what might be called a formal linguistic universal or a principle of universal grammar.

The structure-dependence of lingual operations means simply that the physical analogy of operation within the lingual modality is based on and thus presupposes the spatial analogy of structure, i.e. 'structure' understood as the factual lingual relationship between objective parts of a sentence, or in Chomsky's (1972b: 33) view, the factual lingual relationship that exists between parts of even more abstract forms underlying sentences. It is significant not only that Chomsky (1972b: 30) is here formulating the notion that the spatial analogies within the lingual aspect are necessary, constitutive elements for an analysis of the physical analogies, but that he also very keenly notes the difference between mathematical and lingual structure:

> Notice that the structure-dependent operation has no advantages from the point of view of communicative efficiency or 'simplicity'. If we were, let us say, designing a language for formal manipulations by a computer, we would certainly prefer structure-independent operations. These are far simpler to carry out ... Mathematicians have studied structure-independent operations on strings (inversion, shuffling, etc.), but it has occurred to no one to investigate the curious and complex notion of 'structure-dependent operation', in the relevant sense.

This remark is made by Chomsky (1972b: 29) within the context of showing that the structure-independent operation of certain kinds of question-formation ("Take the left-most occurrence of 'is' and move it to the front of the sentence") yields, if we have the sentence

[1] The dog that is in the corner is hungry

the ungrammatical question

[2] * Is the dog that [_] in the corner is hungry?

However, the structure-dependent operation, that first identifies the subject noun phrase of the sentence, in this case

[3] $_{NP}$[the dog that is in the corner]

before moving the 'is' following this phrase to the beginning of the sentence, yields the grammatically correct question

[4] Is $_{NP}$[the dog that is in the corner] [_] hungry?

(where [_] marks the space or gap left by the lingual constituent ('is') that was moved by the structure-dependent or structurally limited operation). But what makes Chomsky's statements even more remarkable is that his clear distinction between mathematical and lingual structure, a *sine qua non* for the preference given to the structure-dependence of lingual operations, is still pursued only within the limits set in *Syntactic structures* (Chomsky 1957), for "the formal operations of language ... though they are structure-dependent, ... are, in an important sense, independent of meaning" (Chomsky 1972b: 32).

The crucial term again, of course, is 'formal.' It would appear that to Chomsky the content of 'lingual' must ultimately be limited to the technical and (formal) grammatical aspects thereof, since only these aspects can be formalized to the level of explicitness required by Chomsky's methodology. This will again be dealt with below, but it is interesting to note that Chomsky can, apparently without reference to 'meaning,' make a distinction between mathematical and lingual structure in terms of the concept of lingual operation. It is indeed true that both concepts — that of lingual structure and the concept of the lingual operations that depend on that structure — are 'linguistic universals,' in the sense that they reveal the modal coherence between the lingual aspect and two earlier aspects in the order of time, the spatial and physical aspects, respectively. Such concepts are 'formal' to the extent that they are exact *formulations* of methodological concepts that are constitutive in linguistics. But the relationships that are explicitly formulated in terms of such concepts as lingual structure and lingual operation of course refer to a modal coherence that is different from and more than merely formal, and it is in this sense that the modal relation between the lingual, physical and spatial aspects can also be called 'material,' for the relationships that exist between them truly give content to any formal methodological concept that expresses this coherence.

The validity of lingual norms

By calling transformations *normative* lingual operations the critical question of defining what is meant by lingual norm has been raised once again. Transformational grammar is by no means a 'normative' grammar in the traditional sense, i.e. a prescriptive grammar that tells the language user what to do and what to avoid. But transformational operations qualify as normative by virtue of the fact that they are rules and instructions to which lingual facts may be subjected, and as rules they have specified ranges of applicability.

The range of applicability of any lingual norm is the field in which such a norm may be regarded as valid, and this normative validity or normative power is a point that has been raised from the outset by transformational grammar, where it is linked with the normative lingual adequacy of grammars (Chomsky 1970: 28 ff.; also 1957: 34 ff.), and may be explained in terms of the applicability of the rules of such a grammar (cf. Chomsky 1957: 37 ff.). Down to the very last formulation of rule in the generative perspective, the theoretical purpose remains to specify the normative range of applicability of the rule.

Lingual power, as the normative lingual energy to enforce and apply lingual norms, is a physical analogy on the norm-side of the lingual aspect. Because the physical analogies in the lingual aspect presuppose the spatial, the enforcement or application of lingual norms can only make sense within the boundaries of a material lingual sphere.

The general modal principle to which the physical analogies on the norm-side of the lingual aspect direct our attention is that of lingual efficiency. This principle, which is linked to the normative lingual ability to express oneself efficiently in all material lingual spheres, is realized differently on different occasions: to speak in such a way as to obtain the desired effect in an academic lecture differs significantly from effectively expressing one's disapproval as a parent of a child's actions, and so forth. The operation of this principle is illustrated in the factual lingual effects that are obtained by using metaphor and irony. In his discussion of the 'aspect' of language, Robinson (1975: 46 ff.) correctly distinguishes between the effect that a factual command may have, and which points to an external or concrete coherence between language and the physical modality, and the intrinsically lingual effects obtained, *inter alia*, by irony and metaphor — factual effects that are linguistically relevant, since they answer to the principle of lingual efficiency, that asks: "What does an utterance do?" Chomskyan grammar has too narrow a focus to be able to account for this, Robinson (1975: 46) asserts, for if "a sentence has undergone the negative transformation, Chomsky must simply say that it is a negative, but if it is used to affirm something, if it plays an affirmative role, I will say that its 'aspect' is affirmative."

Changes in lingual norms

The validity of lingual norms calls for further specification in terms of another physical analogy within the structure of the lingual aspect, namely that of lingual change. The critical question is whether the validity of a traditionally accepted grammar rule may ever be challenged, i.e. whether a grammar rule may be subject to change. The question is thus not whether such a rule has only a limited range of application or validity since there may be exceptions to it, or because its application is limited, as we have seen above, by certain structural constraints (dependence), but whether the rule itself undergoes changes from time to time.

No-one would deny today that lingual norms, including grammar rules, are also subject to change. Strunk's classicist formulation of the rule for the formation of the possessive case in 1972 still read: "Form the possessive singular of nouns by adding 's" (1972: 1); hence one was instructed to write 'Charles's friend', 'Burns's poems', and so on. Only a few years later, however, Quirk and Greenbaum (1978: 94) had to note that there "is vacillation both in the pronunciation and spelling of these names" so that the written form becoming more commonly accepted was 'Burns' poems', as opposed to 'Burns's poems', which had by then become less common. The various other changes in rule that are evident in the prevailing use of 'will' instead of 'shall' with the first person singular and plural on certain occasions, as well as 'There's four' instead of 'There are four' or 'who' instead of 'whom' not only in the spoken variety of the language, but in written language as well, all are well-known and accepted as correct. The inevitable conclusion that such shifts away from the traditionally accepted grammar rules induce us to draw is that there are changes in the formulated and unformulated lingual norms that result in older rules becoming invalid as lingual norms. This is a dilemma for the prescriptivist grammarian, whose attitude more often than not would express a preference for greater normative lingual stability.

Changes that occur on the norm-side of the lingual aspect, i.e. changes in grammar rule, etc., can permit us to describe the factual process of historical change in language. It is significant that recent studies in transformational grammar are increasingly interested in historical alterations in grammars. The transformationalist hypothesis on historical linguistic studies is that language change is best described in terms of alterations in grammars (Smith & Wilson 1979: 216, 228). The momentum of such change is speeded up and accelerates at different times in the history of a language, notably when the language is subjected to a normative process of opening up. In such circumstances the lingual aspect that qualifies factual lingual usage anticipates the economic modality (cf. Smith & Wilson 1979: 227 f.).

Changes in the grammatical categories of words also signify normative alterations. Such alterations may be occasional ones for obtaining specific lingual effects, as when a noun is used as an imperative (e.g. the surgeon's 'Scalpel!') (cf. Robinson 1975: 50), even though traditional grammar would regard the imperative as a function of the verb. But normative changes in the grammatical categories of words may also be of a more permanent nature. Aranoff (1976: 20, note 13) has noted exactly such a steady drift of words from one grammatical category to another.

Factual lingual maintenance and change

In view of the observations that have been made in the previous section, it should be clear that the analogical physical moment of change functioning on the factual side of the lingual aspect is subject to lingual norms. Lingual maintenance and change, conservation and mutability may be viewed as physical retrocipations functioning on the factual side of the lingual aspect.

Bloomfield (1971: 30 f.) makes some helpful comments on defining various kinds of factual change, and also formulates as one of the fundamental assumptions of historical linguistics that "every language changes at a rate which leaves contemporary persons free to communicate without disturbance" (Bloomfield 1971: 30). The factual lingual moment of change is therefore to be specified still further in terms of another analogical physical concept, namely that of lingual *pace* or *momentum*, since all factual lingual change must take place at a specifiable rate or pace. What is more, lingual change is always counterbalanced by lingual *stability*, by the preservation and retention of older objective lingual elements (De Saussure 1966: 171 ff., also 71 ff.) in the process of making new ones.

Not only must linguistic theory therefore distinguish between various types of change, such as sound-change, analogy, borrowing, coinage, blending (for the last two, cf. Aranoff 1976: 19 ff.), folk-etymology, syncope, obsolescence (or change of objective lingual frequency), as well as syntactic and semantic change (Wells 1971: 11), but it must also investigate the diverse factors that influence the more rapid turnover of words and other objective lingual elements and units. An acceleration of the factual process of lingual change is in the first place related to the material lingual sphere in which the objective lingual elements that are subject to change are used. Code language used under operational conditions in an army may undergo reasonably rapid changes if it is surveyed from an objective lingual angle, even though the various normative lingual systems for developing the code may remain relatively stable. This applies to all languages that fit Halliday's definition of an anti-language, such as the language of the underworld, that has to maintain its status as an anti-language by constantly renewing itself, and is characterized by the rapid turnover of words and other objective modes of expression (Halliday 1979: 180).

Semantic change, as one kind of objective lingual change, may itself be classified into various types such as narrowing, widening, metaphor, metonymy, synechdoche, hyperbole, litotes, degeneration and elevation (Bloomfield 1958: 426 ff.), and may also vary in tempo. At least one factor contributing to fast change is taboo (Bloomfield 1958: 400). Other causes for fluctuation on the factual side of the lingual aspect are the relative frequency of certain objective lingual forms indicating new technical advances and also the lingual effectiveness of, for example, witticisms that wear off after a while and are replaced by even newer forms. The lingually expressive force of vogue words is weakened by frequent use (Bloomfield 1958: 399 ff.; 435). Bloomfield remarks (1958: 403) that one of the most powerful causes for factual lingual fluctuation is the subjective lingual power that prestige or the authority of others exerts.

The elementary concepts of physical analogies on the factual side of the lingual aspect also direct the attention of the theoretical linguist to yet another analogical moment, namely that of factual lingual effect and cause. Again, factual lingual causes and effects are subject to lingual norms and principles. Factual lingual effects and their causes are linked with the elementary concept of factual lingual change, since factual, objective variations in pitch, loudness, speed, rhythmicality (cf. Crystal & Davy 1976: 32 ff.) and so on may figure as objective causes for certain factual lingual effects, as when distinctive changes in the objective tempo of speech are employed to produce different meanings (Crystal & Davy 1976: 34).

Every physical analogy functioning as a lingual retrocipation on the factual side of the lingual aspect is in the last analysis related to the elementary linguistic concept that one may form of the dynamic process in which language is formed. The concept of factual lingual change implies, for example, that there is a dynamic flow that characterizes the factual process of language, and so does the objective relation between factual lingual cause and effect: without a lingual process the dynamic movement from lingual cause to lingual effect would be meaningless.

All the various dynamic processes through which language is formed are subject to lingual norms. This is also the case in the formation of new words. Aranoff (1976: 21) presents the rule that regulates the factual process of regular word-formation in the form of a hypothesis:

> All regular word-formation processes are word-based. A new word is formed by applying a regular rule to a single already existing word. Both the new word and the existing one are members of major lexical categories.

The credibility of this hypothesis rests on the insight that the lingual process, which is a physical analogy on the factual side of the lingual aspect, presupposes a normative lingual regularity or consistency, as well as the factual lingual constancy of already existing lingual objects (words), both of which are kinematic analogies functioning on the norm-side and factual side of the structure of the lingual aspect. This serves to illustrate once again the interrelatedness of the various elementary linguistic concepts and the need for a consistent systematic framework to bolster the significant and worthwhile observations that the theorist wishes to make about language.

10 Lingual development and organisation

Language and biology

Various schools of linguistic thought have paid attention to the analogical links between biotic life and language. Especially, the "genetically sophisticated version of rationalism" (Sampson 1979: 146) that Chomskyan linguistics embodies, claims that at least one of the intriguing reasons for studying language is that one may discover principles that determine the normative structure and factual use of language, and that these principles are "universal by biological necessity ..." (Chomsky 1975: 4). Furthermore, the "theory of language is simply that part of human psychology that is concerned with one particular 'mental organ', human language" (Chomsky 1975: 36).

The 'innateness hypothesis' proposed by transformational grammar must be formulated in such a way that the linguistic theory or universal grammar with which the human mind is endowed can finally be explained by human biology (Chomsky 1975: 34; cf. too 39, 72, 123). This is because the human language faculty is to Chomsky a species-specific, genetically determined property of mind (1975: 79).

The analogical biotic nature of these concepts is unmistakable: only if one relates language to the experiential aspect of organic life, which forms the original field of investigation of biology, can one speak of lingual organ, of lingual development, and of the factual organization of language by means of genetically determined principles of mind.

But the crucial question is of course whether the thesis that language is biologically determined is not merely a partial view of language. If the human mind possesses innate mechanisms that are indeed biologically determined, one would assume that they function according to biotic or biological laws. The problem that arises if this is the case seems to be, if one phrases the question in Chomskyan terms: how do biologically determined mechanisms manage to shape the immense number of completely novel lingual expressions that characterize the creative aspect of language use? If language is characterized by creativity, which amounts to the claim that the design of language is free from stimulus control and always innovative, how do we then reconcile such creativity with the fact that a law, also a biological one, can never allow innovations according to a free design, but can only produce a law-determined uniformity?

The solution to this in terms of a systematic linguistic theory is that one must indeed recognize that the biotic or organic aspect of experience is modally interrelated with the lingual aspect, and that this allows one to speak of analogical biotic concepts like lingual organ, lingual development, lingual differentiation, lingual organization and the like. But the lingual nature of all these analogies makes it impossible to conceive of these analogical moments in other than subjective human terms, which amounts to saying that the human lingual faculty or organ is subject not to natural laws but to cultural principles that allow significant variations in the factual organization of different languages. Biological concepts can function in linguistic theory only if this important qualification is borne in mind.

Normative lingual development and maturity

Normative lingual growth, development or maturation, as an analogy of biological development on the norm-side of the lingual aspect, depends on the kinematic and physical analogies within the structure of the lingual modality that were commented upon in the preceding two chapters. Language development in children follows different phases of rule-governed or *consistently regulated changes* (Smith & Wilson 1979: 208-215). The analogical kinematic concept of normative lingual consistency and the physical retrocipation of normative change are thus constitutive for a theoretical definition of the biotic analogy of lingual development operating on the norm-side of the lingual aspect.

The definition of the normative lingual growth and maturity of the human language faculty as a mental organ in Chomsky also depends upon the analogical physical concept of the initial and steady state of a normative lingual system, since lingual growth progresses from an initial to a steady state. The initial state of language, i.e. the language faculty, is characterized by what Chomsky calls universal grammar. The biotic analogy of lingual growth is clearly what Chomsky has in mind for the discussion of this progression (1978b; emphases added):

> What happens in the *growth of* the individual is that under the triggering and controlling effect of the social environment, the language *organ grows and matures* in him, reaching finally a steady state sometime in the ... late childhood, whereafter changes seem to be rather superficial.

Universal grammar therefore provides a fixed framework for the mental growth of a particular grammar. In fact, Chomsky (1978b) in so many words spells out the biotic analogy when it comes to the acquisition of language, for he remarks that the "metaphor of learning which is generally employed in speaking of the growth of language may be quite a misleading one and that in considering the transition from the initial to the final state, we should rather think of it as *analogous to biological growth and maturation*" (emphases added).

By taking universal grammar as a description of a system of lingual principles or conditions that constitutes the defining quality of the initial state of the language organ, it is clear that Chomsky has in mind the normative growth of the lingual organ, which, though it is itself a factual, subjective human capacity for language, nevertheless has the unmistakably normative ability to order, specify, arrange and organize human lingual experience in the acquisition of a specific language. For it is the systematic organization of the grammar rules of a specific language by this lingual organ to which, inter alia, the factual organization of lingual objects is subjected.

Factual lingual growth and differentiation

Factual lingual growth and differentiation is subjected to normative lingual development. In modern languages, lingual differentiation has taken place, but all languages, ancient and modern, 'primitive' or 'civilized', of whatever substance (phonic, graphic, etc.), are distinguished from animal sounds and bodily movements not only by their great degree of differentiation (Bloomfield 1958: 27), but also by the kind of differentiation. Animal sounds are bound rather strictly to the instinctively-qualified, immediate environment, whereas human language is characterized by the intrinsically lingual functions of displacement and abstraction.

Halliday (1979: 16 f.) insists that the 'nativist' (Chomskyan) and 'environmentalist' positions on language development in children are complementary rather than contradictory, and that one can approach the development of language as a functional differentiation. His statements in this regard are couched in terms that reflect the analogical link between the biotic and lingual modalities on both the norm-side and the factual side of the lingual aspect. According to Halliday (1979: 19), what happens in the process of lingual development is that the child acquires a range of meaning potential:

> This consists in the mastery of a small number of elementary functions of language, and of a range of choices in meaning within each one. The choices are very few at first, but they expand rapidly as the functional potential of the system is reinforced by success ... and this provides the impetus for taking the process further.

Meaning potential and functional potential are two analogical concepts functioning on the norm-side of the set of biotic analogies in the lingual aspect, whereas the factual, functional differentiation of language is a formulation of a biotic analogy on the factual side. Moreover, Halliday's observations make quite clear to what extent a theoretical analysis of the biotic analogy in the lingual aspect relies on other constitutive analogies (retrocipations): compare his use of the terms 'range', 'mastery' and 'number' that reflect the spatial, formative and numerical analogies. One may note, too, how the factual and normative expansion of choice and systematic potential, which is of course a spatial analogy, depends on the physical analogies of factual lingual process and effect. The inescapable analogical coherence of the different modal aspects is again evident.

Furthermore, one can say that the factual differentiation that takes place to make a language a 'developed' one needs not only the above-mentioned constitutive analogies, but is itself guided by the regulative social anticipations within the structure of the lingual aspect.

Halliday therefore defines the notion of a functionally differentiated or 'developed' language in terms of the biotic analogy of function and the social anticipation of sociolingual purpose: "a 'developed' language ... is used freely in all the functions that language serves in the society ...," he remarks (1979: 194). These functions are, *inter alia*, the language used in casual conversation or instruction of children in the home and family, the language used in buying, selling or bartering, as well as the more highly specialized functions such as those of religion, literature, law and government. What have been called typical or material lingual spheres in this study would therefore qualify in Halliday's terms as the more specialized functions of a highly differentiated language, while an 'undeveloped' language would be one that serves only some of the functions listed here by Halliday, but not all. If, with Halliday, one can relate language to the society in which it is used, the biotic analogy of functional lingual differentiation allows one to make the linguistic distinction between differentiated or relatively undifferentiated languages.

In light of these definitions some understanding can be gained, too, of the opposition that the idea of 'inadequate' language has generated. It is certainly true, as the argument goes, that no language is inadequate. Even though the notion persists in the language attitudes of many people, the belief that a 'civilized' language is more adequate than a 'primitive' one has been abandoned by modern linguists, and the very distinction between 'primitive' and 'civilized' languages has given rise to doubts. However, it seems that it is not so much the distinction that one should question as the obviously fallacious grounds on which it is adopted. The concept of functional lingual differentiation allows us (a) to distinguish between languages that are more highly differentiated than others which are not, and so to account for the phenomenon that "English in medieval England was not a developed language, since many of the social functions of language in the community could be performed only in Latin or in French" (Halliday 1979: 194); and (b) also to understand why lingual differentiation is a phenomenon belonging not exclusively to the social anticipatory functions of language, but has a firm basis in the constitutive link between the lingual and biotic aspects of experience.

Any language, therefore, exhibits a higher or lower degree of differentiation, also in its culturally closed or isolated 'primitive' State,

For even a primitive language has to some extent differentiated according to function, although these functions may not yet include a great variety of typical lingual spheres, that provide for the specialized functions of, amongst other things, the various forms of the written language.

It is also clear, however, that the idea of the 'social' functions that language serves or is to serve is a factor that stimulates the process of lingual development (defined now as adding to its range of social functions: Halliday 1979: 195)[10]. Without the normative lingual needs and requirements for language development created by a process of cultural and social differentiation, the constitutive potentialities for a language to become a more differentiated one remain restricted and closed. Normative need for development and factual differentiation go hand in hand: one cannot conceive of the one without the other, because their correlation is an echo within the elementary linguistic concepts that leads us to discover the analogical link between the biotic and lingual aspects, of that complex and crucial alignment between lingual norm and lingual fact.

It is now also possible to attempt a formulation of the normative moment functioning on the norm-side of the set of biotic analogies in the lingual aspect, and to which our factual use of language is subject. This is the principle of lingual vitality operative in the lingual life of the norms that guide our everyday use of language. As a fundamental lingual principle it presupposes the maintenance of lingual norms by competent lingual organs within the various material lingual spheres. But it also takes the analogical moment of maintenance a step further, since it entails a normative lingual adaptability. In view of the biotic analogies functioning on the factual side of the lingual aspect, one is obliged to note also that the normative adaptability of lingual norms is a functional adaptability that enables a language to differentiate and develop to meet the various needs that it has to fulfill in a process of cultural and social differentiation.

Factual lingual organization

The subjective human capacity for using language in various material lingual spheres may in analogical biotic terms be viewed as a lingual

---

10. Bloomfield (1958: 28) emphasizes in this regard that the term 'social organism' is not a metaphor when we speak of the different functions of language in society.

organ. This does not mean that somewhere in the human body one may find a separate organic part that meets this description. Neither the lungs, nor the larynx, palate, nose or tongue would qualify as such an organ adapted specifically for the purpose of producing language. Language, Sapir (1949: 8 f.) said, is not a simple activity carried out by one or more organs. Rather, the production of language involves the co-operation of very nearly all the bodily musculature, and not only the so-called organs of speech, such as the throat, the mouth and the nose (Hjelmslev 1963: 103).

The subjective human lingual organ should therefore be viewed as a subjective lingual capacity for the organization of factual lingual objects. As such a lingual capacity, its production of objective lingual facts moves within the limits of the various material lingual spheres, which in analogical biotic terms are themselves "types of organisation present in language" (Crystal & Davy 1976: 14).

The concept of a subjective lingual organ and of the objective, factual organization of language enables the language theorist to distinguish between lingual potentiality and actuality, as well as between lingually vital and dead elements in existing languages. As biotic analogies these concepts depend on the physical analogy of lingual change: the extremity of lingual loss in the individual, namely aphasia, can be defined, for example, in terms of the rapid changes that the language faculty (viewed from this analogical angle as a lingual organ or potentiality) undergoes (Smith & Wilson 1979: 215). Aphasia involves the kind of lingual change that can be defined as "the breakdown of the rule system governing normal use of language" (Smith & Wilson 1979: 216), which, as a definition, again depends on the analogical kinematic concept of rule-governed creativity or normative lingual consistency. That the biotic retrocipation of lingual organization in its turn allows us to gain some insight into the process of language loss is clear from Smith and Wilson's (1979: 216) remark that we need to refer in an inquiry into this phenomenon to the general organizing principles of grammar:

> What we need to look at is not so much the individual rules of grammar as the organizing principles used to group these rules into a grammar.

As lingually dead elements in any concrete language one may classify archaisms and obsolete expressions. Such expressions lose all lingual life and vitality, and their objective lingual or expressive potential is actualized only when they are revived in specialist terminology. In this respect archaisms and obsolete expressions differ from clichés, the latter having lost only their objective expressive power, but as such are still part of the conventional lexical ranges of adult speakers. The objective lingual potential of words is closely related to the subjective human lingual organ that has to actualize such an objective expressive capacity. Like the complex linguistic concept of lingual norm and lingual fact, the complex relation between lingual subject and lingual object is defined in terms of elementary linguistic concepts: the distinction between subjective and objective lingual potential is only one elementary or constitutive angle from which this relation may be viewed, in this case the set of biotic analogies within the structure of the lingual aspect. The subjective potential (organ) for producing human language and the objective expressive potential of lingual facts to be organized into new expressions are inseparably linked.

It is presumably the objective expressive capacities of words that De Saussure has in mind when he speaks (1966: 166) of the potential existence of words in concrete languages, or of the rating of words in terms of their potential to engender other words in the process of analogical creations, so that one may speak of productive or sterile words in all languages. Through such factual reorganizations of the objective lingual forms of a language its factual lingual growth is ensured.

The subjective lingual organ and the objective organization of lingual facts are subject always to lingual norms, not the least of which is the fundamental lingual principle of adaptability that was mentioned in the previous section. The subjective human potential for producing and understanding language entails a subjective and objective adaptability. The extreme case of a person with a minimal amount of lingual adaptability is where "the lack of a relatively subtle, stylistic awareness has become a more general lack of linguistic awareness" (Crystal & Davy 1976: 6) of the functionally differentiated varieties of language. It is this lingual awareness or sensitivity that forms the subject matter of the next chapter.

11 Lingual volition and sensitivity

Linguistics and psychology

Through the intricate relation between language and feeling linguists approach the long-standing association of linguistics with psychology. Psychology has as its field of study the sensitive dimension of experience and the various kinds of human psychical behavior. The psychical or sensitive aspect of our experience is connected in a multitude of ways to phenomena that are qualified by the lingual modality, and concepts that reflect this coherence therefore abound in linguistic and psychological theory. The field is indeed so vast that the cursory exposition that can be given here of certain of these concepts represents only a brief survey of subject matter which requires further elaboration and refinement. The concepts in question include the relation between language and feeling, the coherence of human expression and emotion, lingual behavior and reaction, the human lingual volition and interpretative intentions, as well as the perception and awareness of lingual facts and lingual norms, to name but a few.

From a systematic point of view, the legitimate analogical links between the psychic and lingual aspects are those that enable the linguist to grasp the constitutive, internal connection between these aspects. This internal association between the psychic and lingual modalities is summed up best by the broad elementary concept of lingual sensitivity.

There is also an external, concrete relationship between language and feeling. It is this relationship that concerns Sapir (1949: 38 ff.) in his discussion of the volitional and emotional aspects of speech. But although human volition is characterized by an emotional urge to express itself, the external, concrete relation between language and feeling, or even the expression of our feelings, does not concern the linguist. Rather it belongs to the psychologist, in whose original field of investigation the study of such phenomena is undertaken.

Linguistic theory has been plagued by psychologistic inroads throughout its history, and the marking out of the boundaries of the two disciplines has not been a happy one. Even the most carefully chosen words used to distinguish between linguistics and psychology may still betray a non-linguistic starting point. Bloomfield (1958: 24 f., 32) provides a good example of this when he emphasizes that linguists are not competent to deal with problems of physiology or psychology, since their study concerns only the speech-signal, viewed then as a 'substitute reaction' to a stimulus that itself prompts a substitute stimulus. The question is whether this kind of argument can succeed in moving beyond a psychological description of language. It is not surprising, therefore, that Bloomfield's behaviorism has been subjected to severe criticism by language theorists (cf. for example Palmer 1976: 52 ff.).

Both structuralist and behaviorist approaches in linguistics are criticized by Chomsky (1972a: 25) for their "faith in the shallowness of explanations, the belief that the mind must be simpler in its structure than any known physical organ," and they are taken to task for simply assuming without argument that language is a habit structure, a network of associative relations or a system of dispositions to respond (Chomsky 1972a: 26). There are conceptual lacunae in the behaviorist approach that prevent it from making the necessary methodological distinctions in linguistic theory (Chomsky 1972a: 72).

Psychologism is evident also in De Saussure's work, particularly in his concept of lingual signs that are constituted of a sensorily perceptible expressive aspect and a signified conceptual component, which, though it is itself not sensorily perceptible, is nevertheless psychical in nature (Van den Berg 1979: 18). And Chomsky himself, even though he has launched scathing attacks against the inroads made by a certain school of psychological thinking upon linguistic theory, claims without hesitation (1979: 43) that "one should not speak of a 'relationship' between linguistics and psychology, because linguistics is *part* of psychology ..." Although Chomsky's position is based on different arguments than De Saussure's, the question is whether, from his standpoint, one can escape the very real dangers inherent in an overestimation of psychological concepts in the field of linguistic inquiry. Does a conflict not arise between the Chomskyan point of view that the language faculty is a species-specific property and the view that this property of 'mind' is to be studied only within the scope of psychology?

Indeed, from a systematic point of view such as the one employed in this study, the special language faculty that humans possess is based on and presupposes normal human emotional life, i.e. psychic and volitional capacities for producing and perceiving. Yet this faculty remains distinct from the latter. The lingual aspect is founded upon the emotional or sensitive dimension of human life, but these modalities are nonetheless distinct, irreducible experiential modi. A person's lingual subjectivity needs all human psychical capacities, and yet cannot adequately be explained in terms of them. Actually the topic is too complex to be dealt with systematically in a discussion of the psychic or sensitive analogies within the structure of the lingual aspect. A serious discussion for example of the acquisition of language by the human language faculty, which is a complex linguistic concept, can only be undertaken on the basis of a reasonably elaborate analysis of the various elementary linguistic concepts. The latter kind of analysis of what Chomsky (1979: 42) calls the 'nature' of the system of language is the more immediate concern of the present study. It is in the last analysis a key not only to a linguistic understanding of more complex linguistic concepts, but also holds the promise of providing a guarantee against an overestimation of the importance of psychology in linguistic theory. The phenomena investigated by psychology can gain their rightful, integrated place in linguistic theory only in a balanced, systematic theoretical perspective.

Lingual volition and intention

One elementary concept of linguistic analysis which articulates the analogical relation between the lingual modality and the sensitive dimension of our experience, and that deserves theoretical attention in linguistics, is that of the lingual volition of the producers of language. Linguistics is in need of a concept of the lingually formative will and intention of the human lingual subject, because any factual lingual expression is the expression of a formative and systematic lingual volition, which serves also as the source of lingual norms. Without a lingual volition or intention, users of a language cannot act as lingual organs and the process of language formation cannot be sustained.

Lingual volition is a subjective volition which has a normative dimension, for it is a drive, urge or desire to organize language appropriately and correctly in accordance with all the various rules that make the factual processes of language possible. Because it employs norms in the construction and formation of language, the human lingual volition is a systematic capacity. And since the human lingual volition anticipates the formative ability of the lingual subject, it is also a manifestation of a lingual awareness and perception of lingual means and ends. It is this awareness that enables the human lingual volition to act as the sounding board for a formulation of the norms for language use.

Chomsky wishes to distinguish between the volitional ability to use language and lingual competence. The latter, also called lingual knowledge by Chomsky, even though it may form part of human lingual ability, is simultaneously more abstract than this ability (Chomsky 1975: 23). Chomsky's concept of lingual competence, as is clear from the explanation given in this first chapter of his *Reflections on language*, is based nevertheless on a psychical, cognitive structure, or could even be a cognitive structure.

If one is to distinguish between lingual ability and competence in a systematic way, the distinction would in the first instance have to be linked to different analogical moments in the architectonic structure of the lingual aspect. It is not quite clear whether this can be achieved, however. Perhaps it would do justice to Chomsky's conceptions to link up lingual knowledge with the existence of a specific cognitive structure (a psychical concept), but the details of his theory of lingual competence and the formal features of language dealt with in this theory seem to suggest that, in systematic terms, the technico-formative sub-structure of lingually qualified objects must also be fully taken into account. Systematically speaking, there is no

Lingual volition and sensitivity

objection to the statement that lingual competence, an intrinsically technical or formative element in the structure of the lingual aspect, is based upon a constitutive psychical element that is evident in a certain cognitive structure.

The importance of the linguistic concept of competence as developed by transformational grammar is that it acknowledges the existence of a pre-analytic grammar (cf. Steensma 1977: 64). This is in keeping with De Saussure's view (1966: 73) that the complexity of the lingual system is such that it can be comprehended only by reflecting upon it; those who use language every day are ignorant of its normative complexities.

Searle, too, acknowledges (1969: 42) that one has to assume that human lingual behavior is subject to rules, even though those who use language may not have any conscious awareness that they are acting in accordance with a rule. And one of the general presuppositions of Cartesian linguistics is that the principles of language are known unconsciously and are also the (normative) preconditions for the acquisition of language (Chomsky 1966: 63).

The existence of a pre-analytic grammar raises the issue of the psychological reality of grammar rules and other lingual norms. That these rules or norms are known unconsciously (Smith & Wilson 1979: 22) is a truth that transformational grammar has once again allowed linguists to see, for it recognizes a pre-theoretical lingual intuition (cf. Chomsky 1974: 40). The primary goal of a generative grammar is to make theoretically explicit the intuitive, unconscious knowledge that speakers have of the language they use (Chomsky 1979: 109). The rules of such a grammar, though mastered and internalized by speakers, are only specified in linguistic theory (Chomsky 1965: 8). Or as Chomsky puts it (Chomsky 1972a: 103-104) elsewhere:

> A person who knows a language has mastered a system of rules ... Of course, the person who knows the language has no consciousness of having mastered these rules or of putting them to use ... Rather, to discover these rules and principles is a typical problem of science.

Here, however, the term 'consciousness' is restricted to mean 'theoretical consciousness.' One may well ask if Chomsky has considered that among the literate and articulate users of a language a pre-theoretical consciousness of norms and systems may well exist. If it does not exist, the concept of human lingual volition itself becomes impossible to maintain. Such a pre-theoretical consciousness can without doubt be made explicit, although its explicitness will in certain instances remain a pre-theoretical articulation that can never be compared with the level of explicitness required for example by a theoretical linguistic perspective like that of transformational grammar. The existence of scholarly and academic works like Strunk's (1972) *The elements of style* points to such a pre-theoretical explicitness, even though they may probably not be called 'theoretically explicit' with any justification, especially not from the point of view of transformational grammar. The criteria applied by the latter would exclude traditional grammatical formulations from the desired level of theoretical explicitness. We return below to both the notion of theoretical explicitness (adequacy) as it is understood in transformational grammar, and to the concept of the psychological reality of lingual norms and lingual facts.

The acquisition of language by the human 'organism' entails, according to Chomsky (1970: 112) "a highly restrictive characterization of a class of generative systems" which, somewhat confusingly, he calls 'potential theories.' And a further problem that can be raised in this regard is whether Chomsky's rigid distinction between competence and performance allows the theory of transformational grammar to have any significant effect on grammars that have as their goal a didactic purpose, i.e. a mastery or control of a language (cf. Chomsky 1972a: 156 ff.), except as forming part of a performance model. It is not at all clear at present which direction will be taken by adherents of transformational grammar who are concerned with language teaching, and the whole question of the impact of transformational grammar remains clouded in doubt by these very issues.

Factual lingual will

The human lingual volition or subjective lingual will is not to be explained purely in psychological terms, even though the sensitive analogies in the structure of the lingual aspect provide linguistic theory with a systematic starting-point for the analysis of this subjective capacity for language. This is why the subjective volition to produce language was called a formative drive in the previous section:

although founded upon the human psychic capacities, it is open to the normative, post-psychical spheres in which human life functions. It is a subjective volition which is led by the lingual function of a person's act-life and is expressed only through the mediation of the formative, cultural ability that the lingual subject possesses.

On the factual side of the set of sensitive analogies in the structure of the lingual aspect, the factual lingual will to understand language functions as the addressee of a normative lingual volition. The concept of lingual will and intention is one of the crucial distinctions between language and what is not language. Behavior can qualify as lingual communication only when the noise or mark that is to be understood is addressed to someone by another human being with the intention or volition to communicate (Searle 1969: 16). To quote Searle (1969: 16-17):

> If I regard the noise or mark as a natural phenomenon like the wind in the trees or a stain on the paper, I exclude it from the class of linguistic communication, even though the noise or mark may be indistinguishable from spoken or written words. Furthermore, not only must I assume the noise or mark to have been produced as a result of intentional behavior, but I must also assume that the intentions are of a very special kind peculiar to speech acts.

The last sentence quoted here is the crucial one. For, if only certain kinds of intentions are adequate for the behavior Searle wishes to call speech acts, it means that these intentions must always be characterized by the lingual (expressive) function of our experience as lingual intentions. Furthermore, Searle's exclusion of natural noises or accidental marks from the sphere of lingual activity does not deny the objective lingual factuality of such noises and marks. They are excluded from the realm of lingual acts only because the human lingual will has not been directed at them to come to some interpretation and understanding of their meaning (cf. Searle 1969: 42 f.). Such objective marks or noises do not participate subjectively in the sphere of lingual activity, since their meaning is only actualized if it is interpreted by someone with the active, subjective will to understand them, even if that meaning is merely a human identification of the noise as the noise of the wind blowing through the trees or the mark as the accidental stain left by a teacup on a piece of paper. Only when the human lingual intention is directed towards natural phenomena and accidental marks, do the latter acquire a humanly meaningful character. Otherwise it would have been impossible for the direction of the wind to have any meaning to those intending to go on a picnic, or to the farmer looking for signs of rain or drought. If the objective lingual factuality of accidental or natural marks made no sense, the professional detective's work would be impossible, and trackers who work as nature conservation officials would have a very difficult job.

The concepts of factual lingual will and normative lingual intention rely on the constitutive physical analogy of lingual effect, since, on the speaker's side, according to Searle (1969: 48), "saying something and meaning it are closely connected with intending to produce certain effects on the hearer." And as regards the hearer, "understanding the speaker's utterance is closely connected with recognizing [the speaker's] intentions." Our factual understanding of another's normative lingual intention thus requires the operation of lingual rules that have lingual effects on the factual side of reality. Therefore the concepts of factual lingual volition and normative lingual intention must also, amongst other things, be related to the concept of lingual convention. The meaning of an utterance is determined by rules, and a theoretical linguistic analysis must, as Searle (1969: 45) correctly points out, "capture both the intentional and the conventional aspects" of the human lingual act of signifying.

The factual human lingual will, that functions as the addressee of a normative intention to be understood, is inextricably connected with such an intention, and the factual (subjective) concurrence between writer or speaker and interpreter may be viewed as a unity of interpretative lingual intention functioning within the perimeter of various material lingual spheres.

The human lingual will is, furthermore, a will to perceive. Lingual perception and awareness are two elementary linguistic concepts that focus the theoretical attention of the linguist on the sensitive or psychical aspect of the human lingual will. The intentional use of language not only presupposes our perceptional functioning, but recognizes the limitations of human perception. Therefore one may observe that "language is constrained by the nature of … short-term memory and mental processing" (Yallop 1978: 71). Even though this constraint is not always discernible in the syntactical formulation that the forms of different languages allow, this characteristic of the factual use of language may be understood as a universal feature which can be formulated in terms of elementary linguistic concepts.

The psychic analogies in the structure of the lingual aspect also enable us to observe that the factual use of language is regulated by a subjective sensitivity to norms on the part of the user. As an analogy of the sensitive mode of our experience in the lingual aspect, this subjective sensitivity requires other analogies for its definition. From a sociolinguistic perspective, for example, our subjective sensitivity to lingual principles is a sensitivity to the lingual context on the part of the language user, or, more specifically, to the lingual norms that govern the specific social context in which language is used. This is a fundamental lingual principle that is of the utmost importance to language teaching, since one of the basic aims of teaching a language is to open up and enhance the development of a lingual sensitivity to norms. The human volition is not, as reductionist psychological trends would imply, mechanically determined, but open to the guidance of norms. It is in the formative process of language education that such norms are formulated and a certain sensitivity to lingual norms is nurtured. The same applies to the intentional disclosure of the originally psychical (Dooyeweerd 1953 vol. 2: 425) phenomena of lingual fantasy and imagination.

The factual perception of lingual objects

Objective lingual forms are of necessity always perceived objects, since the lingual aspect of experience is founded upon the sensory aspect of the human act of perceiving. Even though it is essential for a lingual object that its qualifying lingual function is founded on an "objective optical, auditive or at least tactile sensory image" (Dooyeweerd 1953 vol. 2: 381), the arbitrariness of the objective image of an abstract symbol does not do away with the fact that our perception of language also needs the capacities that humans possess for distinguishing and forming the objective facts of language. Lingual perception is always mediated through the logical and formative aspects of our experience, since a lingual sign or an objective, abstract symbol is in principle distinguishable from other signs and symbols, and is always the product of human formation according to a free design.

There is an interesting correlation once again, in the analysis of the set of sensitive analogies within the lingual aspect, between lingual norm and lingual fact on the one hand, and, on the other, the complex relationship between lingual subject and lingual object. Specifically, to return once more to the conception of the psychological reality of factual lingual units that we referred to above, such factual lingual units must, in terms of the sensitive analogy within the structure of the lingual aspect, be perceptible as units.

It is by virtue of the native speaker's subjective lingual competence in a language, for example, that Chomsky claims that such a speaker is able to distinguish between possible (i.e. grammatical, acceptable) sentences (as objective lingual units) and impossible ones (Weideman 1988: 15). This does not mean that all the factual sentences that native speakers produce will perfectly conform to grammatical norms; quite the contrary. But in Chomsky's rationalist frame of mind such factual lingual units as normatively impossible sentences may be disregarded (cf. Lyons 1970: 39), since we are interested, from a rationalist perspective, only in characterizing the ideal speaker's grammatical competence. Various slips and errors are (empirical or factual) performance factors, i.e. characteristics that actual (and not ideal) speakers produce when they are using the language. It is evident that Chomsky's rationalist perspective forces him to drive a wedge between the norm-side and the factual side of the lingual dimension of our experience. Chomsky's position is nonetheless, once again, one that runs counter to traditional, behaviorist views of linguistics, in that he assigns a crucial role to the intuitions of the native speaker. Where behaviorist approaches are primarily interested in the development of techniques of linguistic analysis, the transformationalist would see the proper task of linguistics as accounting for how well a particular system of lingual rules (in this case: the grammar of a language) characterizes the (normatively lingual) intuitions and grammatical knowledge of a native speaker.

A grammar of a language in this sense means a theoretical instrument which should generate all and only the well-formed (normatively possible) sentences as the factual lingual units of a language. One should note that such factual lingual units as sentences are abstract, theoretically relevant entities. By 'generate' — a technical term which should, according to Chomsky, not be confused with the actual pro-

Lingual volition and sensitivity

duction of factual lingual utterances, Chomsky means: "able to specify in abstract, formal terms." Here a further difference with behaviorist structuralist linguistics emerges: not only should a grammar as such a characterization of a set of normative lingual intuitions be observationally and descriptively adequate, but it must also attain explanatory adequacy (Radford 1981: 25 f.). This means that a grammar has to characterize a language in formal terms and principles that present psychologically plausible mechanisms of mental computation. Such is the force that binds together lingual norm and lingual fact, however, that in much of the psycholinguistic research that was stimulated by generativism, the notion of the human possessing psychologically plausible mechanisms that enable us to discern psychologically real, factual units of language was taken up quite seriously and concretely. In the various so-called 'click'-experiments, for example, the experiments were set up to test the psychological reality, to native speakers, of theoretically distinguishable syntactic units. Subjects were asked to listen for the 'click' sound that had been inserted somewhere on the sound-track of an uttered sentence, and to mark the position of the 'click' on a transcribed version of the same sentence in front of them. Even though the click was intentionally displaced by those who set up the experiment, in other words not positioned on a major factual lingual unit boundary such as that of a clause or a phrase, the subjects tended to hear it on the boundary (Clark & Clark 1977: 53 f.)! They therefore demonstrated the strong psychological or perceptual reality that such factual lingual units have for competent lingual subjects.

As I have remarked elsewhere (Weideman 1985a: 195 ff.), although discourse rules and units seem to be much more obvious and self-evident than the apparently abstract factual lingual units perceptible at or below the level of the sentence, this is a more complicated notion also at this level of lingual factuality than is evident at first glance. Intuitively, it looks difficult to deny, for example, the existence of conversational units such as adjacency pairs occurring at various stages of the conversation, such as the pairs of greetings ("Hello!" / "Hi!") used in opening a conversation, or in closings ("Bye" / "Bye") or even pre-closing sequences ("OK" / OK"), non-topic talk and topic talk sequences. The apparently 'dirty' data used by conversation analysis seems to reinforce this notion. So while there has been much debate, for example, about the psychological reality of rule in syntactic theory (cf. also Smith & Wilson 1979: 21 ff.), speaker and hearer knowledge of interactional rules for language use has apparently been less controversial (cf. McDonough 1981: chapter 4). Yet this is only apparently so, for even though the existence of lingual units such as adjacency pairs seems self-evident, they are nonetheless theoretical constructs. In other words, they rely on a certain level of abstraction and theoretical bias that omits a great deal even of what happens lingually between participants at talk (Goffman 1981: 31 f., 34, 41). One of the examples given by Goffman is especially pertinent in this regard; a favorite sample exchange among interactionists is:

[1] A: What's the time?
B: It's five o'clock.

One of the many problems that arises when we use such (fabricated and decontextualized) samples, Goffman argues, is that it is not evident, merely by looking at them, that B (assuming for the sake of the example that he is a man, though this is irrelevant) looks at his watch — which he is in fact normatively required to do if he wishes to be polite and appear to be giving an appropriate answer — before responding. The theoretical categorization of conversation exchanges in terms of units such as adjacency pairs, in other words, does not (amongst other things) capture the semiotics or lingual expressiveness of non-verbal actions that is normally required between the first ("What's the time?") and second ("It's five o'clock") parts of a pair (which is a factual lingual unit) that in print, i.e. verbally, appear to be immediately adjacent utterances. In fact, the flexibility of talk in being responsive to both verbal and non-verbal 'reference' shows in more than just this one way how misleading the idea of a factual lingual unit such as an adjacency pair (a pair of adjacent utterances such as in example [1] above) may be if we take it as the basic unit of conversation (Goffman 1981: 48 ff.; cf. also the more detailed discussion of these units in Chapter 15).

For such reasons, then, it is necessary that the psychological reality of adjacency pairs must be tested in some way. From the point of view of language teaching, it is even more urgent: since the early 1980s, the second language teaching profession has been seeing the results of conversation analysis in textbooks (cf. e.g. Cook's *Using intonation* [1979] and his *People and places* [1980 & 1981, especially 1981: 19 f.], Weideman's *Making certain* [1985b], Van Jaarsveld & Weideman 1985). One experiment that tried to test the psychological reality of adjacency pairs is described in Cook (1981: 253 f.). He found a high level of awareness of such factual lingual units among learners, and observed also how this awareness affected long-term memory. Cook foresees objections to his experiment on the basis of the small numbers of lingual subjects used, but it is unlikely that a duplication of the experiment will lead to radically different results.

What seems to be a greater difficulty is finding an adequate definition for the factual lingual unit 'conversational exchange.' This appears to be still too general and too wide a term, since sequenced lingual interaction between lingual subjects, even though words can be fitted into it, does not necessarily follow a conversational (i.e. lingual) design (Goffman 1981: 38 f., 71). We first need to answer the question: what is conversational, and what is not? Would giving instructions to an employee by an employer be embedded in the lingual unit we would call a conversational exchange, or would it not be conversational at all? In what way is conversation different from other exchanges, such as lectures, arguments, discussions, trials, interviews, meetings, and so forth? Compare, for example, in this regard the different kinds of exchanges that Sachs, Schegloff & Jefferson (1974: 729) list. One way out of this difficulty is not to label all forms of talk 'conversational exchanges', but to speak rather of interactional sequences that may occur in different kinds of talk.

The distinctions between different material lingual spheres that were made above in Chapter 4 allow us to specify the different types of factual lingual interactions going on in various (non-linguistic) situational contexts in a much more specific way than is possible with a broad and potentially confusing term such as 'conversation.' Moreover, having considered such typification of talk in various kinds of sequenced interaction, we may be able to relate such insight more readily to the specific needs of second and additional language learners, discover defects in existing language course syllabuses, and, eventually, adapt our teaching of lingual interaction accordingly (Weideman 1985a: 199). The identification of various kinds of factual lingual exchange must prepare us, therefore, "to appreciate that the social setting of talk not only can provide something we call 'context' but also can penetrate into and determine the very structure of the interaction" (Goffman 1981: 53), since a particular context of situation may be crucial if we are to understand the language used in it, or to judge the appropriateness of speech acts typically occurring in it (Ferrara 1980: 322 f.). We return below, in Chapters 14 and 15, to a more detailed discussion of these distinctions. What is relevant within the context of the current discussion is what has been termed the 'psychological reality' of the factual lingual units operating within various material lingual spheres; the question here revolves around the perceptibility and discernibility[11] by those who use language within different types of discourse, of these factual lingual entities as lingual units.

The perception of lingual objects is an act of the human lingual subject. As one aspect of the complex relation of lingual subject and object, it may itself involve the highly complicated psychic capacities of the human being as well as the sometimes extremely intricate network of objective, associative components in the meaning of lingual forms such as words. Especially in the sphere of literary language, for example, one finds a complicated interaction between lingual systems functioning on different levels. The well-worn distinctions between denotation and connotation or created and established symbols operating within the same text give evidence of this, and pose a problem of linguistic perception and interpretation. The human ability to discern or distinguish between the denotative or connotative components of objective, perceptible lingual forms may be called a person's semantic competence, which forms part of the relation between the lingual and logical aspects of experience that is discussed in the next chapter.

---

11. The latter is an analogical moment belonging to the set of analytical retrocipations within the structure of the lingual aspect that will be the theme of the following chapter.

12 Lingual identification and distinction

Language and thought

There has been much controversy in linguistic theory about the relation between language and thought. Most arguments are put forward either to substantiate the claim that language presupposes thought, or to prove that the reverse is true. Notwithstanding the persistence of claims in this regard, language is not identical with thought, else discussion of a relationship between them would be impossible.

One way of clarifying this confusing issue is to point out that a discussion of the link between language and thought usually concerns only the external, concrete relation between the logical and lingual aspects of our experience, or rather the concrete acts of thinking and expressing thought. Thinking and expression are human activities, and have a concrete, practical existence in normal human life. They are also unique activities, characterized respectively by the logical and lingual aspects of our experience. But as concrete human acts, thinking and expressing function in all aspects of our experience simultaneously, and consequently a temporal priority of the one over the other is impossible. Arguments that attempt to illustrate that language needs thought or that thought needs language are merely stating the obvious: in their simultaneous participation in all aspects of human experience our thoughts and expressions assume concrete forms. The supposedly pre-rational character of language discussed by Sapir (1949: 13 ff.) and the so-called conceptual components of speech are both themes that concern the concrete, external relationship between logically and lingually qualified acts, but that tell us very little about the internal connection between the logical and lingual aspects of experience, that must be systematically surveyed in linguistic theory.

The set of logical analogies in the structure of the lingual aspect relies on concepts that echo the original *analytical* mode of *identifying* and *distinguishing*. On the norm-side an investigation of the logical analogies in the structure of the lingual aspect yields the concepts of normative lingual distinction and judgment, while on the factual side the analysis attempts to clarify the conditions that enable humans to identify and distinguish between lingual facts. From a systematic angle the analytical mode of experience indeed presupposes the lingual, for our judgments about lingual norms and lingual facts presuppose an original logical modality. It is only in this abstract sense that thought, or rather the logical aspect of thought, assumes a foundational role in respect of language. Rational distinction and consideration, which is not to be identified with scientific, theoretical analysis, functions as the necessary basis for the formation of language only in this qualified sense.

Normative lingual concurrence and contradiction

The original logical principles of identity and contradiction function on the norm-side of the lingual aspect either as measures of the degree to which factual human language may concur with or contradict lingual norms, or as criteria by which we are able to judge whether the human formulations of the norms for using language agree with fundamental lingual principles. Lingual norms are normative conclusions reached on the basis of the logical norms of identity and contradiction.

On the norm-side, the fundamental lingual principle of lingual concurrence implies that the factual use of language should be in agreement with valid lingual norms. As transformational-generative theory has pointed out, our factual use of language may (and does) contain mistakes that defy normative lingual prohibitions, and may therefore be lingually anti-normative in that it does not agree with valid lingual norms. But caution is in order before we exercise normative judgments on correct or incorrect usage. What may be erroneous in one material lingual sphere may be perfectly acceptable in the next. Moreover, the use of language contrary to formulated and accepted lingual norms may become such a constant factor in certain material lingual spheres that the validity of accepted lingual norms is eventually completely undermined, and that other formulations of lingual norms are needed.

Normative prohibition and judgment are inextricably linked with yet another logical analogy functioning on the norm-side of the lingual aspect, namely that of the *imputation* of the act of using language to human beings. Lingually qualified deeds are the acts of responsible people, i.e. people who are responding to lingual principles and norms. The language that they use is imputable to the free human lingual volition to form language. Without the concept of volition, which we considered in the previous chapter, and that of imputation, the linguist is unable to distinguish between meaningful and meaningless lingual facts. Relevant at this point are Chomsky's statements on the resolution of ambiguity. Both the ambiguity and the deviance of certain sentences can be explained by *attributing* a system of lingual norms that allows one but not another extension of an ambiguous sentence (that would consequently resolve the ambiguity) to a "person who knows the language, as one aspect of [that person's] knowledge" or lingual competence (Chomsky 1972a: 32). Attributing a knowledge of lingual norms to someone is in fact the basis of the existence of lingual competence, of possessing the ability to form language, in the cosmological perspective which is being used in this study. The reason for this is that the subjective human lingual ability is directly founded upon the human capacity to form according to a free design, which in turn is grounded in the analytical capacity for identifying and distinguishing.

If we attribute to the hearer or speaker a complex system of rules (Chomsky 1972a: 63), this also means that humans possess a *semantic competence*, which is an ability or knowledge to distinguish and identify the meaning of factual lingual items. Indeed, the human lingual competence is not only of a formal, grammatical nature, but also possesses semantic and communicative dimensions (Habermas 1970; Hymes 1971). Whereas the last two specifications of lingual competence respectively take into account the analogical relation between the analytical retrocipations and social anticipations in the structure of the lingual aspect, grammatical competence relies on analogies relating to the formative aspect of experience.

Semantic competence is also broader than the knowledge to detect contradiction and anomaly, as well as tautology, analytic truth and entailment relations, as Smith and Wilson (1979: 63 f.) point out. There is also the ability to recognize *identity* and *ambiguity* in smaller and larger objective lingual units. However, 'semantics' to these authors seems to indicate conceptual rather than lingual knowledge. It is not quite clear whether Smith and Wilson do indeed honour the distinction between logical and lingual knowledge, yet it is a difference that must be acknowledged and explained in linguistic theory. The conclusions they reach as regards the inadequacy of explaining the objective meaning of a sentence in terms of logical entailment relations (Smith & Wilson 1979: 156-158) suggest that they desire to honour this distinction, and the suggestion that is offered deserves attention. But it is not quite clear whether the concept of ordered entailments completely escapes this dilemma (cf. Smith & Wilson 1979: 158 ff.). Their theoretical intention seems to be sound nonetheless, for it calls for an account of the boundary between language and logic, to which the next section is devoted.

Language and logic[12]

Various approaches to semantics regard the meaning of a sentence as a logical proposition and wish "to revive the old ambition of seeing language as a calculus of propositions ..." (Robinson 1975: 103). This is untenable within the framework of a theory, such as the one that is employed in this study, that distinguishes sharply between the logical and lingual aspects of experience, and considers the relationship between them as an analogical one. In this theory, in other words, any 'proposition' contained in a sentence must of necessity be a *lingual* and not a logical one. In the same way that the objective lingual meaning of a word does not coincide with the logical concept of that which is indicated by it, the objective lingual meaning of a larger unit like the sentence must necessarily be rendered in terms of a *lingual* proposition, if 'proposition' is at all the desirable word.

---

12. Cf. the section on the limits of method-borrowing, above, Chapter 2.

To the extent that semantic theory ignores this crucial distinction, it will lack a proper perspective on what constitutes the objective meaningfulness of words and sentences. At the same time, semantics will also be unable to recognize the more than arbitrary boundaries between logic and linguistics, which are, respectively, the mutually irreducible analytical and lingual modalities. The categories and concepts of logic can only be used in a defined and qualified analogical sense in linguistic theory.

This is a truth that is echoed in Smith and Wilson's (1979: 156) summary of the difficulties encountered in introducing a set of concepts from logic to linguistic theory. They point out that the definition of meaning in terms of entailment is erroneous because there are many propositions which are logically deducible from a sentence that are not part of its (lingual) meaning. They conclude (1979: 157 f.) that the entailment theory of meaning cannot adequately account for the difference between rules of logical entailment and rules of semantic entailment, a conclusion that reflects the theoretical idea that the limits between logic and linguistics, and also the scientific methodology derived from such an idea of what these limits are, are themselves neither arbitrary nor merely theoretical.

It is of course also possible to maintain that the objective lingual meaning of a word or sentence indeed has something to do with the logical analogies in the lingual aspect. For example, the objective lingual identity of a word or sentence echoes the figure of logical identity. There is no doubt that Smith and Wilson wish to formulate this analogical relation; after having asked what type of structure it is that is involved in the semantic analysis of a sentence, they answer that "the structure involved is essentially a logical one, and ... the mechanisms used for deriving it involve the lexical, syntactic and phonological form of the sentence under analysis" (Smith & Wilson 1979: 158-159). By speaking of grammatically specified entailments, Smith and Wilson seem to steer clear of the confusion that results from a refusal to honor the distinction between the lingual (including the grammatical) specification of an entailment on the one hand, and the purely logical entailment of sentences on the other. We say 'seem to', because the authors can, on the basis of this, at least give a more workable definition of lingual synonymy than that proposed by the entailment theory. Where the entailment theory falsely predicts that all necessarily true sentences are synonymous, the concept of grammatical or lingual entailment enables them to "modify the definition of synonymy so that only sentences which share their grammatically specified entailments are synonymous ..." (Smith & Wilson 1979: 170). And in the case of grammatically unspecified entailments one could argue that the lingual (which is more than merely grammatical) specification that a sentence must possess still enables one to honor the distinction between the logical and lingual modes of experience.

A problem that linguists have to face if they disregard the distinction between language and logic is that language "notoriously means, sometimes, what it doesn't say (if 'say' refers to propositional content)" (Robinson 1975: 113). Irony and intentional ambiguity, sarcasm and silence all create objective forms of meaning that are difficult to determine solely in terms of logical propositions.

Nonetheless, linguistics owes a systematic explanation of irony and metaphor to the work of Grice (1975) on logic and conversation. In attempting to answer the question of how conversation is maintained (a question that relies on the physical analogy within the structure of the lingual modality), Grice has shown that participants at talk adhere throughout to the following cooperative principle:

[1] Make a contribution (to the ongoing conversation) such as is required, at the stage at which it occurs, by the accepted purpose or direction of the talk exchange engaged upon.

Grice then proceeds to add some further specifications to this norm, particularly the requirements to be

[2] a. as informative as is required (but not more than is required)
  b. truthful
  c. relevant
  d. brief, orderly and clear

Though maxims [1] and [2] seem merely to be stating the obvious, they offer an explanation for what in discourse analysis or text linguistics may be called non-texts. A good example of a non-text, which violates both [1] and most, if not all of the specifications of [2]

would be the following, taken from a real exchange between doctor and psychiatric patient (Coulthard 1985: 6):

[3] A: What is your name?
   B: Well, let's say you might have thought that you have something from before, but you haven't got it anymore.
   A: I'm going to call you Dean.

Consider, however, what happens when, instead of violating (fully contradicting) the norm, participants at talk intentionally flout a Gricean maxim. Grice observes that, in such a case, the co-participant at talk will adhere to, or at least interpret the first participant's utterance as adhering to, the overriding cooperative principle [1] above, and, by imputing lingual co-cooperativeness, so understand such an utterance as a (mere) flouting (partial, limited and intentional contradiction) of one of the maxims. Thus the metaphor

[4] Maggie was an iron lady

will be a flouting of maxim [2b], but by the overriding cooperative principle [1] be heard as

[5] Maggie was a tough politician

whereas the ironic

[6] You've done a pretty marvelous job this time, haven't you?

is, by the same token, heard as

[7] You've messed the car up pretty badly this time, haven't you?

By means of the lingual norms of imputation and cooperation we therefore have a means of explaining phenomena such as metaphor and irony (Weideman 1988: 68). These are lingual norms that rely on the analogical connection between the lingual mode of experience and, respectively, the logical and social dimensions. This means that linguistics and logic proceed from two distinct, though related facets of our experience.

Another equally significant indication that logic and linguistics constitute two distinct branches of academic enquiry is that words with logically opposite meanings are not necessarily antonyms in every respect, i.e. lingually or semantically. Thus 'come' actually shares the distinction of 'move' with 'go.' Human understanding of the lingually meaningful identity of objective lingual elements goes beyond explanations offered by logical concepts.

Factual lingual identity

The factual identity and distinctiveness of objective lingual facts are regulated by norms. Our semantic competence enables us to identify and distinguish a lingually meaningful diversity of lingual facts. Whereas linguistic theory now recognizes the subjective imputation of a complex system of lingual norms to the human being, it must also stress, as we have seen in the previous section, the objective attribution of meaning by humans not only to lingually qualified objects, but to objective lingual facts in general. Only by assigning an objective meaningfulness also to natural events and phenomena are humans able to interpret their environment. Such facts have an objective lingual factuality that is not founded upon the human formative ability and the intervention of the human lingual volition, but they nonetheless are not interpretable without human attention and the subjective human capacity for identifying and distinguishing their objective meaning. Humans have the ability to read the signs of the weather and recognize the objective lingual indications of seasonal change; a person is able to identify and distinguish between different sets of animal tracks, and is able to say, after sufficient training or practice, whether the tracks are fresh or old. Likewise the doctor must be able to identify and distinguish different disease symptoms from normal, healthy bodily conditions before making an interpretative diagnosis, and the farmer has to learn to identify and understand the distinct meaning of animal behavior at mating time.

The fundamental lingual distinction that can be made in this respect is that between meaningful and meaningless lingual facts. Lingual facts possess a distinct, meaningful identity when they are formed or interpreted in accordance with lingual norms. Without normative regulation lingual facts are meaningless.

The concept of factual lingual identity relies, furthermore, on all the other constitutive lingual concepts investigated so far. A lingually qualified object has a distinct identity, or a distinguishable variety of lingually meaningful distinctions of meaning, only if it is a constant lingual unity operating within specified material lingual spheres, and occupying a determined and determinable factual position in the midst of a variety of other lingually qualified objects in the process of language production. Its lingual identity can only be determined by the subjective human lingual volition and competence to produce and understand language, and it is to the latter that the enquiry turns in the next chapter.

13 Formative retrocipations in the lingual aspect

The internal molding of language

The aim of this chapter is to investigate the internal coherence that exists between the lingual aspect of our experience and the controlling manner of giving a distinct form to cultural objects. It is concerned specifically with what Dooyeweerd (1953 vol. 2: 222) terms the inner formation or molding of language in its factual production by competent users. It is, in other words, an attempt to conceptualize the retrocipatory link between the lingual modality and the formative or technical aspect of experience.

What holds for verbal languages as well as for other semiotic structures is that they possess the "possibility of forming signs and ... very free rules for forming units of great extension (sentences and the like) ..." (Hjelmslev 1963: 109-110). Our formative ability in the case of language is a capacity that functions according to the free design that is characteristic of all cultural activities. Chomsky (1972a: 100) has called this the creative aspect of language use, the "one fundamental factor that distinguishes human language from any known system of animal communication". It can be defined as the competence to form language in accordance with norms and principles of great variety. It is a subjective ability that enables us to give objective form to our lingual expressivity through the medium of sound, ink and paper, paint and cardboard, chisel and marble, muscle and skin, and so forth. As an analogical historical or technical mode of formation, the human formative ability in respect of language is characterized by a controlling design, and by the subjective power of production with certain objective and subjective means towards specified cultural ends. The means may vary greatly, for humans have a variety of objective materials from which to choose in the production of language. They range from the most obvious, the medium of sound, to the most complex typographical and sophisticated electronic means. But all work towards a common goal: that of enabling us to express ourselves through our formative capacity for the production of language.

The subjective human competence to form and mold language has a systematic, normative dimension, for it is in the first instance a capacity to mold language in accordance with lingual norms. Lingual norms are human formulations of fundamental lingual principles, and as subjective formulations are subject to revision and reformulation. But a human formulation of the norms that regulate the formation of language nevertheless exerts a normative influence upon the users of language. Since it is subject to change, the human formative ability is also a cultural or historical ability. Linguistic theory should thus note not only factual changes in the history of the language, but also attempt to explain the development and growth of the human lingual organ, noting especially how the human capacity for forming and producing language develops (or in certain cases fails to develop) into an individualized ability to use language in all material lingual spheres.

The formative analogies in the lingual aspect thus call for an examination of lingual competence on the norm-side and factual side of the lingual aspect, as well as of lingual form and function on the factual side, an examination that corresponds broadly with the fields of investigation of two linguistic sub-disciplines, namely syntax (as the study of the normative structure for the organization of language) and morphology (as the study of the factual forms of lingual objects).

The normative dimension of lingual competence

Our subjective lingual competence functions on the norm-side of the formative analogies in the lingual aspect as a normative command of the language. It is not merely a tacit knowledge or mastery of lingual rules that the speaker is unable to state (cf. Chomsky, 1972a: 190), But a conscious normative competence to form and formulate, reform and reformulate, change or institute, deny or conceive, challenge or call into being lingual norms, at least if we broaden the linguistic idea of lingual rule or norm to include any instruction to which the factual use of language is subject, and not only highly formalized, theoretically formulated rules of syntax.

It is of course true that lingual competence has been studied almost exclusively in syntactical studies. As the study of lingual form and the formal structure of language (Chomsky 1978a: 57; cf. too Carnap 1937: 1-8), or as the theoretical explanation of the grammatical devices that are available for the organization and expression of lingual content (Chomsky 1978a: 57), syntax is universally considered to be the best suited for an investigation of lingual competence. But there is good reason to suspect that the concept of lingual competence includes more than a subjective syntactic competence and the grammatical instructions associated with it. Of this the less well-developed concepts of semantic and communicative competence already provide some evidence. Even quite simple instructions for the use of language, as for example the instructions on filling in a form ("Write in BLOCK LETTERS") or completing a withdrawal slip ("Amount in words") presuppose a competence to use language that goes beyond syntactic explanation.

Neither is it hard to find a reason for the systematic narrowing of the concept of lingual competence to incorporate only an enriched notion of syntactic competence. The concept of syntactic competence exhibits in almost every respect its reliance on formative or technical analogies such as *device, form, formatives, mastery, command, production* and so on. In transformational grammar, for example, syntactic devices are normative lingual structures that are subjectively put to use and realized:

> Phrase structure and transformational structure appear to provide the major syntactic devices available in language for organization and expression of content. The grammar of a given language must show how these abstract structures are *actually* realized ... (Chomsky 1957: 102; emphasis added).

Thus, too, the syntactic component of a grammar contains lingual rules that regulate "the well-formed strings of minimal syntactically functioning units (*formatives*)..." (Chomsky 1965: 3). Numerous other examples can be cited from the literature on syntax, but the point should be clear: it is tempting to reduce the concept of lingual competence, itself an analogical formative moment within the modal structure of the lingual aspect, to syntactic competence, which relies (perhaps exclusively) on the analogical concepts of lingual form, mastery and device. Since the latter set of concepts is also made up of formative analogies within the structure of the lingual aspect, linguists seem to identify syntactic competence with lingual competence all the more easily; if there is any theoretical uneasiness about doing this, the concept of syntactic competence is merely enriched by calling into play the other 'levels' of language, and by offering arguments that are intended to show the preponderance of syntactic considerations over semantic, phonological and morphological phenomena.

It is with this in mind that one should approach the distinction between competence and performance in transformational grammar, since it might go some way towards providing an explanation for what Chomsky himself has frequently claimed to be misunderstood and misinterpreted by other linguists.

The distinction between competence and performance, implicit already in *The logical structure of linguistic theory* (Chomsky 1978a: 7 – the earlier work, though it was published later) and *Syntactic structures* (Chomsky 1957), is first explicitly made in *Aspects of the theory of syntax* (Chomsky 1965). It is a distinction that is compared very often with De Saussure's distinction between 'langue' and 'parole'. Palmer (1976: 7) comments that "for both De Saussure and Chomsky, language or competence is some kind of idealized system without any clear empirical basis ..." The crucial point of concurrence between De Saussure and Chomsky's linguistic theories is thus that both show a rationalistic trend in the systematic idealization of either 'langue' or competence.

Competence and performance are in the first instance distinguishable as the knowledge and use of language (Chomsky 1965: 4). Chomsky's main contribution has been to draw the attention of linguists to the normative dimension of human lingual competence, since competence is a normative command or mastery of language which is part of our lingual subjectivity (Chomsky 1972a: 190). Competence is a command of the language that enables one "to understand what is said and to produce a signal with an intended semantic interpretation" (Chomsky 1972a: 115), whereas performance is the observed use of language.

The interpretation-problem in Chomsky's explanation of the relation between lingual norm and lingual fact that was raised earlier can now be reformulated as follows: what is the relationship in Chomsky's thought between competence, as a normative command of the language, and performance, as the data encountered in the factual use of language?

The remarks made earlier about the complementarity of the linguistic perspectives of sociolinguistics and transformational grammar are again pertinent, for they enable one to make a systematic methodological statement about Chomsky's linguistic perspective on the relation between competence and performance.

Firstly, the internalized system of rules that constitutes lingual competence in Chomsky's thinking is a restricted or limited system which refers only to the constitutive elements in the structure of the lingual aspect, especially to the elements in this structure as surveyed from the technical sub-structure or analogy in the lingual aspect.

Actual performance, as the observed use of language, however, goes wider than this, and cannot be explained simply by application of the lingual principles that make up lingual competence. Other, to Chomsky 'extralinguistic' factors and features, that in a systematic theory would be identified as 'intralingual', yet belonging to the disclosed, anticipatory or regulative structure of the lingual aspect in which the various material lingual spheres figure, combine and are combined with lingual competence to make up performance. Therefore, although lingual performance provides data for the study of lingual competence, the latter is just one of the many factors that interact to determine performance (Chomsky 1972a: 117).

The problem, however, is that competence, linked as it is with performance in Chomsky's view, can still refer to a rationalist conception of the idealized speaker-hearer's lingual ability (cf. Chomsky 1972a: 118). The problem seems to persist if one considers Chomsky's thesis that the notion of competence is a necessary requirement in any theory of performance.[13] If 'universal grammar' is an essential

---

13. It is interesting to note that that Carnap (1937: 8) also held that the

element of a property of mind (Chomsky 1975: 148) and if this property or cognitive structure is actually employed in speaking and understanding (Chomsky 1975: 160), then competence and performance can in principle not be separated; they must remain correlates, though theoretically distinguishable as formulations of the formative analogy on the norm-side and factual side of the lingual aspect.

The problem of the relation between competence and performance becomes more acute, in other words, whenever the distinction between them is employed so as to emphasize the one in favor of the other, or even in stating that we must necessarily start with an analysis of the one in order to gain insight into the other. The question thus is whether one can, from a transformationalist stance, criticize a theory of word-formation (such as that of Aranoff 1976) on the grounds that it is based on actual, attested, existing or used words (that belong to the sphere of lingual performance) instead of on possible words (that belong to lingual competence), especially if the results obtained by morphologists working wholly within a generativist perspective are tested by reference to actual utterances (facts of lingual performance), utterances that can act, as elsewhere in the theory, as examples or counterexamples. If the examples and counterexamples that are produced to test the adequacy of the theory are indeed taken from the experienced facts of lingual performance, then this emphasizes still further the strict, and therefore simultaneous, correlation between lingual competence and performance. But there is no doubt that there is uncertainty about this. It seems that Currie (1975: 56) wishes to draw our attention to this problem when he remarks, after describing the Chomskyan distinction between competence and performance:

> But competence underlies all performance, and, in a strangely circular way, depends on it, since statements about competence are ultimately verified by being part of performance.

In a mimeographed article, Botha (s.d.) also draws attention to the ambiguity, paradox and obscurity in Chomsky's thought on this point. And Robinson's exasperation (1975: 62) is that Chomsky's insistence

---

method that he proposed for arriving at the 'logical syntax' of language would help in the logical analysis of the incredibly complicated word-languages, in what Chomsky would call the theory of performance.

on the theory of performance incorporating a model of competence "still means that competence is made flesh," whereas the abstractness required by the linguistic concept of competence as formulated by Chomsky denies the very possibility of doing this.

In short, although the reality of our experience of language forces Chomsky to acknowledge the strict correlation of lingual competence and performance (the technico-formative analogies on the norm-side and factual side of the lingual aspect), he can still (1972a: 116), with a rationalist bias, maintain that the primary goal of linguistic investigation is to discover the "grammar of a language, as a model for idealized competence ..."

At times, in spite of Chomsky's insistence on the sharp distinction, perhaps even theoretical separation, between competence and performance, he recognizes the necessary correlation between the two, for competence or knowledge can "be *used* to understand what is heard and to *produce discourse* as an expression of thought within the constraints of the internalized principles, in a manner *appropriate to situations* ..." (Chomsky 1975: 13; emphases added). And in spite of the fact that Chomsky's ideas have been labeled 'imperialistic' by some of his critics, presumably because of what they felt was an undue emphasis in his theory on lingual competence, Chomsky himself (1975: 197; emphasis added) asserts:

> The study of language is concerned with the system *and* its use. The linguist is thus concerned with the competence acquired and performance models that incorporate this competence and are concerned with its use.

In spite, too, of his earlier claim (Chomsky 1972a: 116) that the discovery of grammar is the primary goal of linguistic investigation, Chomsky here adds that neither the theory of competence nor the theory of performance need precede the other, in terms of temporal sequence.

Much of the criticism that is leveled against the Chomskyan distinction between competence and performance, in fact against the theory as a whole, is based on opposition to the notion of idealization; much of the response to this is characterized by the notion that such criticism is simply more or less intolerant empiricist reaction to rationalist thought. But there is also the possibility that opposition to the theoretical formalization of subjective lingual competence echoes an opposition to the current fashionability of formalization in various branches of academic endeavor that goes wider than empiricist sympathies. Chomsky's view (1979: 124) that a characterization of lingual competence *must* ultimately be a formalized theory to be explicit could be considered incorrect from the vantage point of theories that wish to avoid the theoretical pitfalls of both rationalism and empiricism. One of the aims of a systematic investigation of the elementary concepts of linguistics is to provide a methodological framework in which, through the interdefinition of linguistic primitives, the analogical relations between the lingual and other experiential aspects can be explicitly defined. To be sure, such a theoretical idea of analytical explicitness differs from the definition given to it by rationalist approaches. The most prominent difference between a systematic, theoretical explicitness such as is proposed in this study and a notion of formalized theoretical explicitness, is the acknowledgement that the formulations given to fundamental lingual principles can never be formalized even into a quasi-mathematical system since the lingual principles to be formulated are themselves not of a formal, but of a material character, in that they are the conditions that first give content to any theoretical formulation.

Mention has been made above of the fact that the concept of the normative dimension of lingual competence in a systematic linguistic theory also differs from that given by the theory of transformational grammar. The normative lingual competence that is part of human lingual subjectivity is a competence not only to know, but also to formulate or reformulate lingual rules, norms or instructions. Some lingual norms are explicit instructions ("Say X and not Y"), while others indeed are a tacit understanding of the lingual principles that govern the use of language in a specific lingual sphere. There is good reason to suspect, however, that the grammatically specified distinction between lingual competence and performance cannot adequately account for the tacit knowledge that the participants in a conversational exchange have of some of the typical norms that regulate the language used in this lingual context. An example in this regard is the norm of non-fluency. Crystal and Davy (1976: 111) point out that too much fluency in informal conversational exchanges tends to be stigmatized; the non-fluent features that characterize this material lingual sphere cannot summarily be dismissed as deviations of lingual performance, since the frequency with which they occur, their distribution in terms of regular syntactic and phonological patterns and their relation to a standard response on the part of the language-user seem to suggest that they are the rule rather than factual aberrations.

In spite of such differences between transformational grammar and the systematic linguistic theory that is developed in this study, they are in agreement on one fundamental point: the normative human lingual competence, as well as the normative power of lingual norms, is not derived from scientific analysis, nor even is their discovery a question of theoretical reflection. Chomsky recognizes the difference between the theoretical description of a grammar as a model of competence and the internalized system of rules, though both are sometimes ambiguously referred to as 'grammar' (Chomsky 1972a: 116, footnote 1).

Other normative analogies

The normative dimensions of human lingual competence are not the only retrocipatory analogies of original formative power in the structure of the lingual aspect. There is also the linguistically important notion of the formative influence of lingual norms. The influence of traditional ways of speaking and writing is a truly normative assurance of the factual continuity of language. It is probably most evident in the way that educators teach others how to write and speak (for it is not without reason that 'traditional grammar' was and is still taught in some language departments at school and university), but it is also manifest in the customary, stereotyped forms and styles that are used and employed in other areas. Some insurance companies, for example, are now trying to break away from the traditional, long-winded style that is customary in most legal contracts, advertising that they are 'straight-talkers'; in other spheres, notably that of the arts and of religious worship, traditional styles of writing and speaking are forever being challenged.

This is possible because lingual traditions or the customary forms and styles in which language is used are not direct sources of lingual norms, but only indirect modes of prescription of lingual norms that presuppose the original lingual competence to do so (Dooyeweerd 1953 vol. 2: 242). A lingual style, tradition or custom may have significant, even lasting influence, but it is subject to formative, historical change and may thus be replaced by other styles. This formative, historical relativity of an influential lingual tradition is increasingly being recognized by linguists and language teachers. The traditional preponderance of one kind of British English pronunciation as the ultimate standard has been undermined by an acceptance, even encouragement of regional and social variation in pronunciation (cf. Quirk & Greenbaum 1978: 6), even though the normative power it has on other levels of language use still has a healthy, integrating influence. Much the same can be said about the normative influence of language academies, grammar books, spelling lists and dictionaries, or of manuals and directives for the use of language in specific lingual spheres. Although very few linguists would today accept that the standards of language prescribed by a language academy or dictionary are criteria of usage for all varieties of the language, the integrating normative influence of such institutions and books is nonetheless recognized. Such standardizing influences have merit in any national variety of a language, as long as there is no classicistic or rationalistic denial of the original lingual competence to use language in a variety of lingual contexts or spheres. There is no single set of normative prescriptions that is valid for the use of language on all occasions, and no grammar book, dictionary or academy can take away or replace the differentiated lingual competence to use language in a variety of material lingual spheres. The most that such standard guides can at present hope to achieve is to touch upon some of the lexical, grammatical or other forms that are common to more than one variety of the language, whereas manuals and directives that prescribe or suggest lingual norms for specific needs in certain material lingual spheres concentrate on the particular grammar and vocabulary of those spheres.

The factual dimension of lingual competence

Throughout the discussion of lingual competence in the previous two sections it has been clear that human lingual competence is not only a mastery of the norms for the concrete use of language, but a subjective, and hence factual lingual command or power to produce and create language in accordance with fundamental lingual principles and norms. As the correlate of lingual competence on the norm-side of the formative retrocipations in the lingual modality, factual lingual competence is a subjective formative mastery employed by the lingual subject to form and produce lingual utterances (objective lingual facts).

Lingual performance, as the objective product of factual lingual formation, must necessarily be distinguished from both the lingual competence to know and formulate lingual norms and the subjective competence or power that the lingual subject has to form lingual objects. But as objective lingual fact, lingual performance is simultaneously correlated, in terms of the lingually qualified subject-object relation, with the subjective human lingual competence.

The subjective lingual competence that someone possesses to use language in a variety of lingual spheres or contexts further echoes its reliance upon the formative sub-structure of the lingual aspect in that it enables us to employ a factual practical style, technique or method of creating language suited to the needs of the occasion. Moreover, one's subjective mastery and command of a language grows and develops: it unfolds and matures in certain developmental phases. This subjective development of the lingual command of a language, like the history of the objective facts of language, can never be understood purely in analogical biotic or organic terms. The acquisition of a first or second language is always mediated through the formative or cultural sphere. The developmental phases that characterize the acquisition of a subjective command of the language are, in an analogical formative sense, cultural developments, not simply because they reflect the opening-up of an ever-expanding objective cultural milieu, but because they are developmental stages in the growth of a subjective lingual competence that are in the last analysis explicable only as developments in a creative command of language. It is in this creative command or control of language that the original cultural manner of controlling according to a free design is most poignantly expressed.

Other formative analogies on the factual side of the structure of the lingual aspect concern the lingual form of lingual objects. Morphological investigation attempts to determine the rules that govern the objective shape of smaller lingual units. In predicting the objective 'creativity' or possible objective combinations of lingual units, linguistic morphology is best guided by strong phonological, grammatical and semantic constraints.

The constitutive structure of the lingual aspect

The systematic linguistic analysis attempted in this study has so far focused on the essential, constitutive structural features of the lingual aspect, entailing an investigation of the retrocipatory analogical relations of this aspect with modalities preceding it in the order of time.

Such a study of the constitutive structure of the lingual aspect, according to Hjelmslev (1963: 19), avoids the transcendent point of view in seeking an immanently-understood, specific and self-subsistent lingual structure. The term that Hjelmslev uses for a science investigating the constitutive, immanent and independent structure of the lingual aspect is 'glossematics.' With an appeal to the formative analogies on the factual side of the lingual aspect, the objective lingual forms that are distinguished within this investigation are called 'glossemes' (Hjelmslev 1963: 80). These terms, Hjelmslev suggests, will prevent the abuse of the term 'linguistics' by transcendent and irrelevant studies of language. The lack of success of such studies - as well as their irrelevance - might be avoided, according to Hjelmslev (1963: 78), if we focus our attention on the essential analysis of objective lingual forms so as to arrive at an 'algebra of language' (1963: 79, 96).[14]

But even though linguistic theory may seek to investigate only the constitutive structure of the lingual aspect, the analysis cannot end there. Hjelmslev therefore acknowledges (1963: 20) a self-consistent broadening of perspective for linguistic theory, in which

---

14. However, Hjelmslev's theoretical intention of avoiding description of 'purport' (which in his view should be left to the non-linguistic sciences) seems to come close to a denial of the objective lingual factuality of non-lingually qualified things and events. He steers clear of this dilemma only by admitting that the 'purport' is functionally related to the 'linguistic schema', in that the "resultants of the non-linguistic hierarchy, when they are ordered to a linguistic schema, (viz.) the linguistic usage," have "function to the linguistic hierarchy ..." (1963: 81). 'Usage' thus manifests 'schema.'

> after analysis, the global totality - language in life and actuality - may again be viewed synthetically as a whole, this time not as an accidental or merely *de facto* conglomerate, but as organized around a leading principle.

It is this leading principle that has been termed the lingual aspect of experience in this study. This aspect leads, guides, characterizes and marks the concrete empirical fact of language for what it is.

After an analysis of the retrocipatory, constitutive structural moments in the elementary modal architecture of the lingual aspect, linguistic theory thus arrives at a systematic juncture where it needs to survey the anticipatory moments within the structure of this modality. In an investigation of the anticipatory analogies within the structure of the lingual modality, the language theorist ventures outside 'linguistics in the narrower sense', outside the explicit or implicit tradition that the linguist's work begins with the division of sentences into clauses, and that linguists may legitimately refer the analysis of objective lingual units larger than the sentence to other disciplines and fields (cf. Hjelmslev 1963: 97 f.). For, from "this point of view the analysis of the text falls to the linguist as an inevitable duty, including the textual parts that have large extension" (Hjelmslev 1963: 98). Hjelmslev (1963: 99) concludes:

> In all this is seen a significant broadening of the perspective, frames and capacities of linguistic theory, and a basis for a motivated and organized collaboration between linguistics in the narrower sense and a number of other disciplines which till now, obviously more or less wrongly, have usually been considered as falling outside the sphere of linguistic science.

Hjelmslev is here theoretically paving the way for more recent developments in sociolinguistics and text theory and criticism. The analyzed constitutive structure of the lingual aspect ('frames' and 'capacities' in Hjelmslev's terminology) indeed forms the complement of the analysis of its anticipatory, regulative structure. To the extent that the latter type of analysis relies upon the former, it takes up the analyzed constitutive structure of the lingual aspect as a motivated basis for 'organized collaboration' between linguistics and other disciplines, since it involves bringing other 'frames' into play, other 'capacities' and theoretical ideas that are not foreign to linguistic theory, but that complement, as broad, specifying yet limiting concepts, the study of the constitutive linguistic concepts.

The study of the constitutive, retrocipatory features of the lingual modality includes, especially in the linguistic theories and analyses done during the latter half of the 20th century, an almost exclusive investigation of the objective lingual form of lingually qualified facts. It proceeds, in other words, from an emphasis on the objective factuality of lingual objects as viewed from the set of constitutive formative or technical analogies in the lingual aspect and other retrocipatory moments related to it. But linguistic theory is certainly not exhausted by this kind of investigation, because, as Searle (1969: 17) puts it, "a study purely of those formal features, without a study of their role in speech acts, would be like a formal study of the currency and credit systems of economies without a study of the role of currency and credit in economic transactions." Although linguistic theory has a great deal to say about the formal features of lingual objects, Searle points out, such a study is in itself necessarily incomplete. And, he adds, there is no single valid reason to suspect that a more inclusive study would be moving outside the Saussurian concept of 'langue'. It would by its very nature remain essentially linguistic study, even though the theoretical focus is adjusted to include not only formal, constitutive features of the lingual aspect, but also its anticipatory, regulative facets.

After the temporary restriction of the field of vision of linguistics, as Hjelmslev calls the analysis of the constitutive features of the lingual aspect, the systematic linguistic analysis given in this study has now progressed to the point where linguistic theory, in his words (1963: 127)

> Is led by an inner necessity to recognize not merely the linguistic system, in its schema and in its usage, ... but also- man and human society behind language ...[15]

---

15. It is clear also that Hjelmslev's structuralism at this point reveals the humanistic undertone that it shares with later developments in linguistic theory, especially transformational grammar. For, at the end of his *Prolegomena to a theory of language* (1963: 127), Hjelmslev concluded that when linguistics has reached the point of recognizing behind language also human society and the person, it "has reached its prescribed goal: *humanitas et universitas."*

Of a recognition of a temporal order, to which the human innate language faculty and factual, formal lingual data are subjected, there is no trace in either transformationalist or structuralist theory.

— the point, in other words, where linguistic theory must begin an investigation of the social anticipatory structure of the lingual aspect.

It is at this point that linguistic analysis ventures beyond expression, which stamps the modal structure of the lingual aspect in terms of its analogies with earlier aspects in the order of time. And in venturing beyond this, in order to come to grips with the way that the lingual mode of experience reflects those that follow it – the social, economic, aesthetic, ethical and confessional dimensions of reality – the lingual modal meaning kernel of expression is deepened and opened up. In the first instance this disclosure is reflected in the social anticipation of shared expression, or human communication, and it is to a preliminary analysis of this analogical moment that attention turns in the next chapter.

14 Discourse, text and other social anticipations

Linguistic concept and linguistic idea

The analysis so far has indicated that the formative (historical), logical, sensitive, organic, physical, kinematic, spatial and numerical analogies within the structure of the lingual aspect are constitutive elements forming a set of analyzable linguistic concepts. The technical term for these constitutive moments is retrocipations, whereas the analogical relations between the lingual aspect and those experiential modes that follow it in the order of time are truly regulative moments, distinguishable in terms of a set of linguistic limiting concepts or ideas. These are formally known as anticipations.

The distinction between linguistic concept and linguistic idea is implicit in Bruns's distinction between structuralist linguistics on the one hand, and the phenomenology of language on the other. From our standpoint the dialectical opposition of these two positions as defined by Bruns echoes the polarity of the humanist motive of freedom and determinism (see above, Chapter 2), but it serves the purpose of an initial distinction between linguistic concept and idea. The distinction and relation between linguistic concept and idea places us before the task of examining, in Bruns's words (1975: 239), the

> ... problem of meaning along two distinct fronts: from the standpoint of man's life of speech within the horizon of the speakable, as well as from the standpoint of how language is made and how its formal elements are organized in the formation of an utterance ...

The first anticipatory moment distinguishable as a linguistic idea is the social anticipation in the lingual aspect. It actually comprises not a single anticipatory analogy, but a whole set of analogical links between the lingual and social aspects. It is a set of anticipations which has been investigated in recent times by various scholars working within the field now known as sociolinguistics. So far, the analysis has indicated that Chomsky's major contribution to linguistics lies, for several reasons that were outlined above, within the theoretical view that the linguist has of constitutive elements within the structure of the lingual aspect, elements belonging to the set of linguistic concepts. The differences between Chomskyan linguistics and sociolinguistics depend on the distinction between constitutive linguistic concept and the regulative idea of language. This is the systematic background against which one should interpret Halliday's remark (1979: 192) that after a period of intensive study of language as an idealized construct, language theorists have at last come to acknowledge that people talk to each other.

It is exactly the distinction between linguistic concept and linguistic idea that also causes Halliday (1979: 4) to remark:

> It was Chomsky's immense achievement to show how natural language can be reduced to a formal system; and as long as the twofold idealization of speaker and sentence is maintained intact, language can be represented not only as rules but even as ordered rules. But when social man comes into the picture, the ordering disappears and even the concept of rules is seen to be threatened.

In this somewhat sketchy formulation of the content of transformational grammar, Chomsky's 'idealization' is no true linguistic idea, but an abstraction necessitated by his rationalistic starting-point and belonging wholly to the formally conceived set of constitutive linguistic concepts. In the theoretical investigation of the anticipatory structure of the lingual aspect, however, the nature of the linguistic limiting concepts or ideas forces the linguist to relate the abstractions belonging to the set of linguistic concepts to the concrete specificity of language-in-use, i.e. to language in its social context. Phrased differently: linguistic ideas are limiting concepts that link the abstractions that linguistic theory makes in respect of the constitutive structure of the lingual aspect to the experienced concreteness of language. Perhaps Halliday is a little off the mark when he concludes that the very concept of rules is threatened by linguistic ideas related to the social anticipations; actually the constitutive concepts of rule systems should be broadened, specified and enlivened by the sociolinguistic perspective. Elsewhere,[16] he does link the constitutive concepts of lingual change and persistence — concepts that depend on the physical and kinematic retrocipations — to the process of lingual interaction investigated by sociolinguistics. But the point is that if Chomsky's theory is not susceptible to the dynamism of sociolinguistic ideas, there is something fundamentally wrong with the notion of formalizing language in the first place, and not with the linguistic idea of rules itself. Lingual rules are norms that necessarily allow choice; there is no reason to distinguish between a grammar of choice and a grammar of rules as long as the grammar of rules has an intrinsically lingual nature.

Just as linguistic concepts are stimulated to become dynamic, specific and relevant to concrete language by linguistic ideas, the ideas themselves depend on linguistic concepts for their theoretical formulation. The whole idea of 'language in its social context' needs the constitutive, analogical spatial concept of place, position or environment. If the lingual aspect had had no spatial substratum, the very possibility of broadening the concept of lingual environment to the specific sociolinguistic idea of context would not have existed. Linguistic concept and linguistic idea are therefore entirely interdependent, and "the inseparability holds in both directions" (Halliday 1979: 13; cf. too Hjelmslev 1963: 127).

Sociolinguistics as a study of social anticipations in the lingual aspect

The numerical, spatial, kinematic, physical, organic, sensitive, logical and formative aspects precede the lingual aspect in the time order of aspects; they lie, in respect of the lingual modality, in the foundational order of time. The first aspect in the transcendental, anticipatory direction to succeed the lingual aspect is the social aspect of experience, and the social anticipations within the structure of the

---

16. Halliday 1979: 92. For Searle's distinction between regulative and constitutive rules, see his *Speech acts* (Searle 1969: 33 ff.).

lingual aspect form the field of investigation of sociolinguistics.

Again, as in the theoretical enquiry into analogical relations between the lingual aspect and other modalities, sociolinguistic investigation must strive to avoid, at first, consideration of the external connections between language and social processes. If working "from the outside inwards, interpreting language by reference to its place in the social process" (Halliday 1979: 4) means that the method followed by sociolinguistic enquiry restricts itself only to external relations between language and social processes, the systematic necessity of enquiring first into the internal coherence between the lingual modality and the social aspect of experience is disregarded. Of course, saying that the internal coherence between the lingual aspect and the social aspect must be investigated first does not mean that external links between the concrete phenomena of language and social life should not be investigated at all. It is merely a call for a systematic postponement of the latter kind of enquiry, a postponement that is motivated by the methodological requirement that elementary linguistic concepts must be investigated first, since the complex concepts such as lingual object and subject, i.e. language and the humans who use it, are explicable only in terms of elementary linguistic concepts. What has been called the 'external relation' between two modalities is really a complicated relationship between concrete phenomena which can be grasped only in complex concepts. While such phenomena as, for example, the global dominance of English and the accompanying political power that this bestows upon users of that language, are certainly of linguistic interest, they cannot adequately be accounted for in terms of a single elementary linguistic concept.

The social anticipations that require attention at this stage of a systematic analysis are anticipatory analogies on both the norm-side and the factual side of the lingual aspect. On the norm-side these structural anticipations generate the ideas of a sociolingual syntax, of communicative competence and of socially differentiated normative types of discourse. Ideas of the appropriateness and informativeness of utterances function on the factual side of this set of anticipations together with communicative performance and the notion of 'text'.

These are some of the linguistic ideas that should be reviewed in a sociolinguistic perspective that wishes to do justice to intralingual phenomena before investigating extralingual features of language use.

Normative anticipations

Since the social anticipations in the lingual aspect are dependent upon the idea of lingual intercourse, communication or interaction, all lingual norms are also norms for lingual communication or sharing, and all lingual facts are from this perspective communicative facts. Like all other regulative linguistic ideas, the idea of lingual communication is an idea of the integrating and dynamic force of the anticipatory opening-up process of lingually qualified things. This is why De Saussure offers the notion of lingual communication as counterpoint to the restrictiveness of provincialism, and defines lingual intercourse as a factor that spreads language and gives it unity (De Saussure 1966: 206; cf. too Robins 1967: 15 ff.) across dialectal splintering.

Apart from this cultural, historical dimension of lingual communication as communication across dialects, however, synchronic linguistics has always recognized the social, communicative side of human language, and especially the humanly shared normative aspect thereof. De Saussure exploited the idea of a social contract to explain this aspect of language: language, he said (1966: 14), "exists only by virtue of a kind of contract signed by the members of the community." This is of course a fiction, like so many other theories concerned with the complex idea of the origin and source of human language. But it is nevertheless of systematic importance, because it indicates the struggle of linguistic theory to grapple with the problem of formulating the elusive idea of the normative aspect of human lingual communication, in which we try to understand theoretically how expression deepens to become shared expression, and how we move beyond expression into the realm of communication with our fellow human beings. Yet it is also true that the idea of human collectivity, the notion that "every means of expression used in society is based, in principle, on collective behavior or — what amounts to the same thing — on convention" (De Saussure 1966: 68)[17] cannot adequately account for the social anticipations on the norm-side of the lingual aspect. Neither can the more modern idea of social structure as the external situation in which language is set do this.

---

17. For the idea of language as a habit, custom or idiom peculiar to the community, cf. De Saussure (1966: 191).

From the angle of the social anticipations in the structure of the lingual aspect, the typical socially structured situation in which language is used is not something external to language or even an incidental addition. Rather, the idea of language in social use requires a consideration of the normative, regulatory effect that the typical social structure has on the factual language itself. The following example, taken from Halliday (1979: 134), contains sentences which in other contexts or on their own can be considered as quite well-formed, but as the text of a radio commentary become absurd:

> Now comes the President here. It's the window he's stepping through ... On his victory his opponent congratulates him. What they are shaking now is hands. A speech is going to be made by him. 'Gentlemen and ladies ... I shall, hereby pledge I, turn his country into a place, in which what people do safely will be live ...'

Halliday's conclusion (1979: 114) that the typical social structure in which language is used and operates is not simply an ornamental background to lingual interaction, as it has tended to become in sociolinguistic investigations, but rather a necessary (normative) factor in the development of semantic systems and processes, is a more convincing approach, since it touches upon the normative dimension of the social anticipations within the lingual aspect.

Equally necessary in the theoretical delimitation of this normative set of anticipations is the linguistic idea of a subjective communicative competence (cf. Habermas 1970, Hymes 1971). Communicative competence, as an idea of an "ability to use language in ways that are appropriate to the situation" (Halliday 1974: 85) is in systematic terms a command of the language that also has a normative dimension. The mastery and control that we have of language is, as has been indicated in the previous chapter, a constitutive linguistic concept that is not exhausted by defining it as a grammatical or syntactic command, but that can be broadened to indicate the anticipatory link between the lingual aspect (and its constitutive formative and logical elements) and the social mode of experience. Thus one is able to speak in analogical social terms of lingual competence as a communicative command or knowledge of lingual norms and principles. Viewed from the factual side, this sociolingual command is at the same time a subjective capacity to use language in accordance with typical (from this analogical angle: socially differentiated) lingual norms and principles.

In the case of the concepts articulated within linguistic theory in respect of syntactic or semantic competence, the subjective human lingual competence is often restricted to a general competence to identify and distinguish objective lingual facts, as well as to a universal grammatical or syntactic command to form and produce the objective facts of language. These are general and universal concepts because they are systematically bound to consider first the concept of lingual competence in terms of the restrictive, constitutive, abstract and general modal structure of the lingual aspect that applies universally to all lingually qualified objects, events, systems, processes and capacities. But now that the systematic linguistic analysis attempted in this study has progressed to an investigation of the specifying and limiting concepts inherent in the anticipatory structure of the lingual aspect, the constitutive, general concept of lingual competence can be redefined and specified in the linguistic idea of a subjective lingual command to produce language in accordance with the typical lingual norms that apply within the different material lingual spheres.[18]

This, in my opinion, is what forms the background to Greimas's idea (1974: 75) of a secondary or sociolinguistic syntax, or what causes Crystal and Davy (1976: 5) to comment on a command or social awareness of language, which is loosely described as the social standards of acceptability in the use of language, or the appropriate lingual 'manners' for the typically different contexts in which language is used.

In the next section attention is given to the determining features of the typical or material lingual spheres, that Greimas (1974: 58 f.), in keeping with structuralist conceptions, called signs or macro-signs.

Material lingual spheres as normative types of discourse

The linguistic idea of a subjective communicative competence to produce language within a variety of material lingual spheres presupposes as its normative correlate an idea of the typical norms that apply within these spheres.

---

18. See above, Chapter 4. This redefinition illustrates the thesis that linguistic ideas form a bridge between abstract lingual concepts and concrete lingual phenomena.

The material lingual spheres, that were discussed in Chapter 4 above as types of socially variable discourse, operate on the norm-side of the social anticipatory structure of the lingual aspect as regulative determinants. Linguistic theory cannot come to grips with the reality of language "understood in terms of the random or isolated sentence but must take into account the larger structure of discourse itself, on the grounds that it is only at the level of discourse that world and speaker become fully present in speech as determinants of meaning," as Bruns (1975: 250) puts it. However, 'discourse' taken up as a material lingual sphere, i.e. as a specifying normative type of language, cannot merely be a structure larger than the sentence, which figures on the factual side of the lingual aspect as lingual object, but is in principle on another, this time normative level. Discourse can rather be defined as a system of typical lingual norms that regulate typical lingual facts on the factual side of the lingual aspect within the defining and limiting context of a socially differentiated lingual sphere. If, of course, one restricts the term 'discourse' to indicate an objective lingual factuality (which is possible, by way of theoretical definition — cf. Bruns 1975: 250 ff.), then it cannot serve also as a term to indicate a normative type.

The phrase 'normative type of discourse' which has been employed here to indicate the normative, determining dimensions of a socially differentiated sphere of language seems preferable to distinguish the social analogy on the norm-side of the lingual aspect from the factual text. Normative types of discourse therefore determine the factual type of text being investigated (see the section below on **Text as factual lingual unit**).

Human speech, as factual lingual utterances, operates as lingual object produced by the human lingual subject, within the "determining field of reference" of a normative type of discourse, and therefore "cannot be conceived except in terms of such a field" (Bruns 1975: 251).

Ultimately, Bruns's argument (cf. 1975: 290, note 36) is in favor of taking up discourse as a normative (in his terms 'hierarchical' as opposed to factually 'linear') type: "... a fully adequate theory of meaning ... must eventually go beyond the syntax of propositions to describe the rules which govern the composition or generation of texts" (Bruns 1975: 252). What is needed in other words, according to

Bruns, is a specifying set of lingual norms for the formation of texts, a grammar of discourse. Such a grammar describing the rules that govern the composition of factual texts will of necessity take its starting point in the linguistic idea of the material lingual spheres, and can be constructed only in concert with a typology of texts (Bruns 1975: 256).

Actually linguistic theory must from the outset provide for more than one grammar of discourse, since the co-ordinated differentiation of language into material lingual spheres is a linguistic idea that proceeds from the assumption that there is a variety of such spheres, each possessing its own specifying set of typical norms. Since no sphere takes precedence over any other (cf. Hommes 1972: 423 f.), the normative specifications of one sphere do not in principle apply to other spheres.

The fundamental difference between the different material lingual spheres in analogical social terms is that they are differentiated firstly into associational, communal or institutional relations between lingual subjects. This differentiation entails that the typical norms that apply within material lingual spheres also possess an associational, communal or institutional nature. Social associations between lingual subjects lack an authority-relationship that would make possible an enforcement of lingual norms (cf. Hommes 1972: 408 ff.). In the sphere of friendly conversational exchange, for example, suggestions of one friend 'correcting' aspects of pronunciation or accent of another can comfortably be ignored or accepted: there is no authority to enforce compliance with lingual norms in the associational bond of equality between friends. In institutional relations, where a relationship of authority exists, the reverse is true. Greimas (1974: 75) acknowledges, for example, that things are not said the same way when a superior addresses a subordinate. Linguistic theory thus has to recognize the typical social differentiations functioning as sets of normative determinants in associational, communal or institutional relations between lingual subjects. In doing so, the linguistically relevant relationship of lingual status (as the typically specified role of speaker or hearer in the subjective lingual relationship between, for example, parent and child, teacher and pupil, client and customer, and so forth) (Lyons 1968: 276) is of the utmost importance. It is an internal linguistic idea, that must be sharply distinguished from the external notion of social status or rank.

Typical specifications of the general modal norm of acceptability

Chomsky distinguishes between 'grammatical' and 'acceptable' utterances by means of the distinction between the constitutive concepts of competence and performance. 'Acceptability' is a linguistic idea associated with the theory of performance, while 'grammaticalness' is its conceptual counterpart in the theory of competence (Chomsky 1978a: 7). In systematic terms 'acceptability' is a general modal lingual principle that receives typical specifications in respect of the social anticipations in the structure of the lingual aspect. In other words, at the very least the acceptability of a lingual utterance depends upon the normative evaluation of an utterance by a second lingual subject (hearer, speaker or reader). Put differently, a lingual utterance is acceptable when another lingual subject judges it to be in compliance with lingual norms and principles that apply in a specific lingual context.

The idea of the acceptability of a factual lingual utterance illustrates the difference between the practical and theoretical idea of language, since it is, in the first instance, a practical idea of language that only receives theoretical explanation and articulation in linguistic theory:

> 'Acceptable' is a primitive, or pre-scientific, term, which ... does not depend upon any technical or theoretical concepts of linguistics (Lyons 1968: 137).

To the degree that grammatical theory, including transformational grammar, expresses a willingness to be guided by the theoretical (linguistic) or practical (lingual) idea of acceptability, it has accepted that linguistics does not investigate only linguistic concepts, i.e. concepts related to the constitutive moments in the structure of the lingual aspect. It then acknowledges that linguistic investigation must be guided by practical, pre-theoretical ideas in its analysis of the theoretical ideas of language, i.e. theoretical ideas of the regulative moments in the structure of the lingual aspect.

Although 'acceptability' is a primitive, pre-scientific normative measure which can be grasped only in the form of a linguistic limiting concept or idea, its regulative sense can be formulated theoretically. Lyons (1968: 137) gives the following explanatory outline:

> An acceptable utterance is one that has been, or might be, produced by a native speaker in some appropriate context and is, or would be, accepted by other native speakers as belonging to the language in question.

To the extent, however, that linguistic theory limits its use of the idea of acceptability only to the grammatical acceptability of a factual lingual utterance, it has in principle not yet abandoned a bias in favor of a theoretical investigation of only the restrictive, constitutive structural elements of the lingual aspect (linguistic concepts), since, in such a case, the theoretical enquiry is focused only momentarily on an anticipation of a constitutive element (in this instance the grammatical-technical sub-structure of the lingual aspect), in the social modality.

It is obvious that lingual acceptability is to be understood in a much wider sense than grammatical acceptability. It also goes wider than a measure only of the acceptability of larger factual lingual objects such as the sentence. One may, for example, also wish to evaluate the acceptability of objective lingual units like the word. In the social sphere with its wide divergence of social situations and lingual contexts, that have been broadly defined as material lingual spheres in this study, the whole question of the acceptability or unacceptability of a taboo word in a specific social situation, not to speak of the age-old question of the linguistic enquiry into truth, or the avoidance of the lie, once again comes into play (cf. Lyons 1968: 140, for a discussion of various levels of acceptability).

An utterance may in other words be unacceptable for more than grammatical reasons. A document drawn up by a subordinate in the institutional lingual sphere of the military may for other than grammatical reasons be lingually unacceptable to the superior officer who has to approve its distribution. A signal message in the army, for example, is a factual lingual text that has to be released by an officer, but it is often drafted by a member of the other ranks. Such a message may be turned down for release, i.e. may in this particular context be lingually unacceptable for many reasons, one of which may be its lack of instructional clarity. Many examples can be given of the typical specifications of the lingual norm of clarity in the sphere of the military. One of the rules of voice procedure over the military radio is not to ask someone to repeat when the signal has not been clear, since, in the case of the artillery, this is presumed to be a standard call for the repetition of a bombardment on a previous target. Hence the unambiguous "I say again" so often used by trained signallers when they repeat parts of coded and partially coded messages.

The appropriateness, relevance and informativeness of utterances

Closely allied to the idea of acceptability are the sociolinguistic ideas of the appropriateness, relevance and informativeness of utterances. These are ideas of the objective characteristics of factual lingual utterances that can be determined only by evaluating those expressions in terms of typical lingual norms.

The notion that these ideas are aspects of lingual communication that involve non-linguistic knowledge and non-grammatical principles, as well as the view that the objective meaning of an utterance is context-independent (cf. Smith & Wilson 1979: 172) is in keeping with the transformationalist distinction between competence and performance (cf. Smith & Wilson 1979: 148), but is nonetheless a mistaken notion. The distinction between linguistic concept and linguistic idea, between constitutive and regulative elements in the structure of the lingual aspect, does not allow a separation of the two, for a linguistic idea of the relevance or appropriateness of an utterance within the context of a material lingual sphere remains exactly that: a linguistic idea. Only if the existence of social anticipations in the structure of the lingual aspect is denied, does the view become tenable that non-linguistic principles enable us to account for the ideas of appropriateness and relevance.

Furthermore, it is the linguistic idea of the appropriateness of an utterance within a social context that enables us to understand more fully the constitutive linguistic concepts of lingual background or setting, lingual process, lingual effect, lingual operation or functioning, and the normative validity of a lingual norm (e.g. a rule of grammar), to name but a few. These are some of the constitutive concepts that are specified and given a more concentrated meaning by this linguistic idea.

To divorce the linguistic idea of the appropriateness of an utterance from constitutive linguistic concepts by means of the distinction between 'grammar' and 'theory of communication' is thus unacceptable. The idea of a 'sociolinguistic syntax' or 'communicative competence' that must make it possible for the human lingual subject to judge the degree of appropriateness, relevance or informativeness of utterances is itself a linguistic idea, for these are social anticipations or analogies on the norm-side of the structure of the lingual aspect.

To some extent it is hard to say whether the usual notion of an interaction between lingual and non-lingual factors that provides the full interpretation of a given utterance in context (cf. Smith & Wilson 1979: 188 f.) can in all cases solve the problems caused by a strict separation between linguistic concept and linguistic idea, simply because the nature of this interaction is never specified. If the interaction is part of the lingual process, which is a constitutive moment in the structure of the lingual aspect, then there is of course no problem, since the process of interaction has been lingually specified. If it is not part of this process, the question of how it is specified and structured remains.

What is clear, though, is that the linguistic idea of the appropriateness and relevance of factual lingual utterances intrinsically involves a normative lingual evaluation or judgment. And although this evaluation may be specified and structured still further by the nature of the social context (material lingual sphere) in which the utterance functions as a lingual object, it nonetheless remains a lingual evaluation, for it is a judgment about the relevance or appropriateness of (a part of) the language used, and can therefore be studied in linguistic theory without any theoretical qualms.

There is more to lingually qualified events and processes than the words themselves, since our lingual interpretation of any lingual process or text goes beyond the scope of the lingually qualified objects found in the text. Interpretation and hermeneutics are impossible without an idea of the objective lingual factuality of facts that are interpreted within a socially differentiated normative type of context. The objective lingual factuality of a text or lingual process, that Halliday terms the semiotic structure of the situation, is specified in terms of the social analogies functioning on the norm-side of the lingual aspect as the meaning and significance of the 'field', 'tenor' and 'mode' of a lingual text within the sphere of reference of a normative type of context (Halliday 1979: 189). Exegesis and hermeneutics can be theoretically accounted for only as activities that involve the anticipatory, disclosed structure of the lingual aspect.

'Text' as factual lingual unit

Linguistic theory is in need not only of a linguistic idea as to what constitutes a normative type of context, but it also has to attempt to give theoretical formulation to the idea of text as factual lingual unit.

To the extent that linguistic theories have tied themselves down to a study of the constitutive structure of the lingual aspect, to what Bruns (1975: 252), following Ricoeur, calls the 'worldless text', a perspective in which lingual subjectivity is at the same time limited to a view of humans as fabricators of utterances whose meanings must be accounted for by recourse to rules governing constitutive, formal lingual units, 'text' as objective lingual unit functioning on the factual side of the social anticipations within the lingual aspect has been discredited, depreciated or simply disregarded as something that is not worthwhile studying in linguistics. Nevertheless, it cannot be denied that texts are produced, are indeed fabricated by the lingual subject, since correlated to the normative communicative command of language (defined also as a subjective communicative competence), one finds the objective products of that competence, i.e. the facts of human communicative performance. Halliday (1979: 114) notices renewed linguistic interest in the imperfections and 'fuzziness' of communicative performance, the objective lingual units of which are texts.

Already in 1943, Hjelmslev (1963: 16) claimed that the objects of interest to linguistic theory are texts. He remarks (1963: 98-99) that linguistic analysis must eventually progress to the stage where the divisions between itself and literary theory are no longer clear and demarcated, and where linguistic theory must further classify "the larger textual parts ... into productions of single authors, works, chapters, paragraphs, and the like ..."

'Text', as a factual lingual unit, is determined by the normative type of discourse in which it functions. Where the constitutive linguistic concepts need word, clause and sentence as factual, objective lingual units, the social anticipation within the lingual aspect explicitly requires the more inclusive, and yet more specific, objective lingual unit of 'text'. The text, says Halliday, is the lingual form of social interaction. He proceeds (1979: 122) to define the objective lingual unity — itself a numerical analogy — formed by the text in terms of the spatial retrocipations of lingual continuity, combination, simultaneity and succession:

> It is a continuous progression of meanings, combining both simultaneously and in succession.

As a factual lingual unit dealt with in the set of sociolingual analogies, text, like all other lingual facts, is subject to lingual norms. This is so because the concept of lingual choice (a logically founded analogy) enters into the picture immediately, as well as the observation that the text is the factual realization of a set of normative lingual potentialities; the meanings that constitute the text are therefore "the selections made by the speaker from the options that constitute the meaning potential; text is the actualization of this meaning potential, the process of semantic choice" (Halliday 1979: 122).

'Text', as used by Halliday, may be literary or conversational, may include both the written and spoken form of the language, since it is what people do, mean and say (1979: 140 f.). And because the realization of the objective lingual factuality of the text needs the factual human subject,

> the essential feature of text ... is that it is interaction. The exchange of meaning is an interactive process, and text is the means of exchange: in order for the meanings which constitute the social system to be exchanged between members they must first be represented in some exchangeable symbolic form ... (Halliday 1979: 139-140).

Both lingual subject and lingual object, as two complex systematic linguistic concepts, therefore require for their own definition the elementary linguistic ideas of, amongst others, text, lingual interaction or exchange and member, as these are specified in an analysis of the social anticipations on the factual side of the lingual aspect. The anticipatory structural moments of the lingual aspect, in which 'text' functions as factual lingual unit, form the bridge between the elementary and complex linguistic concepts. At the same time the linguistic idea of text, through its dependence also on constitutive linguistic concepts such as lingual unity, continuity, combination, simultaneity, succession and choice, is an illustration of the thesis that linguistic ideas and concepts are interdependent.

15 The idea of lingual economy

Other linguistic ideas

This study has been limited to elementary systematic concepts in linguistic theory. The analysis of the social anticipations in the structure of the lingual aspect (a linguistic idea) that constitutes the focus of the previous chapter is intended in the first instance as an illustration of the view that elementary linguistic concepts and ideas are interdependent.

In the development of the systematic linguistic methodology outlined in this study, the investigation of elementary linguistic concepts must be complemented both by an enquiry into the remaining elementary linguistic ideas, and by a systematic linguistic analysis of the various complex linguistic concepts.

Among the limiting concepts that should be reviewed in such an investigation are the linguistic ideas of normative and factual lingual economy (including the phenomena of aposiopesis, abbreviation and catalysis; cf. Hjelmslev 1963: 94 f.), factual and normative lingual *harmony*, lingual *accountability*, lingual *integrity* and lingual *trust*. These are ideas that link the lingual aspect to the economic, aesthetic, juridical, moral and confessional aspects of experience.

The analysis so far has illustrated, I believe, that the analogical connections between the lingual aspect of our experience and the other temporal modalities yield not a single analogy to be analyzed, but normally offer a whole set of retrocipations (in the case of constitutive analogical moments) or anticipations (analogies looking forward to the relationship of the lingual modality with those aspects following it in the temporal order). While the former are analyzable in terms of theoretical concepts, the latter connections are conceptually clarified in terms of linguistic limiting concepts or ideas.

The analysis has also demonstrated that the conceptual understanding of one set of such analogies is not really possible without either implicit or sometimes explicit reference to other analogies.

The current chapter therefore takes an element of another linguistic limiting concept, that of lingual economy, further along the analytical track that has been indicated by the systematic framework adopted in this study. As will be shown, the notion of lingual economy cannot be understood without reference to other analogical relations or sets of relations, but in fact deepens the systematic exploration of these. In a very specific sense, the idea of lingual economy that will be systematically articulated below enhances our understanding of the social disclosure of language in different material lingual spheres, which was discussed in Chapters 4 and 14 above.

The idea of lingual economy

There are, naturally, all kinds of intuitive and practical, everyday notions associated with the idea of lingual economy. One may think, for example, of judgments we make of an interlocutor's loquaciousness or taciturnity, or of the more intellectually sophisticated assessments we might make of the economy of expression that is associated with certain forms of verbal art, in particular poetry, which achieves a remarkable density through its utilization of a number of lingual and other symbolic resources.

Then there is, as the analysis so far has indicated, the further temptation to conceive of the analogical modal link between the lingual dimension of our experience and the economic dimension of reality in terms of the concrete phenomenon of language and its role in the sphere of economic life, in other words in the world of trade, commerce and financial transactions. These are no doubt interesting issues. The way that language acts as barrier to commerce and trade, or the way in which economic considerations influence the power that some languages gain on a global scale, while others stand to lose, are complex issues that are studied within the realm of language

The idea of lingual economy

management or planning, as well as in language politics, and are therefore more properly treated in these sub-fields of applied linguistics. Again, therefore, we would argue that, for systematic reasons, the analysis of these phenomena be postponed until we have come to a better conceptual understanding of the elementary linguistic concepts that concern the abstract modal relationships between these two dimensions. This does not mean that they have a lower conceptual or theoretical status; quite the contrary: such concrete issues are much more complex, and the problems that they throw up need deliberate and sustained attention, and are worthy of consideration from a multiplicity of perspectives.

Instead, I propose to set out below a single illustration of how, in the theoretical approach known as ethnomethodology (cf. Sachs, Schegloff & Jefferson 1974; Goffman 1981), a breakaway school of sociology, we find a theoretically exceptional treatment of the idea of lingual economy. Their analyses enlighten us as regards the wonderfully complicated nature of lingual interaction when our theoretical view ventures beyond the consideration of the expressive kernel of the lingual modality to an analysis of the structuredness of the shared expression or communication that lingual subjects attempt every day. In the illustration that follows, I shall freely use some of the earlier analyses and material that I referred to in the *Prologue* (Weideman 1984, 1985a, 1988; Weideman, Raath & Van der Walt 1986; Weideman & Verster 1988).

A system for lingual sharing

The analyses that the school of ethnomethodology made have been particularly useful for us in gaining insight into the normative dimensions of our communicative ability to function as lingual subjects within the material lingual sphere of conversation. These insights, I shall argue, have taken us much further than the initial, preliminary analyses of Crystal and Davy (1976), where the overall impression is that conversation is 'random', forever edging towards indeterminacy and chaos. Most of the examples cited in this early study are of a lexical and syntactic nature, that is: they use factual lingual units at word and sentence level.

We have noted above, however, that once we take the study of human lingual competence and action beyond the notion of grammatical competence, other considerations emerge, and other levels of lingual object-formation come into play. Thus it is with the analysis of conversation. Far from being random and indeterminate, conversation analyses have shown such talk to have a remarkably tight and economical organization.

Central to this analysis is the idea of turn-taking in conversation. It is of course true that the lingual economy that is effected by means of turn-taking among those sharing in communicative interaction is not limited to conversation. In most forms of talk, done within the various material spheres of discourse that have been referred to above, some normative system of turn-taking is indeed operative. Take for example the allocation of turns at talk in a classroom, that has been investigated by Greyling (1987; cf. too Coulthard 1985) and others. Such is the inequality in this form of institutional talk that in conventional classrooms the teacher normally occupies two-thirds of this scarce resource, in initiating a typical exchange by eliciting information, and ending it by giving feedback to the learner's response. Similarly, in ecclesiastical settings, which make up another institutional context, there may be predetermined and liturgically or ritually specified measures of how turns at talk are distributed. Courtrooms provide yet another example of institutional lingual interaction, and there have even been studies of how audience applause — a non-verbal, but certainly linguistically meaningful action — in all kinds of settings is both allowed, elicited and achieved (cf. Levinson 1983: 301).

For conversation analysts, however, the central problem was to explain how participants at talk manage in a lingual context that is associational, that is a context in which there is neither accepted authority, nor a more or less durable relationship between the members. How, in a relationship that is characterized rather by equality between participants, do they manage a linguistically fair and economical way of distributing access to a scarce lingual resource: a turn at talk? What lingual subjects in the communicative event that we call conversation need, as Levinson (1983: 297) puts it, is

> ... a sharing device, an 'economy' operating over a scarce resource, namely control of the 'floor'. Such an allocational system will require minimal units (or 'shares') over which it will operate, such units being the units from which turns are constructed.

The idea of lingual economy

The idea of turn-taking as a set of norms or a system of lingual economy is such a deceptively obvious piece of knowledge that, before the advent of ethnomethodological analyses, very little attention had been paid to it. The earlier analyses to which we have referred above failed to recognize its potential significance for discovering the organizational structure of conversation, and also the host of explanatory problems that it evokes.

One of the hardest questions to answer, perhaps, is why it is so that turn-taking is central to conversation. When we look at an actual instance of conversation, it is not difficult to observe that one participant talks, stops, that at that point another starts, talks, stops, at which point the turn at talk is transferred to the first speaker, and so on.

One possible explanation for this is that in the roughly equal (in the sense of recurrent) distribution of talk across the turns of different speakers there is evidence of the (social) equality of the speakers. Note that, while the notion of lingual distribution is certainly an articulation of an echo of the economic modality (which is originally concerned with the allocation of scarce resources) within the lingual sphere, and the idea of equality concerns the social specifications of the role of lingual subjects, the concept of lingual recurrence most probably echoes and conceptually broadens the constitutive relation between the lingual aspect and the kinematic. When the opportunity for talk is as evenly and recurrently distributed as in conversation, it is a way of securing, a ratification, of the equality of participants. We return below to the articulation of the idea of ratification or lingual confirmation as a juridical analogy within the structure of the lingual aspect.

To see why this explanation is plausible, we need to compare the relatively equal distribution of turns at talk in conversation with other forms of talk that were referred to above. In non-associational, institutional settings for example, there is often a marked and widespread lack of an equal distribution of turns. The lecture is a case in point, for here one of the participants holds forth for almost any length of time, and, moreover, has the ability to withhold from other participants any opportunity of talking, by employing a number of devices: "Let me just finish this point ..." is a technique often used to counter an interruption signal from one of the other participants, be it in the form of a cough, a raising of the hand, the clearing of a throat or any combination of these. Actually, then, it is not so much the size of the turn that suspends the equality of the participants; it is more likely the presence of an authority to allocate (or withhold allocation of) turns.

The same inequality seems to reign in law courts, religious services and meetings, where there are either ritualized ways of allocating turns, or where one participant has the acknowledged right to allocate turns (be such a person presiding officer of the court, chairperson, or whatever). There are in these types of discourse signs of the authority relationship that ordinary conversation lacks.

One of the most interesting observations that follows from turn-taking or speaker change in conversation is the remarkable lack of overlap between speakers. It has been calculated that less than 5% — a minimal amount by any standard — of talk overlaps between the turns of ratified speakers (Levinson 1983: 296). In the moment of speaker ratification, we find an echo of a juridical analogy in the lingual aspect: once rightfully confirmed as speaker, and acknowledged as such by co-participants at talk, a speaker has a defensible, allocated space in which to speak. What is even more remarkable about the lack of overlap between speakers is that at the same time gaps between speakers' turns are almost immeasurably small — only a few tenths of a second, and sometimes considerably shorter. In spite of speaker change, talk is therefore continuous, always in progress. This is a significant enhancement of our understanding of the concept of lingual continuity, which was preliminarily analyzed in Chapter 7 above. It is an illustration, once again, that the constitutive linguistic concept of continuity is enlivened and developed further by the regulative linguistic ideas that flow from the modal interconnections between the lingual and the social, economic and juridical analogies, since the idea of lingual continuity is now conceived of as a communicative space (the turn) in which lingual subjects share expression or meaning in an economically moderated way that not only allows for the sharing of such lingual space, but rightfully distributes and allocates it.

How can one explain this? Conversation analysts suggest a rule to which speakers are subject that explains both the absence of gaps between turns and the simultaneous lack of overlap, i.e. the continuity of talk:

The idea of lingual economy

RULE: At least and not more than one party talks at a time

This rule has a normative character, and so does not function as a natural law which is inviolable. Indeed, speakers do in fact overlap (marked //) as in

[1] Desk: What is your last name // Lorraine?
Caller: Dinnis.
Desk: What?
Caller: Dinnis.
(Sacks, Schegloff & Jefferson, 1974: 702)

but the amount of overlap either remains negligible, or can at least be remedied, as in the above, since both speakers know that a fundamental rule has been violated, and collaboratively set out to rectify such deviation in their first subsequent round of turns. In this lingual collaboration, we see another dimension of the social analogies within the lingual modality.

That knowledge of the rule above is part of our subjective communicative ability or competence is also evident, firstly, in the fact that we know, within milliseconds apparently, that in the case of speakers competing for a turn one has started first. This will probably be the one who will continue while the other drops out, as in

[2] A: ... I thought he was going to talk us into having to do another complete set of ... set books for that bloody philology // paper
* B: Erm +
* A: If he had I'd // have said ...
* B: the .. the other the other the other + the other man ehm who .. I thought was going to get you wild was Potter.
A: (swears) I'll crown that bastard before I'm finished with him.
(Svartvik & Quirk, 1980: 47, adapted from 786-797; + marks the end of overlap)

Secondly, if there is almost exactly simultaneous talk, we have techniques to snatch a turn or to let it go by either upgrading our tone and pitch, or by fading, as in

> [3] J: But this // person that DID IT + IS GOT TO BE
>   * V: If I see the person
>   * J: ... taken care of
>   (Levinson, 1983: 301)

and

> [4] A: ... It is sui generis ..., you see
>   B: Yes.
>   A: Ehm..
>   B: // But I I +
> * A: THIS IS + this is one of the things that eh one
>   of the many things eh in English structure which is
>   ehm an item in a closed system.
>   (Svartvik & Quirk, 1980: 46 f., adapted from 738-750)

However interesting these observations may be, ethnomethodology requires that we offer a local explanation for them. If, as we have remarked, we indeed, as part of our communicative competence, possess the general ability to recognize and act upon overlap, while striving to maintain and uphold the fundamental rule of talk that at least but not more than one party talks at a time, then it should be obvious that we have some kind of system for achieving this. For if talk must normatively be continuous, then, given the fact of turn-taking or recurrent change of speaker, we must have some means of achieving such change.

How, in other words, do we hand over turns to another in speaking?

One obvious way of transferring a turn at talk to another lingual subject is by nominating the next speaker. But while in other kinds of talk this occurs frequently — cf. parliamentary debates:

> [5] I now call upon the honourable member for Upington ...

or press conferences:

> [6] Mr Jackson, from the Daily Star?

The idea of lingual economy

— it is clear that speaker nomination has to be done much more delicately and subtly in conversation. It would be ludicrous if in conversation we are forever being formally and explicitly called upon to speak. And yet we are called upon to speak, and, if we reflect upon it, are often selected as next speakers in continuing conversation, by means of address terms tagged to questions or statements, checks, and so on:

[7] Are you coming, David?
[8] You've been here before, right?
[9] Beg your pardon?

By looking closely at the data, conversation analysts have, however, come up with a whole system of rules to effect speaker change. They have found that turns form units, the ends of which may act as places for transition. These possible completion points are called transition relevance places or TRPs. With this in mind, one may then formulate the rules for speaker change in ongoing conversation by ratified speakers. They are (C = current speaker; N = next speaker):

RULE 1 (applying at the initial TRP of any turn):

(a) If C selects N in his current turn, then N and no other must speak.
(b) If C does not select N, then any party may elect to speak, and the first party to do so has rights to the next turn.
(c) If C has not selected N, and no other party self-selects under rule 1(b), then C may, but need not, continue.

RULE 2 (applying at all subsequent TRPs):

When by rule 1(c) C has assumed the right to take another turn at speaking, then at the next TRP rules 1(a) – 1(c) re-apply, and so on recursively until speaker change is effected.

(adapted from Levinson, 1983: 298; cf. too Sacks, Schegloff & Jefferson, 1974: 704).

These 'rules' are again normative, that is, orientation points or starting places for the collaborative lingual effort we call conversation. It is clear that the rules must be attended to by both S (speaker) and H (hearer) if they are co-operatively to accomplish a conversational exchange, i.e. transform an S:H relationship into a C:N one.

Instances of rule 1(a) applying at the first possible completion point for a turn are straightforward enough. When we come to a discussion of the turn constructional units called adjacency pairs below, further examples will be cited. Of course, [7] – [9] above will be units at the end of which one may normally expect transition to N.

But what about the operation of the other rules? We have, in other contexts, already looked at examples of this, but another clear example of where self-selection occurs is marked * in the following exchanges (the phenomenon marked ** will be discussed below):

[10]   A: Ih .. is .. is it this year that eh Nightingale goes?
        B: Eh no, next year.
  * A: Ehm sixty / f..
        B: Sixty five + ..
 ** A: Four, sixty five
        B: Yeah.
  * A: I thought it was before sixty-five. || So it's not until next year that // the job will be advertised
 ** B: January I suppose there + may be an interview round about January.
        A: Yeah.
        (Svartvik & Quirk, 1980: 38, adapted from 238-247)

In all the turns marked * in the above, self-selection (as opposed to other, or C-selection) has occurred because there are no N-selection devices present in the preceding turn, and transition takes place at the end (TRP) of this turn. The operation of rule l(c) is also evident in A's fourth turn (marked ||).

The normative character of rules 1 and 2 also provides, of course, for their violation, as in the intentional interruption

[11]   C: Well, I wrote what I thought was a a .. a reason//able explanation

> F: I think it was a very rude letter
> (Levinson, 1983: 299)

which violates the provision for taking up a turn at a TRP.

Moreover, we have, by virtue of the normative character of these rules, an explanation for significant silences. In [12], A's utterances select B as N, but B, in initially refusing to heed rule l(a) finally yields to the normative force of the rule, which is dependent on the connection between the lingual dimension of experience and the physical aspect of energy-effect, only on his last turn:

> [12] A: Is there something bothering you or not?
> (1.0 second gap)
> A: Yes or no?
> (1.5 second gap)
> A: Eh?
> B: No.
> (Levinson, 1983: 300)

Apart from explaining why B's "No" probably means "Yes", the rules for achieving speaker change also clarify the sense that lingual subjects, as speakers, have of significant silences. Yet it is astonishing to see how quickly, under normative pressures for conversational continuity, they become so. Silences between turns are not tolerated in this kind of talk, and call up complaints of the kind

> [13] You're not listening to me!
> [14] C: Mac
> J: Yes
> C: ø
> (2 seconds)
> * J: Hey, trying to waste my time or something?
> (Weideman, Raath & Van der Walt 1986: 97)

Since both the fundamental rule for conversation and the rules for achieving change of speaker are normative, they do, as we have seen, allow not only silence(s), but also overlap. The collaborative nature of conversation, however, provides for specific ways of extricating oneself from the chaos that would result if violations were allowed to stand without remedy. One such remedy, where overlap occurs, is the recycling of the part obscured by overlap, as in [2], [4] and [10] above (marked ** in the latter case), whereby repair is effected.

Repair can also, in the case of inadvertent overlap, be called for in the form of a check, as in Desk's second turn in [1], and effected by the subsequent turn of N.

The existence of (still to be precisely defined) possible completion points for turns presents yet another problem not only for Ns, who have to attend to TRPs to avoid complaints in the form of [13], but also for Cs who for some reason wish to hold the floor, i.e. in formal terms, strive to avoid the application of rule l(b) and to continue talking past possible completion points (TRPs) by rule l(c). Thus C may employ what are known as incompletion markers by conversation analysts: "but", "and", "however" constitute devices for temporarily suspending the normative precedence of rule l(b) over l(c). Such markers, however, are only successful in avoiding application of rule l(b) in some instances, as

[15] B: Joe has goh .. got it of course // and
   A: Has he +
   * B: and presumably those are the two people who do it.
   (Svartvik & Quirk, 1980: 39, adapted from 324-327)

but not in others:

[16] B: That's what it would amount to, isn't it, but I'd plan to get // somebody ...
   A: Well he wouldn't have to hire + somebody you see, he'd have you built in.
   (Svartvik & Quirk, 1980: 39, adapted from 299-302)

In fact, more than a quarter of all interruptions occur after conjunctions (Coulthard, 1985: 64).

Yet other incompletion markers are openings with "since", "if", or, more elaborately,

[17] I'd like to make two comments on that. First .... Second ...

Of course, no 'incompletion marker' can guarantee that C keeps the turn, but they do show up N as violating the norm by interrupting, which may be decidedly anti-normative behaviour (see [11] above).

The most sophisticated solutions to the problem of C wishing to hold the floor occur before story-telling or jokes. These special incompletion markers are called story-prefaces. Stories and jokes are often begun with

[18] Have you heard the one about ...
[19] There were these three girls ...

The suspension of the rules for turn-taking by story-prefaces calls forth another problem for Ns, of course: how do they know that the floor is again open, and that the rules are in operation again?

In the case of jokes the solution is easy, for they have recognizable endings, or punchlines. The laughter that is normative after the punchline paves the way for a resumption of rule-application. But in the case of stories it is of course less easy to perceive endings (which in their turn call for nods, comments, or both) and resumption of talk by rule 2.

A broadening of the concept of objective factual lingual unit

Some of the phenomena of conversation that have been considered in the previous section also concern its lingual wholeness and continuity — specifically the continuous, sequential nature of talk that disallows both gaps and overlap, as well as the beginnings and endings of shorter and longer turns. These two concepts are related, respectively, to the analogies of the numerical and spatial dimensions of experience within the structure of the lingual aspect. In comparison with the earlier discussions of lingual unity (in Chapter 6) and lingual extension (Chapter 7), it should be obvious that the discussion here has significantly broadened and opened up the constitutive notions of lingual objects, restricted as these were to factual units such as morphemes, words and sentences. The conversational phenomena that have been considered in the current chapter were discussed within the context of an analysis that focused on the norm-side of the lingual aspect, specifically on the normative analogies that link the lingual aspect of our experience with the economic. This analysis has allowed us to conceptualize the turn-taking system discovered by conversation analysts in talk among equals as a device or norm for a shared economy of a scarce lingual resource. If we now turn to focus on the factual phenomena that are regulated by this system, we may consider some remaining questions related to the concepts of objective lingual unity and continuity. These questions relate to the theoretical determination of the lingual extent of the objective lingual phenomena of conversation; in short, to their beginning, continuing and ending. The questions include the following:

(a) What is the minimum format of the linguistic unit we have been calling a 'conversation'?
(b) How is this unit begun and ended, and, having arrived at an ending, how can it be re-opened?
(c) Do we know anything about the overall organization of conversation? (For this would be crucial if we wish to under stand and probe further its objective lingual continuity and wholeness).
(d) Finally, by what other means is conversation maintained, i.e. not only systematically and organizationally (e.g. by rules for change of speaker), but in the efficiency and effectiveness of the content of what is said?

A minimum unit for conversation

When, by rule l(a), C selects N and N takes up a turn at speaking, they fulfil their normative lingual obligations — another juridical analogy — so that these two turns (of C and N) constitute what we may call a minimum unit of conversational exchange. Most of these units are called adjacency pairs, i.e. they are paired utterances, and exhibit a particular typology of sequence. Thus (initial and closing) greetings are followed by (initial and closing) greetings, questions by answers:

[20] A: Eh there was a very nice letter in *The Observer* on Sunday I don't know whether you noticed?
B: I didn't see that, no.
(Svartvik & Quirk, 1980: 78, adapted from 1227-1232);

The idea of lingual economy 215

offers and apologies by rejections or acceptances, summonses by answers, complaints by responses, and so on. Again this is an observation that seems quite obviously to match our intuitions about conversational exchanges, but that was first characterized in detail only after receiving the kind of close attention that conversation analysis gave to the data of conversation.

For a conversational exchange to qualify as an adjacency pair, it has to be

(a) two utterances in length
(b) adjacent
(c) produced by different speakers

while the two utterances are moreover to be

(d) sequentially arranged as first and second parts of a particular typology of sequence (cf. Levinson, 1983: 303).

It is clear, though, that adjacency pairs are only minimum units of conversational exchange. What is more, the requirement of adjacency is often too strong, for conversation analysts have also discovered that in actual data the uttering of a second pair part is often postponed by an intervening 'checking' sequence, as in (Q = question; A = answer)

[21] A: Where do you come from? Q^1
      B: You mean where was I before? Q^2
      A: Yes. A^2
      B: History (giggles) A^1
      (Svartvik & Quirk, 1980: 152, adapted from 1-5)

that itself forms an adjacency pair. This postponement of uttering an expected second pair part, however, again stresses the normative organization of conversation: if a second pair part fails to occur, as is normatively expected, the expectation is either retained through the completion of an intervening sequence (technically: an insertion sequence), after which the second pair part occurs, or, in the case of complete failure to occur, it is noticeably absent, as in [12] above. As Weideman, Raath and Van der Walt (1986: 91) point out:

The notion of expectability that one is dealing with in this regard is therefore an idea of the normative expectations inherent in the (sequential) organization of talk.

Within the ethnomethodological framework, what is here called normative expectability is known as 'preference organisation' (cf. Levinson 1983: 307 ff.). In the theoretical perspective adopted in this book, the kind of organisation of lingual objects (adjacency pairs) within the material lingual sphere of conversation echoes in more than one respect the correlation of lingual norm and lingual fact. This correlation has been discussed in relation to a number of analogical moments in the preceding analyses, and, as has been pointed out in other respects, entails a broadening also of our idea of what in a restrictive sense was termed the relation between 'langue' and 'parole' (De Saussure), or 'competence' and 'performance' (Chomsky).

Opening and closing conversations

The discussion above of the lingual objects known as adjacency pairs or minimum conversational units leads quite naturally to the question of what larger factual lingual units one may find within this material lingual sphere. In order to determine what these may be, one may consider the ordering or organisation that is evident in the opening and closing of conversations, where, for example, the expected initial greeting-greeting sequences ("Hello/Hello") qualify as such units, as do the closing greeting sequences ("Bye/Bye"), or

[22] B: Thank you very much.
  A: It's a pleasure.
   (Svartvik & Quirk, 1980: 82, adapted from 1460-1463)

Conversation analysis has also discovered that there are sequences (so-called pre-closing pairs) that normally precede closings, as in the turns directly preceding [22] above (marked below in [23] with a single *):

(23) ** B: So that's how it goes, um, you know. This bloody university will be the death of me.
  A: Yeah. Oh well. If you inherit a university from

bureaucrats what do you expect.
* A: (laughs)
* B: Yes ...Oh well
(Svartvik & Quirk, 1980: 82, adapted from 1449-1459)

It appears that our ending of conversations must again be a co-ordinated, collaborative effort, and pre-closing sequences ("Okay ... Okay/Right") are a means of achieving this.

Moreover, it has also been discovered that participants in a conversation recognize the transition to pre-closing sections because the turn preceding such a section (cf. the turn marked ** in [23]) is marked by the use of idiomatic and proverbial formulae ("This ... will be the death of me"), or by the reiteration of arrangements already agreed upon

[24] A: See you this afternoon then
B: Okay

the giving of regards, as well as the proverbial "All's well that ends well" or idiomatic

[25] Theresa: Yeah, well, things uh always work out for the best
Dorinne: Oh certainly
(Schegloff & Sacks, 1973: 307)

The normative character of the organizational machinery available for closing a conversation is once again evident in that, having progressed to the closing or pre-closing stages of conversation, participants can jointly achieve a re-opening. The subject of how such 'closings' can be 'opened' again was indeed the topic of one of the more well-known studies in conversation analysis (Schegloff & Sacks, 1973). In such cases, the reopening bid is usually marked heavily ("Oh BY THE WAY ..."; "HEY LISTEN, I ...").

It follows, from the discussion so far, that what we know today about smaller and larger objective lingual units within conversation, that is about adjacency pairs as well as about the factual opening and closing sections of conversation, has also given us a clearer picture of the structure of conversation as a whole, and to this we now turn.

The overall organization of conversation

Conversation analysts have also discovered that, having engaged in conversation, we move in a highly ordered way from one topic to another. Thus there are topic boundaries that signal the end of one topic, as well as topic markers that indicate that a new topic is about to be embarked upon, as in

> [26] A: Well that finishes that ehm now what was the other thing I wanted to ask you ...?
> (Svartvik & Quirk, 1980: 38, adapted from 236-237)

or in the following, taken from a conversation that had been going on for some time:

> [27] B: I've got a problem for you my lad.
> A: A problem?
> B: Yes.
> (Svartvik & Quirk, 1980: 44, adapted from 601-603)

The literature on topic opening, topic maintenance and topic transition is interesting in its own right, and excellent surveys of the work done are readily available (e.g. Coulthard 1985). Two final remarks here must, however, suffice for the moment. Firstly, the randomness that stylisticians of a decade or two ago noticed in conversation may have been occasioned in part by the observation of frequent, and sometimes stylistically inexplicable, changes of topic. We know today that such changes are negotiated by means of the complex machinery that is available to speakers.

Secondly, studies have shown that the overall organization of conversation is also normative, in the sense of being a kind of global outline: so speakers may for various reasons skip over some parts, and pay closer attention to others. But we do know that the typical picture that emerges is a progression from one stage to another, and may look something like this (Ferrara, 1980: 332):

(a) initial greeting sequences
(b) howareyou sequences

The idea of lingual economy

(c) non-topical sequences
(d) topical sequences
(e) encounter-evaluative sequences
(f) arrangement sequences
(g) closing greeting sequences

The detailed investigation of this kind of organization will no doubt reveal that the organization tentatively outlined here is normative, and may be violated, flouted, changed or exploited by lingual subjects in the collaborative work that they engage upon in talk. But it will also show that lingual subjects have an orientation towards mutuality in talk, and towards responding in their formation of lingual objects to a system of norms that allows each enough talking space, and the opportunity to share their expression — often called the 'co-construction of meaning' — with selected others.

Some other factual lingual units

Conversation analysis in the ethnomethodological mode does, of course, not have a theoretical monopoly on the identification either of systems for shared expression or communication, on the one hand, or of the observation and isolation of objective lingual facts, on the other.

Indeed, in the discourse analysis literature, we find numerous other instances of factual lingual units, such as the hierarchically arranged (in the sense of 'consists of' relations) lingual objects that Coulthard (1985: 123 ff.) identifies in the organization of discourse in 'transaction', 'exchange', 'move' and 'act', where transaction, the highest objective lingual unit in the hierarchy, is said to consist of two or more exchanges, exchanges consist of moves, and moves in turn consist of a specifiable set or combination of lingual acts. While there may be clear theoretical differences between the hierarchical approach of discourse analysis and the bottom-up perspective of ethnomethodology, (in the sense of taking a view of how talk is locally organized and managed[19]), Coulthard's distinctions do not appear to be so far away from the lingual sequences (adjacent pairs) identified by conversation analysis, for in a real sense we are able to say that

---

19. Conversation analysis, Sacks (1984: 21) remarks, "seeks to describe the methods persons use in doing social life."

such lingual sequences consist of turns at talk (Heritage & Atkinson 1984: 8).

Similarly, there are in the field of discourse analysis the near synonymous concepts of frame, script, scenario and schema that describe the coherence of a given stretch of text (Brown & Yule 1983; cf. also Craig & Tracey 1983), nor should one forget the groundbreaking work done by Halliday and Hasan (1976) in conceptualizing lingual extension and unity in their analysis of lingual coherence.

All of these distinctions attempt to articulate the great variety of objective lingual units that function on the factual side of the lingual aspect once the structure of this aspect is disclosed in the anticipatory direction of time to grasp theoretically not only the restrictive, constitutive analogical moments within the lingual modality, but also to come to an understanding of its social, economic and juridical anticipations. It is as if the abundance of such distinct objective lingual units celebrates the opening up of this modality in the transcendental direction of time. To this author, this wealth of lingual resources has been a constant source of wonder and awe, and an indication that the theoretical apparatus with which we aim to conceptualize all of the resources of language is limited and always incomplete.

The remainder of the agenda

There is little doubt that a systematic investigation of the remaining elementary linguistic ideas referred to in the introduction to this chapter — the ideas of lingual harmony, lingual accountability, lingual integrity and lingual trust — will enable linguistic theory to come to a better theoretical understanding of the multifaceted, and no doubt interesting, complex linguistic concepts of the relation between lingual norm and lingual fact, lingual subject and object, and the idea of the origin, introduction, acquisition, use, development and, in some cases, the loss or extinction of language. That we have barely begun to conceptualize these in a systematic framework such as the one utilized in this study is undoubtedly true. I return in the Epilogue to components of a possible research agenda for such an analysis.

16 A linguistic alternative

What are the prospects for a responsible linguistic approach that does not wish to travel the academic road of either structuralism or generativism? Greimas (1974: 58) observes:

> To be a Hjelmslevian or a Chomskyan is the unhappy question we live with, but it should not have to be asked in linguistics: such a division into sects only shows the immaturity of a scientific discipline.

Palmer, too, points out with some severity that the arguments between Chomsky and his critics are in each case one-sided, with a tendency to be framed in a black and white, yes/no fashion. Linguistics should rather avoid such immaturity, he concludes (1976: 154), and should acknowledge that the arguments cannot be resolved in such terms. One may thus remark, in a more positive sense, that alternative proposals in linguistic theory are today more relevant than ever, especially if these alternatives constitute an attempt, as is the case with this study, to clarify the deep-rooted causes of the academic quarrels in linguistic theory.

In an era of anti-dogmatism, and in a time when no scientific perspective can hope to maintain any academic monopoly, one would hope that there is room for alternative linguistic theories, even if unhealthy academic practices are kindling the fires of a kind of theoretical imperialism. If it is true, for example, as Sampson (1979: 220, note 26) remarks in a footnote, that "one of the most striking practical results of the 'Chomskyan revolution' in linguistics has been to replace an ethos which encouraged a wide diversity of scholars to go their independent ways with a highly authoritarian ethos in which individual scholars' reputation, access to channels of publication, even employment prospects are to a quite unprecedented extent determined by a small coterie who succeed in exacting conformity to a particular 'party line'," the situation is indeed problematic.

It must be admitted today that no single theory can supply a complete systematic explanation for the phenomena investigated by linguistic theory. The linguistic methods and tools that are available at present make it difficult to do this. Chomsky himself has pointed out (1972a: 21) that certain issues in linguistics are so relevant that they remain topical in spite of the narrowness of our methods of analysis. But it is a criterion that applies not only to structuralism, but also to the theory of transformational grammar. Just as the successful employment of the structuralist approach "should have been coupled with a clear recognition of its essential limitations and ultimate inadequacy, in comparison with the tradition it temporarily, and quite justifiably, displaced" (Chomsky 1972a: 21-22), so there is equally no reason why transformational grammar, especially in its more imperialistically inclined tenets, should not include a recognition of its own theoretical limitations.

This includes Chomsky's frequently expressed critique that the linguistic efforts of his academic opposition are not 'explicit' enough to require theoretical attention or comment. For, if by explicitness the linguist merely means 'formalized', then there lurks in the background the unquestioned assumption that in formalization we have found the redemptive method by which to solve our theoretical linguistic problems. By making the method of formalization the central factor in linguistic enquiry, one has then actually closed the door in the face of other theoretical options, and academic tolerance can no longer survive.

Perhaps the time has indeed arrived to unite all "major currents and to develop a synthesis that will draw from their respective achievements" (Chomsky 1972a: 23). But this should not be interpreted as a call for a new brand of eclecticism or even some kind of refined theoretical consensus, for this would merely be postponing the crucially important task of examining the philosophical and religious roots that lie at the heart of the issue, and without which the diversity of linguistic opinion cannot adequately be accounted for. Linguistics is not merely a question of method and technique, but has roots in a diversity of philosophical perspectives that are in their turn related to the sometimes unformulated assumptions of a particular world-view.

If linguistics is to heed the call of questioning its own assumptions, there must also be a greater willingness on the part of the practising linguist to step out of the traditional paradigms of linguistic theory in search of a perspectival, consistent philosophical overview that will do justice to both structuralist or generativist and to rationalist or empiricist contributions. The methodological analysis given in this study is an attempt to do just that.

Perhaps, too, linguistic theory must begin to state not only what its unquestioned assumptions are, but also to examine Sampson's thesis (1979: 191) that "a scientific methodology cannot, as a matter of logic, be shown to be right or wrong, it can only be held as an article of faith." The kind of explicitness that linguistics needs is thus not simply of a formal nature, as linguists have been led to believe, but a clear understanding of its own unquestioned assumptions.

A systematic linguistic framework such as the one outlined in this study is never philosophically neutral. No linguistic theory is. Neither is the philosophical framework upon which this methodological survey is based neutral in respect of a world-view. In an academic way it confesses that reality is orderly, and that the fundamental principles that underlie language regulate our factual production of it.

If there is room for a systematic survey such as this, it has a real contribution to make in facilitating academic communication between schools of linguistic thought that usually fire critically at each other across voids of conceptual misunderstanding. For, although this kind of academic enquiry does not engage in playing the game of linguistic analysis according to the same rules as rationalist or empiricist approaches and the schools of structuralism or transformationalism, but wishes to add some rules of its own, sometimes even questioning the validity of traditionally accepted rules, it nonetheless provides a critical framework for linguistic theory. In this kind of linguistic systematics the different emphases of various schools and approaches can be viewed in a new paradigmatic perspective.

In the preceding chapters some of the systematic concepts that have been and are of linguistic interest to linguistic investigation have been surveyed. As I remarked at the end of the previous chapter, the systematic analysis given here does not claim to be exhaustive. Systematic concepts, echoes of our theoretical linguistic insight into the practical idea that we have of language, come and go; they are discovered and discarded, found again and forgotten. But the framework in which systematic concepts function has a more lasting character, and if the present study has tentatively taken a few hesitant steps towards its formulation, it will have succeeded in one of its major aims.

Epilogue

A tempting question, given my decision to reshape an analysis that had emerged from my own work more than twenty years ago, is whether I would have done the analysis in the same way as before if I had had the opportunity to do it all over again. In one sense, the answer is a fairly easy "No". In the restless world of scientific endeavor (and I count among the sciences both those traditionally termed thus, the so-called 'natural' sciences, and the 'cultural' or 'human' sciences) things are always on the move, always in progress, and questions are never finally settled. Analyses and analytical traditions also move with the times: they are as much subject to fashion and change as other things, and sometimes, in the case of paradigm change, dramatically so. Analyses go out of date, so there is a fair amount of misgiving that I have about some of the analyses that I made above. Similarly, issues and themes come and go. What interests this generation may not be interesting to the next.

However, I hope that there is also some enduring insight in the analyses made before and presented here. In many respects they still provide a challenge, I believe, even to a current generation of academics. And they certainly also provide a platform for the discussion of differences in theoretical approach that I have not seen elsewhere. The reformational philosophy from which the foundational analyses attempted here have grown is often thought of as a narrow, parochial and even dogmatic set of conceptions, out to further its own interests at the apparent cost of others. If that conception is correct, I believe that this philosophy is mistaken, and out of touch with its roots and deepest convictions. My own experience of it has been the opposite:

that it is a philosophy that seeks not only mutuality — science and scientific endeavor is indeed one, despite differences in approach — but also a responsible perspective on the phenomena treated within a scientific discipline. Its research agenda is indeed to challenge, but also to provide a uniting view of various perspectives and theoretical approaches within a discipline. I also believe that its starting points are not entirely out of line with many current approaches. Its basic building blocks are not that difficult to understand either. Simply put, at its very foundation (like many other approaches, as we now freely, under the influence of postmodernism, admit), it

> is based on a pre-theoretical conviction. The conviction is a fairly simple one: that nothing is absolute, and that, though one may distinguish between uniquely different modes of doing and being, all of these are connected to everything else (Weideman 2007).

I shall return below to the point about what constitutes a responsible agenda for linguistics from the particular perspective of this attempt at a systematic, foundational analysis of the field. First, however, I need to deal with a number of misgivings that, if not properly articulated and dealt with openly, may result in a misunderstanding of my decision to go ahead with the project of publishing this analysis.

The first point I need to make is this: doing a systematic analysis of the foundations of linguistics is not doing linguistics. This needs to be clearly stated, even at this late stage, first, as a warning to those working wholly within the discipline of linguistics and who may be puzzled by such an undertaking, and, second, as a clarification to those philosophically interested readers who hope to gain insight from reading an analysis such as this.

The warning is called for, I believe, because neither linguists nor applied linguists are in the first instance interested in the foundations of their fields. They seem to be pre-occupied mostly either with their own theoretical concerns, or, in the case of applied linguists, with the urgency of the language problems that beset us and cry out for solutions. One must accept that.

The downside of such an exclusive focus on one's own field, without an attempt to relate it to larger frameworks and beliefs, is of

Epilogue

course that one may fall victim to one or more of the many academic fashions or theoretical paradigms that present themselves over time. The advantage of working within a specific philosophical perspective is that it directly affects the degree of deliberation and self-consciousness with which one works as an academic. Those wholly occupied by linguistics alone will never feel the challenge that a consciously adopted philosophical perspective brings even to the small details of their work, or the illumination that it provides for some of the most mundane observations within the discipline.

My work within the theoretical perspective of reformational philosophy has enabled me, I believe, to attempt a conscious and responsible framing of even the minutest details of my work as a linguist and applied linguist. Nevertheless, the foundational analyses of these fields that I have done do not themselves qualify as either linguistics or applied linguistics. Though they shed light on linguistic observation, analysis and insight, they are by nature philosophical analyses, and their primary audience remains the philosophically interested among us, or those whose openness allows them to be challenged by issues of belief and perspective.

Working within a specific philosophical framework adds an additional burden to academic work, I believe. Though all of them would probably claim that theoretical analysis is a systematic endeavor, many academics I know abhor systematicity, since it appears to take away their much-prized academic freedom. They do not consider that in contesting one kind of systematic analysis they may unwittingly be victims of another set of beliefs and theoretical convictions.

The philosophical framework within which my academic work has been done has also called up resistance from a number of quarters, both from my own contemporaries and from colleagues whose opinions I value highly. Some of their misgivings may be valid, others less so. However, I do not wish to discuss here the merits or demerits of each separate complaint that one might make against the kinds of systematic analysis attempted in this study. One will probably do more justice to theoretical and confessional objections in the more thorough discussion that one finds in the platform for academic debate provided by a journal article. In any event, most of the objections that are made concern the intentions of reformational philosophy to provide an alternative perspective on our academic endeavors. To these kinds of objections (cf. for example Hoogland 2005: 36; Visagie 2006: 202) one should reply, I believe, that the alternative perspective that is attempted is indeed one of the results of the systematic analysis, but it may, in the times and academic climate in which we live, not necessarily be the most important one.

A much more important outcome of a systematic, foundational analysis is that it sets the stage for communication between schools of thought within disciplines that may be either at cross-purposes, or come to the phenomena within their purview from different theoretical, and sometimes ideological, angles. A systematic analysis done on the basis of the insights generated by reformational philosophy should, if it is to do its job properly, be able to provide a platform for mutuality and appreciation. In short: it should open up rather than stifle communication between various schools of thought.

A foundational analysis is able to do so because it employs a systematic framework in which the varying emphases of different theoretical perspectives can be appreciated. It is my hope that the current analysis has been able to demonstrate in some small way how this is possible.

These considerations may explain some of the misgivings I felt, and articulated in the Prologue to this study, as I set out to revise and reshape it for publication in a form that, I hope, may still be acceptable and even useful to a new generation of philosophically interested academics.

How would I have tackled the agenda for this kind of research if I could start afresh?

There are several developments within the various linguistic disciplines that immediately present themselves for urgent attention in a systematic analysis.

First among these probably is the minimalist turn that transformationalist syntax has taken. It would be a real challenge to discover whether some of the earlier analyses presented above of previous versions of transformational-generative grammar are still useful. A wild guess — a hunch that is based more on experience than any particular insight — is that the earlier analyses may to some extent still provide systematic clarification, especially on the points of difference between transformational syntax and its theoretical competitors, but would be quite wide of the mark in other respects, and would

Epilogue

need to be corrected. Certainly, the analysis would have to attempt to discover a theoretical reason, related to the unfolding structure of the lingual dimension of experience through our analytical work, for new developments here.

The main competitor of transformationalism over the years has been systemic functional grammar (SFG), that builds upon the work of Halliday (1985). As I have shown (Weideman 1988: 21-31), some of the distinctions made by Halliday in creating a sociolingual syntax are as relevant today as before. The insights of SFG form a very important bridge across a major fault line in linguistic theory: that between formal linguistics and sociolinguistic analyses. It is no surprise, therefore, that over the last decade or so, there is renewed interest in SFG. It certainly deserves thorough consideration in a further systematic analysis of the foundations of linguistics.

Related to SFG in many respects, especially as regards its theoretical roots, is the refinement and development of discourse analysis into critical discourse analysis. This is a kind of analysis of objective lingual factuality that unashamedly places issues of power, and how power relations get encoded, on the agenda of linguistics. As I have noted above, the relation between politics and language throws up complex questions. They need systematic attention and treatment.

On the side of approaches that are more empirically inclined, the rise of corpus linguistics has given linguists much food for thought. As the corpora of real language use in a great diversity of settings multiply, we gain more insight into phenomena that linguists may have guessed at fifty years ago, but that we can now more accurately trace and study. The corrective on what constitutes objective lingual facts that corpus linguistics provides, and the many further applications that can potentially still flow from it are both exciting developments.

I have mentioned only a handful of what I believe may become prominent nodes of interest for a renewal of a systematic analysis of the foundations of linguistics. If this is indeed undertaken, and this study has stimulated it at least in some respect, I would be deeply grateful.

Pretoria
December 2006

Bibliography

Abraham, W. (ed.). 1975. *Ut videam: Contributions to an understanding of linguistics; for P.A. Verburg on his 70th birthday.* Lisse: De Ridder.
Aranoff, M. 1976. *Word formation in generative grammar.* Cambridge, Massachusetts: MIT Press.
Atkinson, J.M. & Heritage, J. 1984. *Structures of social action: Studies in conversation analysis.* Cambridge. Cambridge University Press.
Barber, C.L. 1979. *The story of language.* Revised edition. London: Pan Books.
Beeton, D.R. & Dorner, H. 1975. *A dictionary of English usage in Southern Africa.* Cape Town: Oxford University Press.
Berry, M. 1975. *An introduction to systemic linguistics, Vol. I: Structures and Systems.* London: B.T. Batsford.
Bloomfield, L. 1958. *Language.* Revised edition. London: George Allen & Unwin.
Bloomfield, L. 1971. A set of postulates for the science of language. In M. Joos (ed.), *Readings in linguistics, Vol. I: The development of descriptive linguistics in America 1925-1956.* Chicago: University of Chicago Press.
Bolton, W.F. 1972. *A short history of literary English.* London: Edward Arnold.
Botha, R.P. (s.d.). External evidence in the validation of mentalistic theories: a Chomskyan paradox. Mimeographed (originally appeared in SPIL 2).
Brooks, C. & Warren, R.P. 1960. *Understanding poetry.* Third edition. New York: Holt, Rinehart and Winston.
Brown, G. & Yule, G. 1983. *Discourse analysis.* Cambridge: Cambridge University Press.
Bruns, G.L. 1975. *Modern poetry and the idea of language: A critical and historical study.* New Haven: Yale University Press.
Burgess, A. 1974. *English literature: A survey for students.* London: Longman.
Carnap, R. 1937. *The logical syntax of language.* London: Kegan Paul, Trench, Trubner.
Chomsky, N. 1957. *Syntactic structures.* The Hague: Mouton.
Chomsky, N. 1965. *Aspects of the theory of syntax.* Cambridge, Massachusetts: MIT Press.
Chomsky, N. 1966. *Cartesian linguistics: A chapter in the history of rationalist thought.* New York: Harper & Row.
Chomsky, N. 1970. *Current issues in linguistic theory.* The Hague: Mouton.

Chomsky, N. 1972a. *Language and mind.* Enlarged edition. New York: Harcourt, Brace, Jovanovich.
Chomsky, N. 1972b. *Problems of knowledge and freedom.* London: Fontana.
Chomsky, N. 1974. Discussion with Parret. In H. Parret (ed.), *Discussing language: Dialogues with Wallace L. Chafe, Noam Chomsky et al.* The Hague: Mouton.
Chomsky, N. 1975. *Reflections on language.* New York: Pantheon.
Chomsky, N. 1978a. *The logical structure of linguistic theory.* New York: Plenum Press.
Chomsky, N. 1978b. *A theory of core grammar.* Mimeographed (originally appeared in GLOT 1: 7-26).
Chomsky, N. 1979. *Language and responsibility: Based on conversations with Mitsou Ronat.* Sussex: Harvester Press.
Clark, H.H. & Clark, E.V. 1977. *Psychology and language: An introduction to psycholinguistics.* New York: Harcourt Brace Jovanovich.
Cook, V.J. 1979. *Using intonation.* Harlow, Essex: Longman
Cook, V.J. 1980 & 1981. *English for life 1: People and places. Students' book & Teacher's guide.* Oxford: Pergamon Press.
Cook, V.J. 1981. Some uses for second-language-learning research. *Annals of the New York Academy of Sciences* 379: 251-158.
Coulthard, M. 1985. *An introduction to discourse analysis.* Harlow, Essex: Longman.
Craig, R.T. & Tracy, K. (eds.). 1983. *Conversational coherence: Form, structure and strategy.* Beverly Hills: Sage.
Crystal, D. & Davy, D. 1976. *Investigating English style.* London: Longman.
Currie, W.B. 1975. *New directions in teaching English language.* London: Longman.
De Beaugrande, R.A. & Dressler, W.U. 1981. *Introduction to text linguistics.* London: Longman.
De Haan, G.J., Koefoed, G.A.T. & Des Tombe, A.L. 1975. *Basiskursus algemene taalwetenschap.* Assen: Van Gorcum.
De Jongste, H. 1949. Taalkunde en taalbeschouwing. *Philosophia Reformata* 14 (1): 3-42; (2): 49-57.
De Jongste, H. 1956. On symbols. *Philosophia Reformata* 21 (4): 162-174.
De Saussure, F. (Bally, C. & Sechehaye, A., eds.; Baskin, W., tr.) 1966. *Course in general linguistics.* New York: McGraw-Hill.
Die Volksblad. 1976. Gewig bly gewig ... en massa bly massa. 9 April.
Dooyeweerd, H. 1953. *A new critique of theoretical thought.* 4 Volumes. Amsterdam: H. J. Paris.
Ferrara, A. 1980. Appropriateness conditions for entire sequences of speech acts. *Journal of pragmatics* 4: 321-340.
Gleason, H.A. 1961. *An introduction to descriptive linguistics.* Revised edition. New York: Holt, Rinehart and Winston.
Goffman, E. 1981. *Forms of talk.* Oxford: Basil Blackwell.
Greimas, A.J. 1974. Discussion with Parret. In H. Parret (ed.), *Discussing language: Dialogues with Wallace L. Chafe, Noam Chomsky et al.* The Hague, Mouton.

Greyling, W.J. 1987. *The typicality of classroom talk and its relevance for the training of teachers.* Unpublished MA dissertation. Bloemfontein: University of the Free State.

Grice, H.P. 1975. Logic and conversation. In P. Cole & J.L. Morgan (eds.) 1975. *Syntax and semantics 3: Speech acts*: 41-58. New York: Academic Press.

Habermas, J. 1970. Toward a theory of communicative competence. In H.P. Dreitzel (ed.) 1970. *Recent sociology* 2: 115-148. London: Collier-Macmilan.

Haddakin, L. 1955. *The poetry of Crabbe.* London: Chatto & Windus.

Hall, R.A. 1950. *Leave your language alone!* New York: Linguistics.

Halliday, M.A.K. 1974. Discussion with Parret. In H. Parret (ed.), *Discusing language: Dialogues with Wallace L. Chafe, Noam Chomsky et al.* The Hague: Mouton.

Halliday, M.A.K. 1979. *Language as social semiotic: The social interpretation of language and meaning.* London: Edward Arnold.

Halliday, M.A.K. 1985. *An introduction to functional grammar.* London: Edward Arnold.

Halliday, M.A.K. & Hasan, R. 1976. *Cohesion in English.* London: Longman.

Harris, Z. 1966. *Structural linguistics.* First published in 1951 as *Methods in structural linguistics.* Chicago: Phoenix Books, University of Chicago Press.

Hendricks, W.O. 1973. *Essays on semiolinguistics and verbal art.* The Hague: Mouton.

Heritage, J. & Atkinson, JM. 1984. Introduction. In Atkinson, J.M. & Heritage, J. (eds.): 1-15.

Hill, A.A. 1969. What is language? In J.B. Hogins, & R.E. Yarber, (eds.), *Language: An introductory reader.* New York: Harper and Row.

Hjelmslev, L. (Whitfield, F.J., tr.) 1963. *Prolegomena to a theory of language.* Madison: University of Wisconsin Press.

Hommes, H.J. Van Eikema. 1972. *De elementaire grondbegrippen der rechtswetenschap: Een juridische methodologie.* Deventer: Kluwer.

Hoogland, J. 2005. De reformatorische wijsbegeerte in het gedrang. *Beweging* 69 (4): 33-42.

Hulbert, J.R. 1955. *Dictionaries British and American.* London: Andre Deutsch.

Hymes, D. 1971. On communicative competence. In J.B. Pride & J. Holmes (eds.) 1972: 269-233. *Sociolinguistics: selected readings.* Harmondsworth: Penguin.

Jones, D. (ed. A.C. Gimson) 1975. *Everyman's English pronouncing dictionary.* 13th edition. London: J.M. Dent.

Jones, R.F. 1953. *The triumph of the English language.* London: Oxford University Press.

Joos, M. (ed.) 1971. *Readings in linguistics, Vol. I: The development of descriptive linguistics in America 1925-1956.* Chicago: University of Chicago Press.

Lennox-Short, A. 1977. The teaching of writing skills: 1. General principles. *UCT Studies in English* 7. September.

Levinson, S.C. 1983. *Pragmatics.* Cambridge: Cambridge University Press.

Lyons, J. 1968. *Introduction to theoretical linguistics.* Cambridge: Cambridge

University Press.
Lyons, J. 1970. *Chomsky*. Glasgow: Fontana/Collins.
McDonough, S. 1981. *Psychology in foreign language teaching*. London: Allen & Unwin.
McIntosh. A. 1961. Patterns and ranges. *Language* 37(3).
Olthuis J.H. 1979. Towards a certitudinal hermeneutic. In J. Kraay & A. Tol (eds.), *Hearing and doing: Philosophical essays dedicated to H. Evan Runner*. Toronto: Wedge.
Palmer, F.R. 1976. *Semantics: A new outline*. Cambridge: Cambridge University Press.
Palmer, L.R. 1968. *The Latin language*. London: Faber and Faber.
Parret, H. (ed.) 1974. *Discussing language: Dialogues with Wallace L. Chafe, Noam Chomsky et al*. The Hague: Mouton.
Pike, K.L. 1959. Language as particle, wave and field. *The Texas quarterly* 2.
Potter, S. 1953. *Our language*. London: Penguin.
Quirk, R. & Greenbaum, S. 1978. *A university grammar of English*. Seventh, corrected impression. London: Longman.
Radford, A. 1981. *Transformational syntax: A student's guide to Chomsky's Extended Standard Theory*. Cambridge: Cambridge University Press.
Reichling, A. 1947. De taal: Haar wetten en haar wezen. In A. Reichling & J.S. Witsenelias (eds.), *Eerste Nederlandse systematisch ingerichte encyclopaedie* 2. Amsterdam: ENSIE.
Reichling, A.J.B.N. 1962. Grondbeginselen der hedendaagse taalwetenschap. In Reichling, A.J.B.N., Uhlenbeck, E.M. et al., *Taalonderzoek in onze tijd*. Wassenaar: Servire.
Reichling, A. 1969. *Verzamelde studies over hedendaagse problemen der Taalwetenschap*. Zwolle: W.E.J. Tjeenk Willink.
Robins, R.H. 1967. *A short history of linguistics*. London: Longman.
Robinson, I. 1975. *The New Grammarians' funeral: A critique of Noam Chomsky's linguistics*. Cambridge: Cambridge University Press.
Rookmaker, H.R. 1974. Stellingen by natuur en genade in de laat-middeleeuwse schilderkunst. *Beweging* 38 (6).
Sacks, H. 1984. Notes on methodology. In Atkinson, J.M. & Heritage, J. (eds.): 21-27.
Sacks, H, Schegloff, E.A. & Jefferson, G. 1974. A simplest systematics for the organization of turn-taking for conversation. *Language* 50 (4): 696-735.
Sampson, G. 1979. *Liberty and language*. Oxford: Oxford University Press.
Sapir, E. 1949. *Language: An introduction to the study of speech*. New York: Harcourt, Brace & World.
Schegloff, E.A & Sacks, H. 1973. Opening up closings. *Semiotica* 8: 289-327.
Searle, J.R. 1969. *Speech acts: An essay in the philosophy of language*. London: Cambridge University Press.
Seerveld, C. 1968. *A Christian critique of art and literature*. Toronto: Association for Reformed Scientific Studies.

Shaw, H. 1970. *Errors in English and ways to correct them*. New York: Barnes and Noble.
Sheard, J.A. 1954. *The words we use*. London: Andre Deutsch.
Sinnema, D. 1975. *The uniqueness of the language of faith with special reference to the language of scripture*. Toronto: Institute for Christian Studies.
Smith, N. & Wilson, D. 1979. *Modern linguistics: The results of Chomsky's revolution*. Brighton: Harvester Press.
Steensma, G.J. 1977. Language. In G.J. Steensma & H.W. van Brummelen (eds.), *Shaping school curriculum: A biblical view*. Haute: Signal.
Strauss, D.F.M. 1967. *Wysgerige grondprobleme in die taalwetenskap*. Bloemfontein: Sacum.
Strauss, D.F.M. 1970. *Wysbegeerte en vakwetenskap*. Bloemfontein: Sacum.
Strauss, D.F.M., Van den Berg, D.J. & Weideman, A.J. 1979. Some basic semiotic categories. *Anakainosis* 1 (4).
Strunk,W. (revised by White, E.B.) 1972. *The elements of style*. Revised edition. New York: MacMillan.
Svartvik, J. & Quirk, R. (eds.) 1980. *A corpus of English conversation*. Lund: CWK Gleerup.
Tucker, S.I. 1961. *English examined: Two centuries of comment on the mother-tongue*. London: Cambridge University Press.
Uhlenbeck, E.M. 1968. *Taalwetenschap: Een eerste inleiding*. The Hague: De Ned. Boek- en Steendrukkerij.
Van den Berg, D.J. 1979. Die tipering van De Saussure se werk as positivisties. In Riekert, S.J. (ed.), *Studiebrief 1 van die navorsingsprojek: Die gebruik van die algemene taalwetenskap in die interpretasie van antieke tekste*. Bloemfontein: University of the Free State.
Van Heerden, C. 1965. *Inleiding tot die semantiek*. Johannesburg: Willem Gouws.
Van Heerden, C. 1972. *Die grense van die taal*. Inaugural address. Bloemfontein: University of the Orange Free State.
Van Jaarsveld, G.J. & Weideman, A.J. *Doelgerigte Afrikaans (Sts. 8 & 9): Kommunikatiewe oefeninge, aktiwiteite, rolspeletjies en strategieë*. Bloemfontein: Patmos.
Verburg, P.A. 1951. Enkele lijnen en feiten in de ontwikkeling der taaltheorie. In S.U. Zuidema (ed.) *Wetenschappelijke bijdragen door leerlingen van Dr D.H. Th. Vollenhoven*. Franeker: Wever.
Verburg, P.A. 1965. Delosis and clarity. In *Philosophy and Christianity: Philosophical essays dedicated to Prof. Dr. H. Dooyeweerd*. Kampen: Kok.
Verburg, P.A. 1971. De mens in de taalkunde. In *Truth and reality: Philosophical perspectives on reality dedicated to Prof H.G. Stoker*. Braamfontein: De Jong's.
Verburg, P.A. 1976. The idea of linguistic system in Leibniz. Offprint from H. Parret (ed.), *History of linguistic thought and contemporary linguistics*. Berlin: Walter de Gruyter.

Visagie, J. 2006. Key theory and philosophy of mind. In L.O.K. Lategan & J.H. Smit (guest editors). *Time and context relevant philosophy. Journal of Christian scholarship* 42 (Special edition 1): 202-218.

Waher, H. 1984. Chomsky se teorie van 'Government-Binding.' *SPIL Plus* 9.

Weideman, A.J. 1984. General and typical concepts of textual continuity. *SA journal of linguistics* 2 (1): 69-84.

Weideman, A.J. 1985a. Discovering conversational units. *Acta academica* Series B/2: *Fokus op die taalkunde*: 195-207.

Weideman, A.J. 1985b. *Making certain: A course for advanced learners of English*. Bloemfontein: Patmos.

Weideman, A.J. 1988. *Linguistics: A crash course for students*. Revised edition. Bloemfontein: Patmos.

Weideman, A.J. 1991. Faith and objectivity in linguistic science. *Language matters* (UK) 1: 10-11.

Weideman, A.J. 2007. The redefinition of applied linguistics: Modernist and postmodernist views. *Southern African linguistics and applied language studies* 25 (4): 589-609.

Weideman, A.J., Raath, J. & Van der Walt, P.J. 1986: Continuity and discontinuity in talk: Some brief notes on summonses. *SA journal of linguistics* 4 (4): 90-100.

Weideman, A.J. & Van Rensburg, M.C.J. 1984. 'n Kantaantekening by die grammatika van skryftaal. *SA Journal of linguistics* 2 (3): 125-128.

Weideman, A.J. & Verster, L. 1988. "Two roads diverged ...": an analysis of the achievement of partings. *SA journal of linguistics* 6 (4): 55-68.

Weideman, A.J. & Visser, S.F. 1986. A measure of texture: cohesion in English radio drama dialogue and actual conversation. *SA journal of linguistics* 4 (2): 87-105.

Wells, R.S. 1971. De Saussure's system of linguistics. In M. Joos (ed.), *Readings in linguistics, Vol. I: The development of descriptive linguistics in America 1925-1956*. Chicago: University of Chicago Press.

Yallop, C.L. 1978. The problem of linguistic universals. *Philosophia Reformata* 43.

Abstract

If no specific science is philosophically neutral, linguistics must self-consciously strive to clarify its theoretical, philosophical foundations by developing a systematic methodological framework that provides for various elementary and complex linguistic concepts. Since no attempt to do this on the basis of the philosophy of the cosmonomic idea has proved to be exhaustive, this study sets out to elaborate such a systematic methodology by looking first at the expressive character of language and the different material lingual spheres in which language is used. Thereafter various elementary systematic concepts that express the modal coherence between the lingual aspect and the other aspects of experience are surveyed. Amongst others, the elementary linguistic concepts of lingual system, position, constancy, operation, development, intention, identity and form are reinterpreted in a new theoretical perspective. Even though the explicit focus of the study is the constitutive structure of the lingual aspect, attention is also given to language in its social context, as well as to the notions of discourse, text and acceptability, in order to lay the foundations of a systematic theory that provides an alternative viewpoint in the sphere of philosophical linguistics.

www.ingramcontent.com/pod-product-compliance
Lightning Source LLC
Chambersburg PA
CBHW031241290426
44109CB00012B/386